The Invisible Way

Changing your life from within

Anil Giga

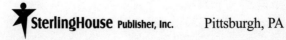 **SterlingHouse** Publisher, Inc.   Pittsburgh, PA

Other titles by Anil Giga

Seven Colors

The Invisible Way

Shiraz,

Best wishes,

Amin Loja 23/1/07

SterlingHouse Books

ISBN 1-58501-103-7
Trade Paperback
© Copyright 2007 Anil Giga
All Rights Reserved
Library of Congress #2006926299

Requests for information should be addressed to:
SterlingHouse Publisher, Inc.
7436 Washington Avenue
Pittsburgh, PA 15218
info@sterlinghousepublisher.com
www.sterlinghousepublisher.com

SterlingHouse Books
is an imprint of SterlingHouse Publisher, Inc.

SterlingHouse Publisher, Inc. is a company
of the CyntoMedia Corporation

Cover Design: Jamie Linder
Interior Design: Kathleen M. Gall

Please contact the author at:
www.anilgiga.com
rainbow@anilgiga.com

Printed in Canada

This book is dedicated to my family
whose constant support and encouragement
was a source of great strength.
I would especially like to thank my wife,
Yasmin,
for all the arduous work she did
turning my scribbles into readable script,
and without whom this book would not have been possible.

And finally, to the one who knows.

Wait till you look within yourself
And see what is there
Oh seeker, one leaf in that garden
Is worth more than all of paradise

Rumi

TABLE OF CONTENTS

INTRODUCTION

The seventies were a great time to be in England. It was the time of the Chelsea fashion scene, Carnaby Street and Sgt. Pepper's Lonely Heart Club Band. The Rolling Stones, Led Zeppelin and Cat Stevens rocked the halls of Earls Court while the old blues legends played the harmonica in the basements of the Soho nightclubs. Like so many people, I really thought that this was the center of the universe.

I was about 25 years old and had a successful advertising company. I had an arrogant swagger about me and if you had talked to me then, you might have concluded that this kid had it all! Deep down within me, however, were questions that kept me up late into the night. Despite all my worldly success and achievements, which had come to me at a very young age, I knew that this was all superficial and meaningless. I was trapped in a labyrinth with no way out and haunted with the knowledge that something inside of me was dying.

At first, I sought to read everything I could lay my hands on; later, it was self-indulgence and waywardness that preoccupied me. I wore a mask that hid a deep torment and did not know how to remove it. On September 7, 1979, everything changed when I met a spiritual master whose council I sought. "That which you seek is within you, and the way is invisible."

For the next six months, I journeyed along this invisible way, a path of animated objects and spiritual beings, during which time I lost all my worldly possessions. My home, my business and my wealth dissipated as the prince became a pauper. In the process, however, I discovered my soul and was able to remove the mask. I had never felt so wealthy and full of abundance as I did then. Today, 26 years later, all the wealth and more has returned, but it is insignificantly pale in comparison to the knowledge that we can all shape our destinies and write our own future.

I arrived in Canada in 1980, a penniless immigrant, and worked hard to acquire the skills to help people plan their finances. I pursued my career in this endeavor with diligence and commitment, helping my clients plan for everything: retirement, estate, taxes, vacations, and even the children's education. Leaving no stone unturned, I lived the life of a planner, believing in the truism, "If you fail to plan, you are planning to fail."

On the May 3, 2000, everything changed yet again. My wife and soul-mate, Yasmin, was diagnosed with an incurable disease and was rushed to the hospital, marked for death. I had spent my whole life planning, but how could I have planned for this? "What would you do today, if you were going to die tomorrow?" she asked. Agonizing days filled with pain and helplessness followed as I searched my soul for direction, for light.

The turning point came nine days later as I wheeled Yasmin into the surgical room. Unable to give me any guarantee of life, the surgeon said sympathetically, "Go home. I will call you when the surgery is finished."

I saw Yasmin's grace-filled face fade into the distance; she was clutching her rosary beads. Walking toward the car, I held my daughter's hand and looked up at the heavens, praying for hope that Yasmin would come home.

When we reached my isolated car, parked at the far end of the hospital lot, I was astonished to find a brand new baby's blanket sitting on the hood of the car. I looked around to see if there was someone who might have left it there, but there wasn't a soul in sight. Deep inside, I understood what this meant. Turning to my daughter, I said, "Mom is coming home." The events that unfolded from then on were surreal. Watching the one you love suffer in pain is not easy, but harder still was finding hope during the agonizing nights when death seemed easier than living, for such is the effect of chemotherapy on a fragile human body.

It was during these days of struggle and outward despair that I found the missing pieces of The Invisible Way. I had learned much since I was first introduced to this way, and the time had finally come to walk along a path that was invisible to everyone around me, and yet was as clear before me as the beautiful sunrise that laid out a yellow shimmering road, inviting me to write and create my own future.

Today, as Yasmin and I gaze out at the lake from our backyard, I am humbled to think that we actually wrote this script, and that we had been empowered with the responsibility to choose our future all along. The world we live in is a paradox for most people who harbor a profound discontentment about life. We see this manifest in a host of ways: alcoholism, violence, drug abuse, depression and a struggle for power both at home and at the work place. These are just some of the malaise that tell the story of the conflict inside of man entangled in this merry-go-round we call life. The paradox exists because, as human beings, we are the highest being gifted with the faculties of reason, intellect and choice and empowered to create our own condition. The way really does exist for us to shape our destiny, but we have forgotten how to use our gifts, so we just lament in desperation.

Visit the public libraries and you will find thousands of books lining the walls. Stop by the bookstore, where new releases are stacked on the shelves in abundance. Yet universities churn out treatise after treatise on every subject conceivable, and now with the advent of the information and Internet era, the disposition of knowledge doubles every month. Our appetite for a sense of meaning grows each day, and our yearning for happiness multiplies as we find ourselves suffocated in a world troubled with tragedies, divorce, terrorism, sickness and despair. If a path to happiness exists, how come we cannot see it? Because the path is invisible! To see it, we have to detach ourselves from the outward form long enough to nurture the gifts we all possess, because they are the keys that will enable us to see the unseen.

If there is only one more book you ever read, read the book that is etched within you, because this is a book about your past and present. Each waking day, we are writing the pages to the later chapters in our life. Yes, our future is being written by us this very moment and our destiny is in our hands. The greatest gift we have is the gift of choice, which empowers us to become the co-creators of our future. Our action, behavior and intentions and the myriad of choices we make each day, are all coded into a script that becomes our life in the future. Remember, each day, we are all faced with two choices—to either accept our current condition and life or take the responsibility to change it.

Is it possible to change our life and future? Absolutely! In the pages that follow, I will share with you the practices and insights of the Invisible Way. These will enable you to create a core transformation and change your life from within.

CHAPTER 1

Reflections from the Visible World

What is life? Who am I? What on earth am I doing here?

Have you ever asked such questions of yourself? Have you ever lost someone you love and wondered what the point was? We are born and we struggle to achieve in life those things we are told are important, like nice homes, cars and investment portfolios. But if you knew you were going to die tomorrow, how important would these things be? We live our lives acquiring things we would discard in a heartbeat for an extra day of life. What about sickness and disease? Have you ever seen someone you care about suffer? Did it make you wonder why? And what about you? Have you ever found yourself disillusioned with your life? If you have more questions than answers and often hear the echoes of discontent from deep inside of you, you are not alone. Life is like a jigsaw puzzle. When all the pieces are there, everything makes sense. Unfortunately, most people have just a few pieces and sadly, not only do they create a fictitious picture, but they actually build a life on it.

I was introduced to the Invisible Way in 1979. It was perhaps the most significant moment in my life because it empowered me to discard the prejudices and conditioning of my physical upbringing and to see and experience life for what it really was. How things are and what we see are a world apart and, unless we get this, our death, too, will be meaningless and just another item in the obituary column.

Rumi, the mystical poet, wrote:

> The bird is flying on high and its shadow is
> speeding on the earth. Some fool begins to chase
> the shadow, running so fast that he becomes
> exhausted.

In our everyday lives, the use of reason and logic are almost indispensable because they are a barometer for all the decisions we make. We like to see things in black and white, or as right and wrong. The Invisible Way, however, will take you into a dimension of reality that is overwhelmingly greater than anything we experience in our physical world and therefore, our reason and logic are blunt instruments in this endeavor. Let me give you an example. When we go to sleep, we often dream. And while we are dreaming, everything seems very real. We have feelings and emotions, we laugh, cry and are even gripped with fear, but suddenly, we awaken and we realize that it was only a dream. At this very moment, you are reading this book, but is this moment real? Think about it. How do you know whether this moment is real or a dream from which you will awaken when the alarm goes off? Is this moment real or is it a dream? Can we really tell until we actually wake up?

All of us have people we love—family and friends who we care about, and many of them have passed away. I was in a meeting one day at a senior's home, and I saw a blue wheelchair in the corner. The memories came flooding back because that wheelchair once belonged to my father and I used to take him out and about in it until we donated it after he passed away in 1982. I asked myself, "Did he really exist or was that just a dream?" "No, no," I told myself, "he existed." I thought about the picture album that had captured some of our time together. What if there was a flood and all the pictures were destroyed? Did my father still exist without the pictures? I wondered. Yes, I told myself, he existed because I can still remember him and had memories of our time together. But what if I got sick with Alzheimer's disease, and had no memory of the past and no recollection of my father ever having existed? I could not even recognize my own daughter if she stood in front of me. So I asked myself, "Did my father exist?" The fact is that to others he may have existed, but to me, in that condition, he never existed.

I had a friend who I knew and worked with for more than 20 years. One day he suffered a brain aneurysm. Sadly, he lost his short-term memory and never remembered the times we met. Therefore, how can we base what is real and what is an illusion on biological things like eyes and memory? Our eyes can and do deceive us because there are so many things that exist which we cannot see, like wind and microorganisms. It is like the mirage in the desert; the eye can see water and trees where none exists.

The Worm and the Apple—There was a worm in an apple. His view of the world was that it was moist and white. He worked himself through the apple, thinking what a wonderful world he lived in. Then one day, he worked himself to the other side and discovered a whole new world and landscape.

As physical beings, we have a very limited perspective. Like the worm, we see only that which is immediately in our face, and we think this is the whole picture. So our conclusions are based on the limited experience of our five senses. If we were to put on yellow sunglasses, the world would appear yellow, and if we had red sunglasses, we would see red in everything. The next time you see a rainbow in the sky, try this simple exercise: Put a red film over your eyes and observe how different the colors are and which ones became invisible. As human beings, we utilize 4 percent of our brains. We need to ask what we would see and how different things would appear if we used the other 96 percent. What we are experiencing each day is a very small part of reality. In fact, it can be said that our five senses have imprisoned us into this illusion of time. As Einstein once said "Time is an illusion of our five senses." It is something man has created; in reality, time does not exist.

Have you ever seen a magician do some tricks? He creates illusions that make things appear and disappear. An illusion is exactly that—something that is not real. This is why a mirage is called an illusion, because the image we see is not real. The fact of the matter is, we are surrounded by illusions. For instance, we see the sun, and we say, "There is the sun." Well, actually, when we see the sun in a particular place, that is also an illusion! This is because it takes eight seconds for the light from the sun to reach us on earth, which is 96 million miles away. Since the sun is also moving at 65,000 miles per hour, by the time we see the sun, it is actually in a different place, 520,000 miles away! The stars that we see up in the sky may not even exist because it takes centuries for the light to reach us, during which time hundreds of stars are dying, just as new ones are forming. So what we see may not even exist. All we are doing is perhaps taking a glimpse into the past. In that context, what is human life? Is it real or just an illusion? Just like the magician who made the rabbit disappear, you and I will one day vanish. Our life is an optical illusion, a shadow of something else. Look around at the countless people we have loved and known. They just disappeared. This is why the ancient sages would tell us that we need to awaken ourselves from this state, because one day, the alarm will indeed go off and we will realize that life was the dream and reality is something different altogether.

The sacred text states:

> Hast not thou turned thy vision to thy lord,
> How he doth prolong the shadow!
> If he will, he could make it stationary!

I had a friend, a hardworking individual who worked 30 years at the railways fixing trains. I met him on his 65th birthday and he seemed happy because he was finally retiring from work. "Now" he said to me, "I can do all the things I have wanted to do. I can travel, read and spend time with my grandchildren. Best of all, I get my pension check each month." A month later, and rather sadly at that, I was at his funeral. Later, as I sat down to console his wife, she showed me some mail that lay on the kitchen counter. "That is his first pension check," she said. "He did not even cash his first check."

Life is like that! It is like a dream and it goes fast. But we are so consumed by it that we choose to ignore what is inevitable.

N. Balagha states:

> People in this world are like travelers whose journey
> is going on though they are asleep. Beware of the

world; it is dishonest and deceitful, it is unfaithful
and mercenary. What it gives, it takes back.

If I am provoking you to think outside of your traditional comfort zone, that is a good starting point. The way to transform ourselves from being puppets to the master puppeteer is invisible, and in this journey, we have to unlearn everything and let go of all the so-called truths that we have built a life on. The physical life that we are so consumed with is a temporary phenomenon; the wise sages will often tell you that life is just six days long, so live as if five days have passed.

The King in the Desert—There was a king who loved to hunt in the desert. One day, he was with his hunting soldiers and got separated from them. He soon got lost, and after having spent countless hours under the hot sun, he was terribly thirsty and desperate. He came across a small tent where a traveler appeared to be resting. He crawled to the entrance, begging for water, and an old lady emerged. The king introduced himself and demanded some water. The old lady told him he may be a king, but he was not her king and to go away. The desperate king than begged and changed his tune, promising anything in return for water. The old lady asked whether he meant it when he offered her anything, and the king nodded. "Very well then," the old lady said, and asked the king his name and age. The king said his name was Wagt and he was 45 years old. The old woman said, "The meaning of your name is time, and I want you to reflect on your last 45 years." The king obliged and thought about his life while focusing on the milestones. After he had spent a few minutes on this, he looked at the old woman again, who said, "I will give you water if you give me your last 45 years." The king, who was so thirsty, readily agreed. After the king had nourished himself, he felt stronger and was able to wait until his soldiers found him. As he got on his horse to leave, he turned to the old woman and asked her what it was that she was trying to tell him. The old woman looked up to the king and told him, "I asked you to reflect upon your life and, it took you two minutes. Then you traded it for some water. If you are not careful, your next 45 years also will pass in two minutes and they,

too, will be equally worthless, so always remember your name."
King Wagt thanked the woman and promised himself to make the
rest of his life worthwhile. So began the transformation of a pauper into a king.

When we reflect back on our lives, we know it has gone very
quickly, just as the rest of our lives will go. Time is so precious, yet
we are either preoccupied with dealing with the past and all the
baggage of regrets and hurts that we carry, or we are busy planning
the future. The most important time we have is now; the past is
meaningless except for what it has taught us, and the future may
not even arrive! The present is all we really can count on and it is
measured in seconds. Alas, we are busy trying to add years to our
life rather than add life to our limited years. If we keep doing the
same things, if we are to live our life in the same way and listen to
the same clatter of noise, chasing the same illusions, the future will
not be any different than our past.

The Dream Car—There was once a man who had been to the
car show where the latest model cars were unveiled. He saw a
beautiful sports car and immediately fell in love with it. He went
home and confessed to his wife the dream he had of owning the
sports car, and began to put money away each month. Eighteen
months later, he had enough money, so he walked into the car
dealership to purchase his dream. He told the salesman what he
wanted and the salesman looked back and said, "I can get you that
car, no problem, but look at the new version. It's refined and modified, and what's more, it's faster and comes in a convertible
model." The man took one look and fell in love, forgetting the
dream he had come to purchase.

Reflection is indeed hard. Why else would we be shopping for
dreams in malls and department stores? It is a contradiction only
humans can explain; unfortunately, it is something that starts at a
very early age.

From a very young age, we learn about collecting and about
ownership. At first, it is the little toys we get from our parents and
family, as well as the doll houses and electronic gadgets, and as we
get older, our habits are ingrained. Instead of toy cars, we want real

cars, and the doll houses are now replaced by real homes. The fact is our whole life revolves around ownership, and often it becomes our goal in life. Life's current just takes us. Sometimes we do question ourselves; after all, the life we lead often leaves little time for anything else. But these voices from within are soon drowned out because we look around and see that everyone is doing the same thing! We turn on the television, we listen to the news, we read magazines, go to the cinema, browse the Internet and we come across the same messages: Owning and perusing that dream of material aspiration is what will bring meaning and joy into our life.

In addition, people with whom we are familiar, superstars, movie stars and rock stars, come into our living rooms and validate the idea that our life should indeed be one of striving for the things of this world and, rather coincidently, they even recommend the right model car, vacation, resort or neighborhood that is just perfect for us.

When the inner voice does resurface again, questioning the value of all this personal sacrifice it is soon overwhelmed by these external messages. Messages that tell us if we drink their beverages, it will make us feel good; that if we visit their destination resorts, we will feel happy and relaxed; that if we wear their clothes, we will feel good about ourselves; that if we own their goods, it will make us wealthy, and if we eat their foods, it will make us thin. We are given the perfect recipe to achieve happiness, and we are constantly reminded that it is a formula that works. Deep inside, is that not what everyone wants—to feel good, beautiful, young and happy? And so we find the resolve and determination to follow the sage advice.

We follow their wisdom, we drink their wine and eat their foods, we buy clothes with their names written on them, we visit their vacation places and own their cars and then we wait, and nothing happens, except time continues to tick away.

We lived our lives according to that "perfect" formula for happiness, and years went by, even decades, and it seems that the happiness and contentment that we sought was still far from our reach. We look around and find that, though time has moved, we haven't.

Problems still surround us because sorrow visits us all and disappointments stand at every corner. This is when we realize that the world's recipe for happiness and abundance is not working and that we have been betrayed, let down and fooled. The fact is, none of us will ever cash our pension checks! Why? Because we are trapped in the matrix of illusion, where here and now has absolutely no value. The only important ideal in this world is "there" and our life is based on the plans we have to get us to "there." Each and every day, the plan to take us "there" unfolds. The minute we awake in the morning, we hear the clock ticking, and we are in a hurry. We rush to work, agonizing over every red light or traffic jam: we rush to get the kids ready in the morning and dropped off to school or daycare and dash to the programs and commitments. And as Einstein explained, "The faster we live our lives, the quicker does time pass!" Finally when we get "there," whether it was getting kids through college, finding a spouse or that dream home, we find that "there" is better than "here," so we devise yet another plan that will get us "there," and the clock continues to tick. We are always going to be heading "there." It is only at the end of our lives when we realize that life was just a game and the "there" was actually a piece of real estate called a grave and that the only thing of value was the "here," which we squandered away.

The Commander—An army commander in the midst of a great battle decided to attack the enemy even though his forces were heavily outnumbered. Although he was confident of victory, his men were filled with doubts on the merits of this battle, which he felt could affect the outcome of the war. On the way to the battlefield, they passed a temple and he stopped his army there and prayed with them. After the prayers, the commander took out a coin from his pocket and told his men that he would flip the coin. If the coin fell to heads, the army would be victorious, and if it fell to tails, they would suffer defeat. He tossed the coin. It came up as heads, and the commander declared that the destiny of victory had now revealed itself. The men were overjoyed and so full of confidence that they attacked the enemy with uncommon zeal and were victorious. After the battle, the subordinate officer told the commander that he was told it was not possible for anyone to change destiny. The commander declared that as correct and showed the officer his coin, which had two heads.

We live in a world where people's lives are constantly and sublimely controlled and manipulated. Like the soldiers, we ignore the doubts emanating from within, we become easily swayed by the illusions of this physical and material world, and we allow others to take charge of our destiny. It is in our hands then to free ourselves from the strands of the puppeteer and create the life of meaning and fulfillment.

The Tourist and the Sage—A tourist was traveling through the orient and he came across a learned Sufi master. "How may I find the Invisible Light?" he asked. The Sufi master replied, "First you must seek enlightenment." "What does it mean to be enlightened?" the tourist asked. The master asked him to stand in front of a mirror. "Now, find a way to look at the back of your head in the mirror, and when you do, come and see me, and I will answer your question." The tourist stood in front of the mirror and struggled for an hour to find the method to see the back of is head. He went side to side and explored every angle conceivable. He finally gave up and returned to the Sufi master. The Sufi master sympathized and said to the tourist, "You are one dimensional. No matter how hard you try, you will never see the back of your head in the mirror standing before you. An enlightened one is he who is multidimensional." "One more question if you don't mind," said the tourist. "How do you become multidimensional?" The Sufi master looked up and said, "When you are able to see beyond your own ignorance, the unseen way becomes visible."

This is our plight; we are one dimensional. Our material world that consumes our attention from birth to death is but only one dimension in a multidimensional world and consequently, we are imprisoned by our own ignorance. We see this virtual world out there, a world of sights, sounds and neon lights. The Internet, television and radio beam images of an ideal world where families live in perfect homes, drive perfect cars and share perfect relationships.

That is the "there" everyone idolizes and strives for, but what is wrong with this picture? It is not real. It was created by copywriters and advertising agencies who hope that we will want their perfect "there" so much that we will sacrifice our life, time and resources to buy it.

The Necklace—King Wagt learned that his daughter had lost her favorite pearl necklace and was extremely sad. He offered a huge reward to anyone who found it. One day, a poor farmer saw the necklace in the nearby river and dived in to retrieve it in the hope of securing the reward.

However, no matter how hard he tried, the necklace was always out of his reach. He informed the king of his dilemma, so the king arrived with some of his best divers so that his daughter's necklace could be rescued. One by one, the king's divers jumped from the tree into the water, but each attempt failed. The king was visibly agitated that the necklace that would make his daughter happy was visible but not attainable. A stranger who sat under the tree, observing all the frantic commotion, called the king and said, "You are looking in the wrong place." The king did not understand the stranger. After all, he could see the necklace. "That is an illusion. The real necklace is somewhere else. Look above." The king did not appreciate the riddle, but thought about it and looked upward. There on the tree branch dangled the necklace. He realized that everyone was looking at the reflection of the necklace in the water and thought it was real. And so King Wagt learned that the world is full of illusions and thanked the stranger.

Most of us have been to a cemetery; death after all is certain. Many families like to put a phrase or message on the tombstone of their beloved. Some of the messages can be quite inspiring. One stone I came across had the word "IF" written on it. I could not understand what it meant, so I went close and in very small lettering the rest of the message read "I have another chance."

As long as we are caught up in this matrix of illusion and deception, we will end up thinking the night before death that perhaps, if we have another chance, we might live life differently.

When we get past our ignorance, the unseen way becomes

visible. I knew a man who was really obsessed with the stock market. He had a television and the only channel you would find turned on was the stock channel with all the ticker symbols. Day in and day out, he followed the stocks, the markets and the ticker as it scrolled across the screen. Years went by, and all day, that was all he watched. I visited him recently; his health was not so good anymore and the television was turned off. But when I looked at the television, I could see the stock channel images engraved on the screen. I turned on the television and surfed some channels, but the images of the stock channel were burnt into the screen. How many years would it take for that to happen? I asked myself. But more importantly, how many years of one's life passed in this pursuit?

Our life becomes like that TV screen; we are so absorbed in this one dimension, that after a while, it becomes ingrained in our minds, and that's all we see. Important moments in our lives, like quality time with family and the spiritual impulses that emerge from within, are always overshadowed. Think about it, and you will realize that we have all been there. We have a particular worry, and it stays with us when we go home to our family or out socially. Our mind remains consumed by the problem. We are there with our family, but our heart and mind are not because the stock channel is always on! The cliché, "Stop and smell the roses," really speaks to this because, in reality, we can never switch off the channel in order to appreciate the subtler things in life.

84th Floor—A woman lived on the 84th floor apartment. One summer, she went away on a vacation. When she returned, the elevators were not working. She was anxious to get into her apartment and was not willing to wait for them to get repaired. So she started to climb the stairs with two heavy suitcases. By the time she got to the 18th, floor her arms were fatigued and she decided to the leave the suitcases there, thinking she would come and pick them up again later. She continued to climb, and by the time she reached the 84th floor, she was completely exhausted and tired. She got to her place and reached for her keys and remembered that she had left them in the suitcases on the 18th floor! She was left with regret. The staircase represents our life. The keys to happiness and meaning in our life lie in the wisdom and practice of the invisible way. Each one of us has only so many years, and time does not allow us to go back and get the keys later.

The Poet Hafiz writes:

> Where is my ruined life and where the fame of
>   noble deeds?
> Look on my long drawn road and whence it came and
>   where it leads.

We live in a multidimensional world, and unless we overcome our own ignorance, the path to this multiplicity will never open up to us.

But how is that possible when we are so wired up? We get a cell phone or a pager and hook ourselves up to text messaging; laptops, voice messaging, email and the Internet. We plug our technology in the car, at home and the office, content to be plugged up because that important call or message is so important that we cannot afford to miss it. Impulses from the seen world are hardwired into our mind; unless we unplug ourselves, how can we open ourselves up to this unseen dimension?

There is a wise saying, "You cannot put two swords in the same sheath." As long as our illusions persist, our life is an imitation based on our conditioning. The challenge remains to become centered so that we are able to recognize what is real. By removing our illusions from the sheath, we create the space for reality to manifest. This is not easy. Unplugging ourselves is a tall order that requires a process that can free us from the ingrained conditioning, hence enabling us to look beyond the mist. For instance, when we lay to rest someone we love dearly into a grave, are we able to see life beyond the grief? When we see a loved one injected with the harshness of chemotherapy day in and day out, could we, for a moment, see better days ahead? When our life is surrounded by conflict and chaos, could we find hope in this darkness? And when the sun is shining and we are blessed with a loving family, could we imagine the gathering storm that sits around the corner, ready to throw our lives into turmoil and so mold our character?

What is life, anyway? Is it a tragedy? A comedy or just random confusion? Is what is happening in our life right now real, or are we about to be awakened from our slumber?

Do we ever wonder why the beautiful pearl is found in an ugly oyster shell at the bottom of the ocean? Why is precious gold found in veins on rocks miles below the earth's surface? And why are diamonds found hidden in coal inside the mountains? Does it occur to us that precious things are all hidden from our sight? So, too, are the unseen reality and the multitude of dimensions hidden. And so the question arises, where should we look for the treasure? The answer and the insights lie in the wisdom and the practice of the Invisible Way.

CHAPTER 2

Wisdom of the Invisible Way

What you are about to read may surprise you and even shock you. The Invisible Way is an ancient practice that has existed long before churches were built and cathedrals included stained glass windows; before the mosques and the beautiful minarets; and before the magnificent Hindu and Buddhist temples. Even as the great prophets and wise men of old walked the earth and their words were being recorded as scriptures, sacred texts and institutionalized as religions, their closest confidantes were being introduced to the Invisible Way. This unseen way was being practiced by the closest disciples of Krishna, Jesus, Buddha, Abraham, Moses, Mohamed and countless others who understood the wisdom that transcended all borders and barriers of religious dogma. It was the "way," the only way to go beyond the form into the very essence that enabled them to experience the secrets of the divine.

Through their personal quest, they had attained the realization that the divine energy that sustained and supported creation was manifest in their own heart. The real purpose of the enlightened souls was to awaken our consciousness to this. Buddha, for instance, who lived some five centuries prior to the birth of Jesus, was known as the "awakened one." If we were to go back further still and look at the revered figure of Abraham, the great prophet who lived some 2,000 years before the birth of Jesus, we would find that he, too, was "awakened" to the "inner dimensions."

"So also did we show Abraham the inner dimension of and metaphysical realities behind the heavens and the earth, that he might have certainty."

These great souls have left for us the sacred and timeless templates of the Invisible Way upon which they walked. What we learn from them is that, instead of accepting our fate, we can change it. We are empowered to change our circumstance, to discover our true destiny and attract into our life all the spiritual abundance happiness, love and fulfillment that money cannot buy.

The Inheritance—Peter was often seen at the homeless shelter lining up for a meal ticket. Most of his day was spent rummaging in the garbage bins of the downtown Calgary restaurants, looking for empty beer and pop cans, which he sold each day at the bottle depot. The few dollars he received came in handy to buy cigarettes and coffee. It was not an easy life; temperatures in winter sometimes dropped to minus 20. When he died, there was no one at his funeral except the local church priest and a few of the church volunteers. The priest, a friend of mine, showed me a letter they had found among Peter's belongings. It was a letter from a lawyer's office. The letter was notification that he had inherited quite a sum of money from the estate of his brother, who had never married. Peter had never collected his inheritance, most likely because he could not read.

Just think how different our lives will be at death. We have all inherited spiritual treasures beyond our wildest dreams, yet at the time of our death, will our inheritance remain sealed, too?

We are all struggling and striving each day to make ends meet, so busy, collecting "beer bottles and pop cans" to get by. How different would life have been for Peter if he had collected his inheritance? Our life can change; the greatest of all treasures has been left to us by the enlightened souls. Of course, we need to understand and interpret the divine language, but in this book, it is all done for you.

The Greatest Treasure—God sat on his throne after he had created the world. The angels gathered around him, in awe of his handiwork.

"Please share with us your knowledge of creation" the angels beseeched him.

"That knowledge I have bequeathed to the highest in creation," God responded.

"Who may that be if not us?" the angels inquired petulantly.

"The Human Beings," God answered.

"Why may that be?" the angels queried.

"Because I made them from my own breath," God answered, observing the puzzled look on their faces. "Where would you have me put the knowledge of everything?"

"Hide it under the ocean," replied one angel.

"No, it is too dark," God said, shaking his head.

"In the mountains, then," suggested another angel.

"No, it is not safe there," God responded. The angels fell silent. "I have hidden it in the human heart. It will be safe there. It will always be available. For in the heart is an Invisible Light that will illuminate the way to the knowledge of creation."

If there is one thing that is absolutely true, it is the perennial wisdom that the knowledge of everything exists inside each one of us. For us to go inward, we must first let go of all our preconceptions and unlearn all that we have been taught. The physical world has blinded our perceptions to the infinite possibilities that exist within.

We can see this is interwoven in the lives of two enlightened mystics, Hafiz and Saint John of the Cross, who have much in common. Hafiz was born a Muslim but chose to go beyond the boundaries Muslims jurists of the day set and became a Sufi. Sufism is one of the mystical dimensions of Islam, rooted in the esoteric wisdom of Ali, cousin brother and closest confidante of Mohamed, prophet of Islam. Sufism is a path of personal experience to the knowledge beyond the physical dimension. Hafiz was denounced and branded a libertine and was even denied a grave.

The essence of the Invisible Way was very evident in Hafiz's poetry. In his life, he had to endure great personal sacrifices and difficulties to go beyond the barriers established by his religion.

Mine enemies have persecuted me,
My love has turned
And fled from my door
God counts our tears
And knows our misery.

Today, the mystical poetry of this once ridiculed soul is found in most Persian homes. His "Divan" is canonized, and was the inspiration for European thinkers like Goethe.

Saint John of the Cross, on the other hand, was a Christian with a Jewish heritage. He, too, went beyond the religious dogma of Christianity, for which he endured much, including imprisonment. Today, this mystical soul is a saint and revered.

Both men had much in common, although they lived 200 years apart. They were both mystics who, through their personal search and inner development, experienced the real.

The following verse from Saint John's "The Spiritual Canticle" may describe the ethos of the Invisible Way.

Whither hast vanished
Beloved, and haste left me full of woe
And like the heart has sped
Wounding, ere thou didst go
Thy love, who follw'd
Crying high and low…

These great mystics refused to be limited and bound. Creating boundaries is, of course, a human pastime. We build districts, cities, countries, and cultures, then we create languages, rituals, codes and laws. We have imprisoned our own thoughts by our boundaries and lost sight of the essence. The mystics broke the boundaries and in the process discovered a world that existed beyond this world of repossession, a world in which they were empowered to co-create.

Hafiz writes in the Divan:

What is wrought in the forge of the living and life.
All things are nought! Ho!
Fill me the bowl
For nought is the gear of the world and the strife!
One passion has quickened the heart and the soul,

> The beloved's presence alone they have sought,
> Love at least exists. Yet if love were not,
> Heart and Soul would sink to the common lot,
> All things are nought!

The pearls of the Invisible Way have long come from the poetry of the mystics. This became the medium of choice to express their experiences and knowledge of the real, enabling them to go beyond the barriers of dogma in the most timeless way. In any case, those enlightened ones who tried openly to share the secrets of the Invisible Way were persecuted and often killed. We see this in the life of the great eighth-century mystic Mansur Al-Hallaj, a Sufi who preceded Hafiz. He talked about the divine nature of man and had the spiritual experience of the vision of god. In his poetry, Kitab Al-Tawasin, he wrote:

> I am he whom I love
> And the whom I love is I
> We are two spirits
> Dwelling in one body
> If thou seest me
> Thou seest him
> And if thou seest him
> Thou seest us both.

Mansur talked openly about our latent divinity, introducing the concepts of our dual nature, that is, physical and spiritual, and as a consequence he was imprisoned for 11 years and later killed. Legend has it that as Mansur's bleeding body was thrown into the water, the blood oozed out and formed words that read: Anal Haqq—I am the truth.

Therefore Hafiz writes:

> The image of water and clay (man) is an illusion
>   upon the road of life.

When reality manifested in his inner self, he was finally able to distinguish the illusion from the real. Let us take a closer look at why Hafiz calls our physical life an illusion.

As human beings, we exist within the perceptible and imperceptible, which are the seen and unseen worlds. There are laws in place that determine how both realms operate. As advanced as we are, most of our progress has been limited to the understanding of laws that operate in the seen or physical world. Through the tools of science, wise men and women such as Einstein, Newton and others, have over time, discovered the laws that operate within our physical world. The laws of gravity, aerodynamics, thermodynamics and relativity are examples. They permit us a deep understanding of our environment and enable us to progress. Without question, the knowledge of these laws is at the root of all our advancement. Since these scientific discoveries are validated by empirical observations and scientific experiment, contemporary scientists have been able to spring-board further research, thereby continuing the progression of our understanding. Scientific research, however, is conducted and understood predominantly through our five senses of touch, sight, sound, taste and hearing.

When we turn our attention to man's understanding of this imperceptible, unseen world, unfortunately we fall short. In fact, one could make the case that we have actually gone backward. The unhappiness, discontentment and conflict so prevalent in our modern and technologically advanced society speaks volumes of a civilization that just does not get it.

The unseen world, often referred to as the spiritual dimension, exists; that is no longer disputed, even by the most ardent of skeptics. In addition, there is a consensus that through the ages, prophets, sages, mystics, wise men and women have brought us knowledge of the laws of this spiritual dimension. Why, then, is there such a deficit in our understanding of spirituality and the spiritual laws that operate within the unseen realm?

There are two reasons that can explain this. First, the tools of science and the rational thought that enabled us to understand our physical environment are inadequate in helping us comprehend spirituality, largely because spiritual laws cannot be validated by empirical observations, nor proven with scientific experiments. Using science to understand spirituality would be like trying to catch the moon by reaching for its reflection in the water. As long as we remain fully intoxicated by our material existence, spiritual comprehension is impossible. Furthermore and regrettably, the contemporaries of the great prophets and sages of old have had much of their work marginalized because it does not stand up to science. This mystical knowledge brought to us by Rumi, Ibn-Araby, Attar, Saint John of the Cross, Teresa of Avila, Hafiz and many others are examples. We have a tendency to create a science out of everything. Just because it helped us discover planets and cures for diseases, it seems to have become a panacea for everything, and so we created this concept of spiritual science. This probably explains why so little progress has been made in understanding spirituality.

We are so advanced that we can travel to faraway planets and see stars that are invisible to the naked eye. Yet, what do we really know about ourselves? Not much. This is because spirituality is not just about knowledge, but also about attainment. Since much of this is practical in nature, the theory is a very small part. We can see that the esoteric dimensions introduced by Buddhism, Hinduism, Sufism and indeed all mystical paths, are all rooted in practice and personal experience, because practice always precedes the theory when it comes to attaining spiritual knowledge.

The second reason is that the five senses we are endowed with are incapable of grasping the spiritual reality. The spiritual dimension just cannot be understood through these faculties. Yet, it is now becoming increasingly accepted that we have faculties that go beyond these five senses. Only when we cultivate them do the possibilities open up for us to have perception of the unseen realm and insight into the laws that govern it. It is this knowledge of the spiritual laws that can empower us to progress spiritually. However, since this knowledge is founded essentially on personal experience, once again, it falls short of the scientific test of rational thought.

This is the paradox of our society. We know that the spiritual dimension exists and that it plays the larger part in fashioning our destiny, but because it cannot be measured and tested with our five senses, it is largely ignored, and all the while we are slowly being suffocated. Ironically, we know our shortcomings but choose to be imprisoned by them, like the alcoholic who knows the harm he is doing to himself and his family, but chooses to remain imprisoned. In all fairness, more and more people are looking for a way out of this quagmire, and the spiritual wisdom brought to us over the ages is finally gaining respect.

Rumi writes:

> The drunken man is he who sees that which is not:
> To whom what is really a piece of copper or iron
>   appears to be gold.

We are so intoxicated by our material world that we are unable to differentiate reality from illusion. As shocking as it may seem, knowledge exists of the sacred templates that govern our existence. Specifically, the blueprints of mankind's spiritual destiny collected over centuries of esoteric contemplation are now within our grasp. Yes, the truth, happiness and joy we long for are within reach, and all it takes is for us to cultivate our "other" senses—the ones that enable us to perceive the unseen.

The ancient sages and wisemen were able to cultivate their inner vision, open their third eye and experience the unseen realm. Their quest helped them to understand the laws that govern this spiritual dimension. Today, we do not need to retreat into the mountains or some monastery, sacrificing our whole life in search for the sacred truths. They did it and now we have it. We owe them a lot, least of all to use it; after all, the idea that humanity would benefit was their deep hope and aspiration.

> Wake up, come out of the stupor of ignorance and
>   do not be lead away by this vicious world.

As you can see, the Invisible Way is not some secret I have discovered, but an approach that has existed since the beginning of time. All I have done is identify the specific practices all the wise souls had in common and present them to you in such a way that they can be incorporated in our daily lives. You will learn these in the practice of the Invisible Way. The tools to open your inner vision and the empowerment to change your life from the inside out are now in your hands. But as we learned, this is a personal quest requiring practice. There are no magic buttons or shortcuts; either we accept our fate or seek to change it.

These practices are founded on five spiritual truths. These insights are not conjectures or theories; rather, they have all been validated by the greatest spiritual minds that have ever graced earth. (You will find this validation in the final chapter). These insights, in other words, are infallible.

A thorough understanding of these truths is very important because they will provide us with a context and backdrop to the practices of the Invisible Way, which will follow. It is here that I will introduce the actual practices, or a step-by-step guide on exactly what it is we must do and how we should do it in order for our inner senses to develop and for our third eye to open and discern the Invisible Way.

Ultimately, the conviction of this less-traveled path can only come when we practice it. I cannot emphasize that only personal practice will lead to attainment. No amount of understanding and knowledge of the subject will move you even one inch forward. It is practice that will develop your insights and enable your third eye to open. It is practice that will take you into the inner dimensions where the knowledge of everything lies. That is when you stop reading everyone else's book and start reading the only book that needs to be read—your own. And this lies within you!

CHAPTER 3

The First Insight

Everything in the Physical World Is Repossessed

The first insight of the Invisible Way explains that everything in the physical and material world will be repossessed. It is a principal that speaks to the temporary nature of the world we live in. We enter the world naked without possessions, and we leave at death in a similar way.

Sandwiched between our birth and death is an allotted time during which a certain amount of abundance comes into our life. This abundance takes many shapes and forms; our families, wealth, friendships, and opportunities are examples. However, problems, difficulties and disappointments also are abundances in disguise. As we begin each day by awakening and end each day with sleep, these abundances are either entering into our lives or leaving them. In other words, as new things are offered to us, other things are taken away and repossessed by the world.

Everything that comes into our life is exactly what we needed, although not necessarily what we wanted, because our wants are based on illusions we discussed in the first chapter. Irrespective of the labels we have assigned to the circumstances that come into our life, all that enters is an abundance that is designed to transform us.

This world is not a place of permanent settlement.
It is a passage, a road upon which we travel
toward eternity.

Every breath we take is another step toward the
    inevitable, death.
Yet within each breath lies also an invincible life
    springing forth from within,
Calling us to grow from every experience.

The situations that come into our life are measured exactly. There is a plan that is unfolding with an ultimate goal of pushing and prodding us to grow, learn and change. The fact is that everything around us is evolving toward perfection. The seed is evolving to become a tree, the caterpillar struggles to become a butterfly, and we are also evolving. It is these experiences that develop and transform us.

The Green Golf Balls—There was a man who seemed very concerned about his lazy teenage son. To motivate him to do better at school and perhaps go on to have a successful career, he promised his son a reward of his choice if he did well in his 11th grade class. The son seemed to be interested, and agreed on the condition that his father gave him whatever he asked and did not question him about his choices.

He went about changing his lazy habits and began to put some effort into his studies. The son did extremely well in the class and, as promised, the father asked him what reward he wished for himself. "I want a green golf ball," the son said, and the father, though baffled by the request, obliged.

The son entered grade 12, which represented a critical time for any student wishing to enter the university. The father offered the son a reward of his choice for each diploma the son aced. Once again, the son rose to the challenge. He did extremely well in six diplomas. The father was thrilled and asked the son what he wanted for each diploma. The son asked for 100 green golf balls for each diploma. Again, the father was inquisitive, but kept his promise and did not ask why he had requested this particular reward. He provided the son with 600 green golf balls.

The son entered the university and Father, sensing that his strategy was motivating his son to become academically successful, offered the son a similar reward of his choice for each successful

year completed. The son once again rose to the challenge and graduated. During each of his undergraduate years, he requested 1,000
green golf balls for his reward and the puzzled father provided it.

The son entered law school with a similar arrangement and
graduated with a law degree. His chosen reward was 10,000 green
golf balls.

The son, having finished his education, went off to work and
secured a good position with a local law firm. The father, in the
meantime, was continuing to be bothered with the requests of
thousands of green golf balls his son had made since high school.
One day, the father decided that, since the son was now working,
he would ask him why he had always requested green golf balls. So
he waited for his son to arrive home from work, but that day,
tragedy struck. While traveling home, his son got into a car accident. The family rushed to the hospital and learned that their son
would not make it from the injuries. As his son lay on the bed, close
to death, the father asked him, "Tell me son, why, why did you want
all the green golf balls?" The son looked at his dad and said, "Father,
I wanted the green golf balls because…." But before he could complete his sentence he died, taking the secret with him.

We spend our entire lives collecting things. Our lives are a
struggle, and each waking day is spent in the pursuit of material
things and consumer durables symbolized by the green golf balls.
Ownership of things motivates us to strive to collect. At death, we
leave all our green golf balls behind for others who also are caught
up in this illusion. The secret of why we sacrificed our lives to collect things that were left to others dies with us and all that remains
is the death certificate and in time, that, too, vanishes.

We are imprisoned in the world of repossession because our
overwhelming attachments to material things have turned us into
techno human beings. We live a life that is totally ignorant of our
real essence and in the process, we have become detached from it.
Just take a look at a bird in a cage the next time you see one. The
bird is safe; it is provided food and looked after, so it must be happy,
we assume. Technically, we can surmise that the bird is indeed
happy. But is it? It has wings, it can soar in freedom in the sky; yet

its wings are clipped and its destiny is denied. Furthermore, the bird has forgotten it can fly, and so it accepts its fate in the cage. Yes, technically the bird is happy.

Not long ago, we built robots so that they could perform tasks we programmed. The idea was to have them act and follow our instructions precisely and to accomplish job functions. Today, we have created technologies that are now turning us into the robots. Our individuality is being drowned in a world where we are being programmed to act, behave and respond in an exact way no matter which part of the world we live in. The world and our life in it has become clinical. We go to work in droves every morning, we complete our tasks and we come home. On the way home, we pick up our homogenized, processed and pre-packed foods, shrink wrapped in chemicals and preservatives. Two minutes in the microwave and dinner is now ready for the robot who is fed and greased. Then we sit in front of the television, and the mind is switched off so that we can be brainwashed by the messages. We are told what to buy, where to buy it, how to live and where to live, not to mention what to wear. All the values and rules of our consumer society are downloaded, auto programming is completed, and we sleep, ready for the next day. We are a robotic society conditioned to believe that bigger is better, more is a good thing and that we must tirelessly pursue these ideals at any cost. As members of the consumer society, we are told that it is our duty to strive to upgrade our homes, our cars, our vacations and our clothes, in the name of a higher standard of living. We push ourselves because we are under some illusion that it will bring us that cherished idea of happiness and peace, a purpose in our life.

So we acquired all these luxuries—the cars, homes and consumer durables—and we ate good foods and found pastimes that have given us gratification and watched movies about how others live and find happiness. We created computer games that enabled us to fantasize about ourselves as super heroes, sports personalities and rock stars. Our worldly attachments have indeed turned us into techno human beings because we are technically happy. We have everything we need at our fingertips and, just like the bird in the cage, it is assumed we are also happy. But are we? Technically we are. After all, we are the remote generation. One minute we are in an African jungle, the next we could be seeing a live feed of the aftermath of a terror attack. Click, and we have moved from the misery and pain of the victims to watching master chefs compete in the art of cuisine. Our lives are instant; everything happens in short sound bites as we surf the channels. If we have seen it on television, it has to be true. That is the world of repossession. Nothing is real, not even our lives! We pride ourselves on wearing clothes with other people's names on them because someone told us it is a designer label. We appear more interested in other people's lives than our own. Why else are we so preoccupied with soap operas and the meaningless lives led by Hollywood actors? What can they possibly teach us about ourselves? It seems we want to be anyone but our real self! We read books of their lives, are engrossed in their personal struggles and successes, we wear clothes with dead actors names and faces on them, but when are we going to be us? Do we even know that behind and beyond the world of repossession exists the real us?

There is a book hidden deep within us that tells the tale of our past, present and future. It is the only book that needs to be read, because it is the book about us. Most people will never read this most important book because they are caught up in the illusion of the world of repossession. This is a world where everyone is technically happy, a world where everything, including our dream, fades and disappears, living only regret and a lament, if only....

But what if there was a switch that enabled us to exit this world of repossession? What if we could change the channel of our existence and emerge into the realm of infinite possibilities? The enlightened souls who practiced the Invisible Way tell us this is our latent potential.

The Beautiful Maiden—There was a man who saw a beautiful maiden in the market place and instantly fell in love. For days on end, he patiently waited to catch a glimpse of her when she returned to the market. He had no thoughts other than of her, and felt alive only when he saw her. After two months, he had the courage to go up to her and express his undying love for her and showered her with praise. The woman interrupted the man's praises and said, "You are so kind, sir, but you know, my sister is just coming behind you and she is much prettier than me. I am sure you will find her even more beautiful." So the man turned around to look at the prettier sister. At that moment, the maiden smacked the man and said, "If I was the girl of your dreams, if you pledged your undying love to me, why is it that the minute I mentioned someone prettier than me, you turned around?"

This story is a metaphor about our life in the world of repossession. We spend our lives chasing dreams that disappear, only for us to replace them with more dreams. And no matter how many times life smacks us, we still do not get it because our habits are ingrained.

More than 14 centuries ago, Ali, considered the wellspring of Sufism and other esoteric traditions, wrote:

"Hear me once again that this world is perishable and destructible; its phases change quickly, often leaving nothing but sad lessons behind them. A proof of the mortality of everything in this world is the fact that there is destruction and decay everywhere. Calamities attack every one without missing a chance, and sorrows visit without allowing a single chance of escape. Here every lying being shall have to pass through the doors of death, every healthy person shall have visitations of disease and every happy individual shall have to face sorrows some time or the other. In its desire for destruction this world behaves like a glutton whose hunger is never satisfied or like a drunkard whose thirst is never quenched. Of sorrows and unrelenting severeness of this life, it is enough to visualize that those who amass wealth seldom enjoy it, those who build homes rarely live in them. They always leave this world in such a way that they cannot carry their wealth and property with them. The sharp, sudden and violent change of circumstances in life are sights to take lessons from. We find have-nots becoming so rich that they are envied and millionaires turning paupers overnight because of disappearance of wealth and visitation of affliction. What a place is it where neither death can be averted nor the past can be brought back?"

Fourteen hundred years later, we are still caught up in this matrix of repossession. Furthermore, we have surrendered control of our lives to doctors, psychiatrists, and psychologists who are supposed to help us make sense of it all. Of course when that fails, people often try to escape this illusion by taking drugs, alcohol and other feel good prescriptions, thereby replacing one illusion with yet another. We are preoccupied in trying to possess things that can never be owned, and as a consequence we are programmed to remain trapped in this inevitable unhappiness.

The King's Master—King Wagt visited a master and was very impressed by the wisdom he taught, so he attended as a student on a regular basis. One day, King Wagt approached his teacher and told him that he was awed by the quality of the master's wisdom and asked if there was anything he could do for the teacher in return, as his wealth was beyond measure. The teacher said that there was one thing the king could do for him. The king said he would oblige any requirement or wish. The teacher asked that the king not come to any classes any longer. The king was shocked at the request and asked what he had done for the teacher to wish this. The teacher explained that before the king joined the group, the students were focused inward in search for the Supreme Being in the hope that they might be graced by him. Now, the teacher explained, the students looked outwardly toward the king in the hope that he might grant them some gift. They were distracted by his presence because they hoped to receive a reward.

All of us are distracted by the rewards this world can offer us, and unless we banish the rich king from our minds, we will continue to be trapped in the world of repossession.

The seventh Dalai Lama said:

> Hundreds of stupid flies gather on a piece of rotten
>   meat enjoying they think a delicious feast
> This image fits with the song of the myriad of foolish
>   living beings
> Who seek happiness in superficial pleasures
> In countless ways they try
> Yet I have never seen them satisfied.

Two children were having a conversation. It had been raining all morning and the plans their mother had made to go to the zoo were about to be cancelled. "Please Mum, can you go talk to the weatherman?" one child asked. The mother seemed puzzled, "Why?" she asked. The child looked up to the mother and said, "I always see the weatherman on television and he tells us if it will be sunny or rainy. Just ask him to make it sunny; it will happen if he says!"

It is easy to sit back and be very amused at how little children see the world and how they could empower the weatherman to such a lofty status. Yet how would we feel if a couple of adults were having the same conversation? Would we still feel amused, or would we feel genuinely sorry at how misled they were? The fact is most adults do the same thing, and chances are, you do too! Think about it. All the weatherman did was to forecast something that might happen based on his understanding of science. How different is his forecast from the commercials that boast weight loss from eating certain products, or the promise of an improved swing using certain golf brands? The child reached his conclusions by watching television, but the questions to ask are, how different are our habits? Where do we get our information before we make our adult decisions?

Each and every day, we allow faceless and nameless people to influence the decisions we make because we have made them and their views so important. Just like the child, it is more than likely that we discovered these personalities through television and other marketing strategies they used to make themselves larger then life. The television ministries of Jim and Tammy Faye Baker, not to mention that of Jimmy Swaggart, are good examples of how anyone with good marketing savvy and a sweet tongue can catapult themselves into our lives and gain hero status. They preached the word of God, asked for money and contributions in his name and demanded that viewers live up to a moral and ethical standard, one to which they themselves could not measure up.

Nowhere is this dichotomy more apparent than in the area of self-improvement. We create demigods, allow them to influence every decision we make, and when we are frustrated and disillusioned, we turn on ourselves, seeking to improve our lives and find some meaning and happiness. Ironically, we repeat our mistakes and look at the weatherman again. Yes, the one who can tell us what habits we can incorporate into our lives, the magical steps we can take that will make the clouds and rain disappear so that the sun can fill our lives. More books are written about self-improvement than any other topic, it's big business. Who is the author of choice this year? We have seen him on TV, attended his seminars, and bought his tapes and book, all neatly stacked on a shelf where we have a collection dating back five years. Somehow, his or her message is different; this time the results are sure! "Ask the weatherman," said the child. "He will bring sunshine into our lives," and he can fix our life!

Finding happiness and meaning will continue to be illusive as long as we look to the "weatherman" to provide it. We can read all the books, listen to all the tapes and even follow all the sage advise, but at the end of the day, our life will continue to be what it is today, and change in it will prove to be temporary, snapping back like a stretched rubber band.

Imagine you are standing by a railway track. In the distance, you see the train approaching and before long, the train is right in front of you. You admire the sight, but soon the train is gone, faded into the distance. The train does not stop where you are sitting; it is programmed not to. This is exactly how the abundances come into our life. We see them coming, we can admire and even enjoy them for a while, but soon they leave us. Sometimes the abundance appears as a speeding train; we get a momentary glimpse and it is gone. Other times, it is like a slow freight train that lingers in our view longer.

We cannot stop these "trains" from arriving nor leaving; furthermore, what is arriving and leaving our lives right at this moment is something we have absolutely no control over. (However, we do have a measure of control over what arrives and leaves in the future).

As mentioned previously, whatever situations and circumstances, wealth or poverty, that enter our lives is exactly what we need. The important thing to remember is that everything that comes into our lives will eventually leave.

Our dilemma is that somewhere along the way, we forgot how it all works. We decided which abundances or approaching trains we liked and which ones we disliked. For instance, we would term landing a great job as good and losing a job as bad. In other words, not only have we already labeled everything, but we fight vigorously to win and hold onto the good and discard the bad. And when we are unable to do this, we are devastated, disappointed and feel a sense of failure and loss. We forget that the train does not stop, nor can we take it home. Abundance comes and leaves; this is the way it is programmed. Instead of enjoying the sights and blessings that enter our life, we stress ourselves by trying to hold onto them. And as long as we do this, we also are programmed to find disappointment.

In the world of repossession, life's phases can change very quickly. One day we could feel content with our life, and the next day, we could well be scratching our heads, wondering what happened. We can plan for a hundred years, but we need to awaken to the fact that we actually do not even know what will happen in the next few moments.

I remember the way the technology stocks were appreciating during the NASDAQ Bull Run. I had a client who had about a million dollars that I managed on his behalf and had it allocated very conservatively because I knew that he was nearing his retirement years. One day, his banker introduced him to their investment brokerage department and convinced him of the tremendous profits that could be made in technology stocks. He had a new dream, and his investments, which were appreciating at 8 percent, were no longer adequate. Like so many others, his portfolio was caught up in the "tech wreck" and he ended up deferring his retirement. Life rarely gives us what we want, but it will definitely give us what we need. I remember reading a story in the paper about Prince Charles. As a young man decades ago, he attended a private school for the rich and wealthy. At the school, he had a friend,

Clive Harold, who was also from a rich family. After school, Prince Charles' rich friend became a very successful businessman who had everything: a wife, children, status and untold wealth. But when Prince Charles was touring a homeless shelter some years later, he saw his school friend again. The man had lost everything, his wealth and family, and was now homeless.

The story of King Midas tells us how this king loved gold above all things and wished that everything he touched be turned into gold. One day, his wish was granted and he found great satisfaction into turning worldly things into gold. But one day he sat to eat a meal and found his food turned to gold. Later still, tragedy struck as he turned his beloved daughter into gold. Everyone wants possessions without realizing it is the possessions that possess us.

People often think life has no value because all of their financial plans and other goals were unfulfilled. Why would I be worthless tomorrow if I lost all my possessions and my dreams are unfulfilled? Am I a lesser person? If I gave you a $100 bill, you would acknowledge its value straight away. But what if I crumpled the bill, threw it in a muddy pool and than gave it to you all wrinkled and dirty? Is that note still worth a hundred bucks or is it worth less? Of course it is still worth $100. Similarly, no matter what life may do to us in the world of repossession, each one of us is very precious regardless of what we attain materially. We can only discover our real value when we look beyond this temporal existence. Now we could just as well go through life as if this temporal world and our self-importance in it were all there was, but sooner or later, the world of repossession would leave its mark on us.

Kheir, a Sufi poet who lived in the ninth century, wrote:
> Be humble
> Only fools take pride in their station here
> Trapped in a cage of dust, moisture, heat and air
> No need to complain of calamities
> This illusion of life lasts but a moment.

As a young kid growing up in England, my favorite band was the Beatles. When you look at how their music evolved over time, it is easy to see their personal transition from the world of repossession. In one of their earlier songs, they sang about how the best things in life are free; however, what they wanted was money. Ironically, the song the Beatles recorded together after John Lennon's death was titled "Free as a Bird" and George Harrison's legacy was that fabulous album titled "All Things Must Pass."

In the world of repossession, all things do indeed pass.

Think and reflect on how our life is built on owning the things of this world, everything from homes to automobiles. Everyone is advised to write a will and create an estate plan, so we do. A major part of any will is an estate plan. Perhaps we should stop and wonder what an estate plan is. It is a list of things that we spent a lifetime collecting, which we are leaving behind for others to benefit from after we die. All the abundances that come into our life will ultimately be repossessed.

The Ashtavakra Gita states:

> Look upon friends, possessions, wealth, mansions,
> wives, gifts and other good fortune as a dream or a
> magic show lasting only a few days.

The next time you visit a cemetery or pass by one, think of all the people who are buried there. Ask yourself what happened to their cars, homes, possessions, investments and even family. Everything was repossessed, that's how it all works. Even the things we have in our lives right now belonged to someone else before us.

Looking for the Camel—King Wagt, whose spiritual senses were aroused by a stranger's wisdom, went upstairs to his beautiful roof garden to find God. Once again, the stranger appeared and called out, "I am looking for my camel; have you seen my camel?" The king was rather agitated by the intrusion and responded, "This is the roof of my palace, and you must be stupid. Why would you look for a camel here?" To this, the stranger replied, "No more stupid than you, looking for God on your roof." The stranger disappeared.

The world of repossession is deceiving. It's the wrong place to find anything, especially truth. This does not exist in the outer, tangible world but occupies a sacred space inside. The place to look is inward and the way is invisible.

What if we were able to determine the abundances that came into our life? What if we could cherish the blessings that entered our lives? What if we could see the sunrise in every sunset, the rainbow in every rainfall? The practices of the Invisible Way will free you from the world of repossession and empower you to create the life you want, starting from the inside out.

CHAPTER 4

The Second Insight

*We are Spiritual Beings in the Midst of a
Temporary Human Experience*

The date November 11, 1979 will forever remain etched in my
memory. On that day, I was blessed with an important piece of the
jigsaw puzzle, one which took my personal quest in a completely
new direction, "inwards."

That morning, I sat in rapt meditation in what had become a
routine start to my day. My mind seemed unusually calm and subdued. Still waters run deep they say, and indeed, deep within me,
I felt a tremor that shook me. I sat and did not allow myself to be
disturbed from my meditative state. I felt myself rise and float; I
offered no resistance and the next moment, I saw a limp body in
front of me. I looked closely and saw that it was me! How ugly I
thought, and if I am here, what is that body? I wondered how I
could move if my body sat on the bed, how could I see if my eyes
were there in front of me and how could I breath without the me
I saw on the bed. Looking around, I saw my room and at first
everything appeared the way it should be, but I felt very sensual
and noticed that something was different. The walls and other
images of form were vivid and animated because I was floating
straight through them. I was confused, and a momentary fear
gripped me. I drifted further through the ceiling and out into a glo-
rious openness where that fear melted into a sublime sense of
security. I felt so free, yet invisibly connected to some divine pres-

ence. I knew where I was, though no words were heard or spoken. I knew that I was not alone, yet could see no one. A warm breeze rubbed against my face, and I rose higher and higher above earth where the sun, moon and the stars lived in a harmonious existence seemingly connected to my presence. They knew me and danced with joy. I felt a tranquil affinity with them and shared their joy and laughed with them as a little child would when gently tickled. The awe and wonderment had hardly sunk in and I was drawn back, against my will, into that lump of clay I used to consider me. I tried to resist, but was powerless as an invisible force gently pulled me into my physical body. I opened my eyes and felt calmness within, the likes of which I had never known, and tried very hard to hang on to it for as long as I could. I realized that life would never be the same again. My real journey had just begun, finally.

One thing I have learned after decades traversing the Invisible Way is that one should always minimize discussion of personal experiences and attainment. This is because these experiences are blessed moments fashioned to speak to us at our own level and capacity, often in personalized symbols and metaphors. Sharing and discussing such experiences indiscriminately can only lead to misinterpretation, confusion and may even lead to negative consequences, which I will discuss later in the book. I have made an exception to this general rule for three reasons. I wish the readers to become aware at the outset that the knowledge of the Invisible Way found in this book is rooted in practice. This is particularly important because in the spiritual quest, practice is everything; practice always precedes theory, unlike science, where theories are the backbone of practical application. Secondly, the particular experience I have shared with you is generally considered to be an early signpost of progress along the Invisible Way. Furthermore, it is an experience that is unambiguous and one readers are likely to be familiar with, as near-death and out-of-body experiences are commonly written about by numerous writers. One that was thrust into the mainstream by Shirley Maclaine's best-selling book and movie, *Out on a Limb*. As the world hungers for meaning and spiritual understanding, such experiences are no longer treated as figments of people's imagination, but as serious encounters between man and his real self.

It is, however, important to keep a context for the experiences Shirley Maclaine, myself and others have discussed. In the vast, expansive world of spirituality, such experiences are mere breadcrumbs. For the seeker there awaits an infinity of majesty, splendor and grace, not to mention an intimate encounter with the self and the divine origin, which cannot be communicated with words. Finally, it lays a firm and solid foundation for the second insight that, "We are spiritual beings in the midst of a temporary human experience."

I must add that all personal experiences are accompanied by knowledge and wisdom of the Invisible Way. This spiritual knowledge is what can and must be shared as we have seen in the examples of the wise souls, whose legacy is the wisdom they left behind, sometimes at a very high personal cost. Therefore, I will refrain from focusing on specific experiences and share with you the depth of the spiritual understanding that I could extract from them and from that of those great masters of old.

We are spiritual beings, and our spiritual personalities are represented by the soul in each one of us. Different mystical traditions have assigned different names to this personality, like, the spirit, Ruh, Athma. In this book, I will be using "Soul" to describe our spiritual personality.

Paul Brunton in his book, *The Quest of the Over Self*, explains
In other words, the real man himself, the soul if one wishes to call it such is emphatically not his body.

Our human body cannot exist without the soul. In fact, without the soul, the human body is worth less than an animal. It is the soul that makes us what we are and gives us life. The human body is just a vehicle through which the soul can journey into the physical dimension of time and space. When we take a closer look at the word "spiritual," we see it is from the word *spiritus*, meaning that which gives life or the breath of life. Hence, it is a word that refers to the very essence of that which brings meaning to life.

As the mystical poet Khusraw writes:
> Your body was a shirt
> But for your soul
> Now see its fabric
> Torn and worn out, look.

The origin of our soul is the spiritual realm. In fact, everything in the physical world has its origins in the spiritual world. All of us, before we manifested as physical beings, had an existence as beings in the spiritual realm. However, much more relevant is the understanding that it is also our destination. "We return from whence we came."

When we look at the word religion, it comes from the Latin word *religre*, meaning back to the origin. Man's religion, though often misinterpreted and misused, is rooted in humanity's noble quest to find its origin.

What becomes obvious is that the soul is not physical in nature, neither will it die when our body does. In other words, our soul will outlive our physical death. This than brings us to spirituality 101: Our soul is our real self.

There is a dimension that exists beyond the physical world we can touch and see; it is a realm where time does not exist. We can call this the spiritual realm because it is real and permanent. The human being is made of two substances: the form and essence. The essence is the real self of the human being; it is spiritual, timeless and eternal. The form is the physical human body, temporary in nature and alive only because this soul exists within it. The death of the human is simply the separation of the soul from the physical body. The entrance of the soul into the body is called birth and its exit is called death. This allows the transition from one state of being to another. Therefore, death becomes a gateway to the higher states of existence. This is why the ancient Sufis describe experiences that enable the soul to temporarily leave the human body as "die before you die." Similarly, the spiritual realm is the essence, whereas the physical creation is the form. The essence of our physical lives is rooted in our spiritual lives, and the foundation of physical creation is the spiritual one.

The Baby and the Mask—A baby was born, and from the time of her birth, a mask was placed on her face. She grew up seeing the world through the mask, but also seeing her image portrayed by the mask. One day, the mask came off, the world looked different, and in the reflection of the mirror, she looked different. She saw herself and knew that this peasant girl was indeed a queen.

From the time we are born, a mask is put on our faces, too—the mask of society. We are conditioned to the norms and prejudices of the time, and boundaries and limits are established and we are encouraged to conform. Society has created a picture of what is and how things are and that is the world we see through our mask. We never stop to question these limits and boundaries, and if we do, we are marginalized and ridiculed.

One person is a farmer; the other is a doctor. Then there is the policeman and the fireman, or a wife who chooses to be a mother. Is that what we really are? A name, a title, a job?

"Son, you can grow up and be a doctor or a dentist," we tell our children. Did we live a life of 40 to 50 years just for this? Is it not ironic that, as human beings, we have made so many advances in science, medicine and technology, we can even walk on the moon, but we still know very little about who we really are?

As long as we look at the world through a mask, how will we ever see and experience the real picture? Sometimes people have after-death experiences, while others find epiphany in the tragedy they face. These are just those moments when the mask accidentally came off, but most people are simply content to live their lives with the mask on. Death, which is part of our perishable world of repossession, will ultimately remove the mask and disclose to us our real self and true origin. If you travel the Invisible Way, it is because you consider life very precious and believe that it exists so that it can be used to remove the mask now rather than at death or by some accident. We all have this one opportunity to discover our destiny and live a life of real meaning and fulfillment, regardless of our profession and career.

Have you ever wondered what happens after we die? This body we see in the mirror, is that it? Will everything that we are simply disappear into darkness while our limbs are buried or cremated, or is there a part of us that transcends this ordeal? Have you wondered why the act of throwing mud at someone, considered insulting while they are alive, becomes a sacred ritual when they are dead? The real self within us is not physical, but spiritual, and hence is not subject to the physical laws of creation. There is a part of us that lives beyond death. We are spiritual beings; our physical experience is a very small part of the whole picture, yet we live as if this is all there is. If we want to make our temporary human experience worthwhile and meaningful, then we have need to understand and connect with our real self and remove the mask.

Let us take a closer look at our real self, the soul within. It is made of the same substance as that which created it; in other words, our soul, being spiritual in nature, is made of the same substance as the creator, God.

The mystic Bistami writes:

> I thought that I had arrived at the very throne of
>   God and I said to it,
> "O throne, they tell us that God rests upon thee."
> "O Bayzid," replied the throne
> "We are told here that he dwells in a humble heart."

The soul within us is the life energy that makes life possible and death inevitable when it is absent. This is why all births come with a label: "Discard the body after use." Death, too, has a label: "Discard the body and continue." In the same way that we start each day by putting clothes on our naked bodies, only to discard these clothes later, this world and our physical body is a garment for the soul which will be discarded, but the journey and life of the real self, the soul in us, continues.

Now you might start to ask a lot of questions that go beyond what you may be accustomed to. In addition, you might ask, where was "I" prior to manifesting in this physical form? In other words, what is the journey of the soul? Let us explore this.

We live in a world where there is the creator and there is creation. It is the creator that is the source of all life. Therefore, anything that is alive must have an aspect of the creator in it, otherwise it cannot be alive. Because our soul is the microcosm of the macrocosm, it has a spark of the divine and consequently, the latent potential to be divine. This is what the mystic Mansur Hallaj experienced when he proclaimed, "I am the truth." Let me give you an analogy. Human birth begins as a sperm in the womb of the mother and therefore, this sperm is a human being in potential. The embryo evolves through various stages of development until it emerges into the world as a human being. Similarly, the soul seed enters the physical world, which is its womb, divine in potential. It progresses through different stages, minerals to plants to animals and finally into human. When the soul reaches perfection, it is divine and merges with the macrocosm. Sufis call this *Fana Fillah*, the annihilation of the self in God.

Imagine water evaporating from the ocean, becoming a cloud, turning into raindrops which have an apparent, distinct identity. Ultimately, the raindrop falls, returning to the ocean and becoming one with it, and in the process, each loses its identity and separateness. Similarly, our souls have come from the universal soul. The physical world is the womb, which provides the soul with the opportunity to develop and finally return to its origin. Consequently, it becomes obvious that we are spiritual beings in the midst of a very temporary human encounter. It should not escape us that we are spiritual beings now. This does not happen after we die, and our spiritual journey is also now, regardless of whether we are aware of it.

Rumi, a master of the Invisible Way, describes his experience in this well-known verse.

> I died as a mineral and became a plant
> I died as a plant and turned to animal
> I died as animal and became man
> What fear I, then, as I cannot diminish by dying
> Once when I die as a human, I'll become an angel and
>   I shall give up angelhood
> For not-being, Adam, calls with an organ like voice
> "Verily we are his, and unto him is our return."

In the world of repossession, everyone is focused on our

worldly life and physical journey, where we spend all our precious time trying to understand and find meaning, oblivious to the fact that the real journey that needs understanding is the journey of the soul. Relatively, since physical life is very finite and limited, whereas our spiritual life is infinite, it should be obvious that our spiritual life is the real and permanent one and our physical life is the shadow and temporary. Therefore, the life experiences we need to focus on are those that care for the soul, those that enable our soul to continue its development to perfection and ultimate annihilation, when the subject merges with the object.

Jesus, who left us so much wisdom on the care of the soul, pointed the way when he said: "Neglect not the gift that is in thee."

Khusraw the Persian poet wrote:

> Your body was the shirt but for your soul
> Now see its fabric torn and worn out, look,
> Open your eyes from sleep,
> From senseless sleep,
> And seek yourself and find yourself my friend

The Builder—John was a house builder by trade. He worked for a local construction company and was very thorough in his work. His supervisors were very pleased with John's work ethic because he gave every job his best effort and never cut corners, always taking pride in his work. He was never lazy and earned his pay. At the end of each day, John enjoyed going home to his wife and children and tried to be a good husband and father. John had been with the company 25 years and one day, his boss approached him with a special assignment. He was told that there was another house that needed to be built for a very important client and, since the scheduling did not allow constructing this house during the normal business hours, they requested that he build this house for the special client after work and on weekends. This bothered John a lot because it would mean less time with his family. He was also expected to do this without extra pay. With a sense of loyalty, John did his master's bidding and began work on building the house. However, because of his resentment, his heart was never in the job. He cut corners, took little pride and always rushed so that he could return home. The house was completed, but it was not up to his usual standards. John informed his boss of this and handed him the keys, glad that it was done so that he could return to his normal life. Two weeks later, his bosses called him into their office and informed him that they were very grateful for his dedication to the company and gave him a set of keys as a gift. He looked at them and realized that the gift they gave him was the very house he had built for the special client!

Of course John had regrets; if he had known that he was building a house for himself, he would not have cut corners and would have put more effort and love in his work.

Caring for our soul is what we do while we are busy living a life and fulfilling our responsibilities. Being spiritual is not a goal that we put off for the future because we are spiritual now. We often choose to cut corners and put off doing the very things that are most meaningful, caring and nurturing to the soul, which is the only thing that remains after everything that was so precious to us, including our families, is repossessed.

And while we are busy doing whatever it is that we are doing, our soul by its very nature is on a journey toward enlightenment. Everything we do or don't do is affecting that journey negatively or positively. Just like a bud that used to be a seed but is now going to blossom into a flower, or the embryo that was a sperm and will be born as a baby, our soul had previous stages and is evolving toward perfection. All the experiences that come into our life are attracted to it in equal measure to enable the soul to continue its development from the potential to actual.

We are spiritual beings in the midst of a temporary human experience. Unfortunately, we live completely opposite. Imagine you just came onto earth for the first time and that you have not seen a single creature. Suddenly, you see circling around you on the floor what seems like a black flying bird. You can see its form and its shape and you start to chase it without success. Quite rightly, you will conclude you have seen this black bird creature. In the absence of seeing a real bird or a recollection, how could you even know what you saw was indeed just a shadow whose existence is completely dependent on a real bird that has a form and identity of its own. The fact is you will convince yourself that you saw a bird, even though in reality, you did not because we are prisoners of our senses. Similarly, we are spiritual beings who have an existence and an identity and our physical bodies are a shadow that cannot exist without that identity. Our physical bodies also depend on this spiritual form and cannot exist independently. Just like the shadow of the bird that will disappear as soon as darkness falls, our physical bodies, too, will disappear.

The Monkey and the Jar—There was a hunter who was asked to capture live monkeys in a certain jungle. As we all know, monkeys are not the easiest animals to catch as they come in groups and climb trees faster than they can be caught. However, the hunter returned from work with the required number of monkeys. People were astonished that he had been able to complete this task so quickly and asked for his secret. He explained that it is always easy to tempt the monkey with his favorite food. The hunter found out that a certain berry was the favorite of the monkeys of that forest. He tied some bottles on a string and put a few berries in them and waited. The monkeys descended from the trees and were attracted to the berries. They were able to put their hand inside the bottle; however, once they closed their hand around the berry, they were not able to pull their hand out of the bottle. The closed fist trapped the monkey's hand inside the bottle and the only way the monkey could escape was to open the hand and let go of the berry. But the hunter knew that the monkeys liked the berries so much that they would not let go! This way, he was able to catch as many monkeys as he desired. He allowed the monkeys' attachment to the berries to trap them.

This beautiful story is a metaphor for the plight of human beings. We have allowed our attachments to worldly desires to trap us. Take a look around you, and you will find that each one of us has found our favorite berry, and just like the monkey, we are not prepared to let go. Our physical life is built on the need to fulfill our desires, and society has evolved to assist us in this pursuit. For some, owning a nice home, a car or other physical possession represents these desires, and for others, it may be a relationship or a life partner. Others find the fulfillment of desires in gambling, becoming intoxicated or changing the way they look. We live in a world of instant happiness; society is geared to ensure that whatever your desires, they can be fulfilled and available instantly.

Hundreds of lenders will lend us instant cash so that we could own our dream home and drive the car we always wanted now. Liquor stores are open 24 hours for our pleasure, as are massage parlors and red light districts. The classifieds boast huge dating agencies, not to mention the information we can download on the foreign brides who can be mail ordered. We have built huge gambling cities, and plastic surgeons stand by to give you a tummy tuck or a new face. It's the Pleasure Island of *Pinocchio*, a land where we no longer have to struggle and strive for the things we want, because they are available now, by dialing a toll free number or clicking the mouse. We have our fist tightly closed around these readily available favorites, and in the process, it is we who are trapped. We are so attached to materialism, that it has imprisoned us. It can be said that attachments and desires are the root of all suffering and until we let go, we will never experience the freedom to discover the beauty and truth that lies beyond.

Letting go does not mean giving up our material comforts and escaping into a monastery. Being spiritual does not require that we abstain from enjoying life and wealth; rather, it is a way of living that incorporates three principles.

First, we are spiritual beings and the abundances that come into our lives come for a reason; it's all right to enjoy these gifts, but we should not lose sight of who we are. Second, don't be greedy. Share a part of your abundance, for the only part that is really kept is that part which is given away. Finally, always remember that we are just traveling through this place called earth. Don't get too attached to the blessing and abundances that enter your life nor gauge your success or failure by their presence. Always remember we can never own any of these abundances; just use them for a time and feel blessed.

The Buddha said:
> Not in the sky, not in the midst of the sea,
> Not if we enter into the cliffs of the mountains
> Is there known a spot in the whole world where
> Death could not over come the mortal.

Of course, the problem is that we live our lives as if we are physical beings who have occasional spiritual encounters. The moments of soul-searching we confront during personal problems are indeed the whispers of the real self, calling out to us to discover our real essence. Those may indeed be difficult and troubling times for us, but it is the depths of these emotions that pry open the doors to the inner path. We have become so attached to the physical world of the five senses, that we go out of our way to obscure that inner voice. It is always easier to drown ourself with alcohol or drugs than follow those deep feelings to their core. We are just not willing to detach ourselves from the physical world. Like the monkey, freedom is really about letting go, but instead, we are snared up in this illusory world. Emotions that come from strife are almost always deeper, which is why it is easier to have tears of sadness than of happiness. The fact is, as long as we live just as physical beings, we are really choosing to live a life that has a sad ending written all over it. Why? Because that's not who we are, and the inevitable time of reckoning will arrive when we will discover that what we saw in the mirror was indeed only a reflection of the real, a shadow, so to speak.

The next time you plan a vacation to some sunny hotspot in the hope that it will help you out of your malaise, or go on a shopping spree because you feel down, consider waiting a couple of weeks. If you do go, you will find that you escaped and felt temporarily gratified, but soon you returned to the same old rut with a lighter wallet, only to try something else. Each attempt is designed to disappoint us until we reach the end of our allotted time on earth, only to look back at the trail of disappointments and the wreckage that was our life. This is when all the things we collected and strived to own because we thought they would bring us happiness is passed on to someone else. The title on the home, family car and investment certificates are changed, and all memories of our existence slowly vanish like a portrait thrown into a bonfire. If we live our lives impervious to the fact that its existence depends on the spiritual being within, then it is just a technical happiness guaranteed to reveal itself as such in the ultimate betrayal. Just look at where you live right now. Through history, there have been countless people who have lived in that exact space and whose aspirations were likely no different to yours. Plato once said, "This is the great error of our day, that physicians separate the inner being from the body."

The Stranger—King Wagt walked through his palace admiring his beautiful hallways and the mass of gold and precious stones that illuminated them. The stranger appeared again. The king was disturbed. "Who are you and what are you doing here," the king asked.

"I have just come to check into this hotel for a night as I was passing through," the stranger replied.

The king was visibly insulted. "This is no hotel, you fool. This is my palace"

"Who lived in this palace before you?" he asked the king.

"My father," the king replied.

"And before him?" the stranger asked.

"My uncle," the king said.

"And before him?" the stranger asked.

"His father," replied the somewhat agitated king.

"So it is a hotel. People have checked in and checked out." With those words, the stranger disappeared, leaving the king to contemplate the wisdom.

Life is indeed like a hotel. We check in and we check out and nothing we strived to collect or own goes with us except that which we give away.

The mystic Rumi writes:

> Generations and generations have gone.
> But these divine attributes are permanent and
>   everlasting.
> The water in this channel has been changed many times;
> The reflection of the moon and stars remain unaltered.

Our life passes, and so does time, but the soul remains. If you have sat in a car at a traffic light, you may have felt your car was moving, when in reality, it was the car in the other lane. Similarly, during our life, we see passing landscapes through the evolving of time, which we segment into days, months and years. However, since our physical life is such a minute part of our soul life, spiritually we are actually standing still as time moves. In other words, although we are under the impression that our life is really moving, actually it is not.

What becomes clear is that the care of the soul becomes the primary purpose of our life, and as I mentioned earlier, it's all about the soul. The soul is the reason we are alive and not a lump of clay. It is the seed of everything, and the circumstances that enter into our life enable it to evolve into perfection.

The dimension beyond the world of repossession can only be experienced and understood by our real self, which is empowered as a consequence of its latent divinity to create for itself the life it wants. Caring for the soul is about empowering ourselves to become the co-creators of our life. Our existence commenced in the ether where there is no concept of time and space; it was a world of infinity. When our soul is allowed to enter the physical realm into a human body, the human form becomes alive, just as a toy does when a battery is inserted into it.

Each soul on its entry into this physical space is given a "Vardan," or a promise of allotted time in this realm. In other words, the exact time period of our physical life is predetermined. This time period is set on the basis of the number of spiritual breaths. At the conclusion of the allotted breaths, physical death occurs and the soul returns to the spiritual realm having kept its "Vardan," its promise of return. It may be hard to accept for us being so advanced scientifically that the timing of our death is predetermined. (Under certain circumstances, this preordained death can be altered, and discussion of that subject may take me beyond the nature of this book). However, when we examine the countless accounts of individuals' death experiences, we find a common thread. Even though they had left their bodies and were quite happy to continue to move toward the divine light, in most cases they are informed that it is not time yet. There is a higher law at work that determines the time of return for every soul.

As humans, we are preoccupied to find ways to prolong death and we mistakenly believe that we can do this through medication and physical activities. The only affect food, medication and lifestyle has is on our health, but not on death. A person who smokes all his life will die exactly on the day the promise of the soul to return is met. Of course, it could be that the last few years of his life may see him in a wheelchair with iron lungs or a respirator, because it was his choice to put toxins in the body. Similarly, a person who is careful about health and works out will likely enjoy a better quality of life. Death itself, however, is predetermined. This is a spiritual principle, and one needs to be mindful because there are other complexities at work that may change this general principle. One of those is the impact of karma through the exercise of our freewill, which I will discuss later in the book. Our death can be changed—it can be shortened or prolonged simply because we are empowered to make choices—but it's a dangerous and slippery slope, as you will see in chapter seven.

Ali writes:
> Every breath that you take is a step you put forward
> toward death
> Everyone who is born has to die and once dead he
> is as good
> As he had never come into existence.

I understand that we can come up with numerous arguments in debating this issue. All I can tell you is that spiritual laws that exist in the ether are the foundation of what transpires here in the temporary physical realm. As I mentioned, the "Vardan," or promised return of the soul measured in the allotted spiritual breaths, can be altered, thereby extending or shortening our human life. But that cannot be done here in the physical and temporal realm which, in the context of creation, is the shadow.

Din's Death—There was a man named Din and, upon meeting an enlightened soul, he was informed that his death was written for the third day of the month. Din decided that he would leave town and travel to Samarkand to avoid the angel of death. On the second of the month the angel of death visited the city where the enlightened soul resided. In a conversation with him, the enlightened soul asked, "Have you come for Din?" The angel of death looked at his list and said, "No, I am not supposed to pick him up from this city. According to my list, I am picking him up from Samark and tomorrow!"

Our soul's entry and exit from this physical world of repossession is measured by the number of spiritual breaths that are allotted to each person. The spiritual breaths convert to physical time in our material dimension. As a consequence, time works backward. We are given our full allocation of time at birth and it then starts counting backward until it reaches zero, at which time the promise of the return (Vardan) is completed and the being in the black coat comes to fetch us. It is very similar to the New Year countdown from 20 to zero, at which point we exit one year and ring in the new. Our allotted time is counted down in a similar fashion, at which time our soul exits the physical realm and enters the spiritual one.

Rumi writes:

> Everything you see has its roots in the unseen world
> The forms may change, yet the essence remains
>   the same
> Every wonderful sight will vanish
> Every sweet word will fade
> But do not be disheartened
> The source they come from is eternal
> Growing, branching out, giving new life and joy
> Why do you weep
> The source is within you

Time is the most precious thing we have and in each moment, it is being counted down and repossessed. It's a gift we can use to empower our real self, and it is in this endeavor that our destiny is fulfilled. Yet most of us make a living out of wasting time. We sleep too much and what we do not use in earning a livelihood is wasted in escapism, movies, soap operas, video games and television. These are useless endeavors in the grand scheme of things simply because they run down the clock.

Khusraw—The Persian poet writes:

O you who have been sleeping at night

If you have rested

Do not think that time too has been resting

The Adept and the Master—A man, hearing the impulses of his inner self, visited the Sufi master for the master's advice. "I feel this prompting from within, how do I satisfy it?" he asked the sage.

"Listen to it," the Sufi master responded.

"With my responsibilities to the family and work, I don't have time," the man replied.

Just then an old man passed by carrying a heavy suitcase. "Why don't you help him with his heavy load?" the Sufi master suggested.

The adept obliged and carried the bags for the old man until they reached the old man's home. Having accomplished his task, he returned to the Sufi master who asked him: "What did you see?"

The adept did not have any answer; in fact, he seemed a little confused by the question.

"Go back to the old man, and don't return until you can tell me what you saw."

Reluctantly, the adept went back to visit the old man. He sat with him, trying to seek the answer to the question the sage had asked. Afraid to go back without an answer, he sat with the old man for hours. Finally, the old man stood up and, since his sight was very weak, he came close to the adept to thank him for his help. The adept looked into the old man's eyes and responded in kind, and just at that moment, he knew the answer. He returned to the Sufi master, who asked him once again, "What did you see?" The adept replied, "I saw myself."

The Sufi master was pleased with the answer and said, "My friend, the gap between you and that frail old man is measured in time. Use it wisely." Upon hearing this, and no longer able to get the image of the frail, old, wrinkled man from his mind, the adept changed his ways.

We are spiritual beings; we have a body where there is a sacred space, and within it is our real self, the soul which is the microcosm of the divine. We have time now during our very short physical encounter to realize this. What, then, should we do with this time? It is ours to use to assist our real self in reaching its potential, and in this is the awakening of our divinity. Caring for the soul is the starting point in this worthy endeavor.

The late Aga Khan the Third in his memoirs writes:

> Man must never ignore and leave untended and
> undeveloped that spark of the divine which is in
> him. The way to personal fulfillment, to individual
> reconciliation with the universe that is about us,
> is comparatively easy for anyone who firmly and
> sincerely believes as I do, that divine grace has given
> man in his own heart the possibilities of illumination
> and of union with reality.

Aware that time was a thief, great mystics expressed diligence, constancy of purpose and made untold sacrifices to develop the divine spark within and experience reality. Rabia the Mystic attained great spiritual heights and, as she writes, it came from making the spiritual quest her most important purpose.

> I am fully qualified to work as a doorkeeper
> For this reason, what is inside of me I do not let out:
> What is outside of me, I do not let in.
> If someone comes in, he goes right out again.
> He has nothing to do with me at all.
> I am a door keeper of the heart, not a lump of clay.

If we are looking for purpose and meaning, these will not be found in the illusive world of repossession. The path is beyond, inward and invisible.

CHAPTER 5

The Third Insight

We Have Two Centers

What should be obvious after reading the previous chapters is that everything in creation has two aspects: physical and spiritual. As human beings, we represent the pinnacle within creation. This is because our spiritual aspect is significantly developed, making us the only species within creation that has free will and choice. The following dialogue from my first book, *Seven Colors*, elaborates on this idea.

Jonathan interjected, "So you have creation, which has a physical and spiritual realm. How do we humans fit into this picture?"

Mami answered, "There is a perfect order within creation. From the lowest plant life to trees, from the lowest animal life to humans, from the cycles of rain, the tides, the orbits of the sun and the moon, there is a perfect balance. In addition, there is a hierarchy, and right at the top of this chain of creation is the human. He is the highest within the created world. We call him the Ashraful Maklukat."

"What does it mean?" Jonathan inquired.

"The highest created being," said Dirum, who was learning as much from this as was Jonathan.

Mami continued. "The human being is unique within creation. We are endowed with the faculties of the perceptible world and the imperceptible world. We are, in other

words, physical and spiritual. Our physical self is perceptible and lives within the laws of this physical world and in
this state; we are no different from the cow, the goat, the
lion, and even a tree. In fact, at this material level, we are
made up of the same recycled elements as the tree or dog,
that being carbon, hydrogen, oxygen, nitrogen, and so on.
It is said that a cow is worth more dead than we are
because its leather at least has value, like its meat. However, our spiritual self is imperceptible and conforms to
spiritual laws."

"Tell me more about our spiritual self," Jonathan
persisted.

Mami obliged. "The essence of our spiritual self is the
soul, although different people have somewhat different
terminologies. It can be referred to as the spirit, the soul,
the athma, but these are just semantics."

What is it made of? Where does it come from?"
Jonathan interrupted.

Mami took a breath and continued. "In the same way
our physical bodies are made of the same substance as the
physical world, our spiritual essence is made of the same
substance as the universal soul, which sustains creation.
As we can draw on the energy of the physical realm, we
can do the same with the spiritual. This is what makes us
unique and separates us from the animals."

Throwing yet another log on the fire and clasping his
hands over the warmth, Mami continued. "The physical
and material realm with which we are so familiar is temporal and finite. It is limited in space and time. Our physical aspects, our bodies, are also subject to the laws of this
realm. We age and our bodies decay, as does everything
else, and so all that we have is temporary.

"The spiritual realm, on the other hand, is infinite and
eternal. It has dominion over all physical things because it
existed before physical creation and will exist long after.
However, the most important aspect is that the soul in

man is made of the same substance as the universal soul, which sustains both realms within creation."

"So," Jonathan said, trying to understand, "the soul or spirit within each human is made of the same substance as that of the universal soul which sustains the creation at all times?"

"Exactly," Mami replied. "Look at this fire. If the fire is the universal soul, than these sparks of fire that emanate from it are the souls. The closer the souls are to the fire, the brighter they glow." Mami tossed on another log, creating a flurry of sparks.

"I understand!" Jonathan exclaimed. "It is so clear! I mean, now that I think of it, it makes so much sense. The closer we are to the universal soul, the more illuminated we become, and the more enlightened we are, the greater is the experience of meaningful happiness. Yet why is this idea of spirituality still very much an enigma?"

The warm glow of the fire in the darkness reflected on Mami's face as he responded. "It is hard to see the darkness in the bright glow of the sun. Similarly, can we feel the air inside the depth of the ocean?" he asked.

Dirum, Jonathan and Gulam shook their heads in response.

"Then how can we feel the existence and the reality of the spiritual realm while we are fully intoxicated in the material one?" Mami asked rhetorically. "The very tools of science and rational thought that enabled us to understand our physical environment and make so much progress in it are turned toward the understanding of the spiritual environment. Yet these are blunt and useless instruments in this endeavor.

"How can we turn to scientific research to learn about our own spirituality? How can worldly knowledge, which negates the existence of the soul, help us in knowing our true essence? It forces us to live an exoteric existence very ambivalent to our esoteric essence. The consequence,"

Mami continued with some passion, "is that those sharp points of distinction between the physical and spiritual have become blurred, the real nature of man's essence has become hazy, and we have instead the emergence of the techno-human being."

The critical component in any discussion of harmony and equilibrium is, of course, balance. Balance rules every part of our creation, and we see this very evident in nature. Plants and animals thrive when operating under an environment of balance. Consider a beautiful garden and how the balance between the quality of the soil, the variety of flowers seeded, watering and sunshine enable the garden to look, feel and be healthy. However, the balance in the garden depends on the gardener. If the gardener is not centered within himself, he will not express balance in his work; consequently, the garden will not be as appealing. We can see that the imbalance in our ecosystem is not only endangering many species of animals, but also causing some of them to become extinct. Even within our own physical makeup, there is a fine balance. For instance, our own heart beats at a balanced, predetermined rhythm. During our lifetime, our heart will beat about two and a half billion times, yet between each beat, it rests and finds that equilibrium before it continues. We know very well what happens when the balance is lost in the heart's rhythm. Our body, which contains billions of cells, is also precariously balanced, and sickness results when that equilibrium shifts. The next time you are out, gaze upward at the sun and moon. In perfect equilibrium, they hang over us. Yet if the sun were just a little closer or a bit further afar, our planet Earth would become inhabitable.

Balance governs all things; it is programmed into everything because it is a spiritual law. Whenever we identify distress, it is certain that the cause was a shift in its equilibrium. Natural disasters have plagued our planet in recent years with immense suffering and human tragedy. We can identify the changing weather patterns and global warming as the cause. However, we need to take this thought a little further.

Why do we have so much conflict in our world? The wars, terrorism, clash of cultures, the increase in natural disasters, inflict turmoil in our world and personal lives. This is a question that does not need an elaborate answer. The Talmud says,

We do not see things as they are

We see them as we are.

The world is our garden and everything that is happening in our garden is our handiwork. When our own internal balance shifts, we are plunged into inner conflict. Subsequently, we express this conflict in our physical world through our thoughts, intentions and actions. In other words, all the problems we see and encounter in our physical world emanate from distortions created by the shift in our own personal equilibrium. Fixing the problems in our society starts by restoring the balance, and since man is the only species within creation that has choice, it all starts with us. This choice empowers us to change ourselves and consequently our life and the world we live in.

The Student and the Carrots—A student asked his spiritual teacher how he could go about changing his life so that he could reduce the personal conflicts he felt. The teacher decided to demonstrate the problem by asking the student to deliver four bags of carrots to a certain orphanage. He put three large bags of carrots in the student's left hand and one in his right hand. The student walked a mile to the orphanage, delivered the carrots and returned exhausted. Upon returning, the teacher allowed the student to rest sufficiently and then gave him another four large bags of carrots to deliver to another orphanage some two miles further than the previous one. This time the teacher placed two bags of carrots in each hand. Sometime later, the student returned, having completed the task.

The teacher asked the student why he seemed more tired after the first trip, which took longer, even though it was a shorter distance. The student acknowledged that the first trip took longer and more tiring but could not explain why. The teacher explained that in the first trip, because he had placed three bags in one hand and only one in the other, the balance with which the student walked had shifted, creating greater stress on his body. During the second trip, however, the weight was balanced and his physical task was consequentially easier. The answer to reducing personal conflicts lay in creating an inner balance between our physical and spiritual aspect.

Conflict in our lives is a consequence of the shift in that inner equilibrium. The story speaks to us about the cause of all our personal distress.

This introduces us to the third insight, "We have two centers," the physical and the spiritual. We know that our spiritual identity, defined as the soul, is more important; therefore, caring for it should be the primary purpose. However, it is equally critical to understand that our physical identity is what enables us to do this. There is little the soul can do to evolve into perfection without the assistance of our physical self. Our physical and spiritual selves at any given time are two sides of the same coin and interdependent. In the absence of the soul, our physical self is lifeless, and without the body, our soul is choiceless. When the two come together, we are empowered with free will and choice. The interaction and balance between the two determines everything.

The center of our physical self is the ego, and mystics generally term our ego center as the lower self, which is endowed with the natural survival skills. Decisions that affect our ability to survive, procreate, seek pleasures, comforts and gratification are rooted in the ego center. We share these instincts with all other species, although ours are more developed. Simply observe animals in the wild and their natural instincts to survive. Lions will work together to hunt, yet they also will fight each other in protecting their own dominance. Larger birds will scare away the smaller ones from morsels of food. These are the laws of the jungle, as we understand them; it is a matter of survival. By its very nature the personality of the lower self or ego center is selfish. It has to be. How long would a selfless lion or a kind crocodile survive in the wild, if it put the needs of other animals before its own? Similarly, our lower self and ego center's selfish personality enables us to adapt to our environment and survive.

As spiritual beings, we also have a second center, which is the soul center and mystics refer to this as our higher self. We under-stand from chapter three that our soul is a microcosm of the macrocosm, and therefore divine in essence. This is the permanent part of us and does not die when our physical body does. By its very nature, the higher self or soul center is selfless, with divine quali-ties of generosity, kindness and nobility. The human being's opti-mum performance occurs when there is a balance between the higher and lower self. When our selfish impulses of personal sur-vival are in equilibrium with our selfless and altruistic ideals ema-nating from the higher self, we have a balance that does indeed empower us to create for ourselves the life we want.

Here we are able to enjoy the abundance of life, the luxury and comforts, because they are underpinned by the ethic to help oth-ers also achieve it. We can see this in the diagram:

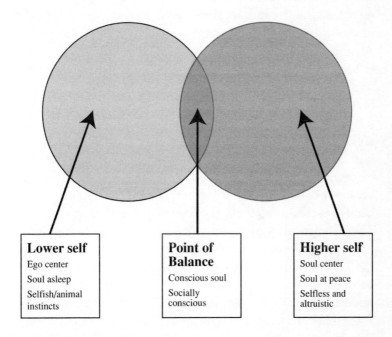

Lower self	**Point of Balance**	**Higher self**
Ego center	Conscious soul	Soul center
Soul asleep	Socially conscious	Soul at peace
Selfish/animal instincts		Selfless and altruistic

As we can see from the diagram, when we are centered on the lower self (A), to a large degree we are completely detached and veiled from the altruistic impulses of the higher self. Consequently, an individual centered on his or her lower self would be predominantly selfish in character. Simply put, when our ego is centered in the lower self, it loses its connection to the higher self, and the material world we live in becomes our only reality, just like that of the animals. This is the world of repossession described in Chapter Three. Although, as with everything else in creation, we were originally fashioned in fine balance, this equilibrium has now shifted. It is easy to see how this may happen.

From the time we are born, we are immersed into a raging, fast-moving river called life. Consider what a parent deals with after the birth of a child in the western world. Issues of health and school begin, as well as non-stop childcare. From the doctors' appointments, education, and extracurricular activities to the adult challenges of finding jobs and dealing with sickness and other disappointments, we are caught up in an endless chase. Life is a struggle as we skip one hurdle to the next—a roller coaster of vicissitudes. All this consumes us; all our actions, creativity, thoughts and encounters are focused on our material world where our ego reigns supreme. It is a world where we are pushed around, so we push back. People step on us, and we respond by becoming assertive. We feel the wrath of others' anger and consequently, we pass on the anger. We are absorbed in trying to get better, accumulate more and stash away as much as we can, as if we are in some road race that we are trying to win. In the process, the fine balance shifts and, because we are engrossed in the feeling of self-importance, we are blinded to the fact that our ego has isolated us from our real self. The vibration changes, the balance shifts and the music emanating from the higher self begins to fade.

Inflated with an exaggerated image of our self-worth, we are conditioned, stressed and traumatized and finally submit to the supremacy of our lower self, the ego center. We are spiritual beings in the midst of a temporary physical encounter, but the shift moves us to believe we are physical beings who occasionally have a spiritual encounter. For instance, when someone close to us dies, or we face extreme problems and disappointments, we have moments of spiritual self-searching. Sometimes, no sooner have the problems passed than we return to our comfort zone in our lower self. Other times, we may see these major events in our lives as opportunities to shift our lives back toward the center.

Wind Against the Sail—It was a windy day, and as the student sat with the master out in the yard, he asked why people have many problems and tribulations in life.

"Have you ever seen a sail boat? How does it reach its destination?" the master asked.

"It uses the wind," said the student, after pondering the question.

"Surely, a strong wind is troublesome and causes many boats to sink," the master noted. The student was confused. "Yes, that is true," he replied, "the wind is indeed the greatest problem for a boat."

The master explained. "The boat that uses the wind correctly, by having it push against the sail, will move forward, and the boat that seeks to have the wind go harmlessly by will have no direction and likely sink or become lost. Life's problems, my friend, are like the wind. They are there to aid us in our journey. It all depends on how we set our personal sails. We can allow the problems to teach us and help us understand something about ourselves and grow from this, or we can allow the same problems to sink us into confusion and hopelessness. Problems and circumstances come into our life to push us to shift our balance, and these are indeed opportunities in disguise."

Although most people exist between the lower self (A) and the soul in balance (B), there really is no instrument to measure where one is; however, the general rule is that you can tell a tree from its fruits. Our actions speak volumes about who and where we are. Through choice and the exercise of our freewill, we are empowered to make decisions that would slowly move us toward our balance, the point where harmony exists between the vibrations of the higher and lower self. Two objects rubbing against each other cause friction. Similarly, when the higher and lower self are not in harmony, the consequence is internal conflict. However, we must move because it is the only way to create lasting change and attract blessings and abundance beyond our imagination into our life.

Shifting our center from the lower self will mean diminishing the power of ego, which we never easily relinquish. The reason why so many people change after they have encountered serious tragedies and problems explains that the heart ultimately has the power to subdue the mind.

The Fallen Eagle—An eagle soared high in the sky. The monarch of birds, she was fearless and enjoyed her freedom to roam the skies. Feared and admired, she reigned supreme. One day, unexpectedly, an arrow struck the eagle and the monarch of the skies fell to the ground in disbelief. "How is it possible for an arrow to reach me so high up in the sky?" she asked as she struggled on the ground. She took a closer look at the arrow that had fatally struck her and discovered that it was made from her own feather.

Our ego is our worst enemy, and as long as we remain under its domination, we can never discover our own celestial state. It is an idea that is explained beautifully in the parable of the devil. Whether one believes in the devil in the context of religion or as a metaphor for all that is negative and bad, it is interesting to look at the story of how the devil came to be the antithesis of god. He was known as Ibliss, and was one of the most learned angels.

God created Adam with his own divine breath. He than asked all the angels to prostrate themselves before Adam. All the angels did so except Ibliss, who considered himself better and higher in status to Adam. Because of his rebellion, God banished Ibliss, who became God's nemesis, Satan. The real message in the parable is that, despite being so learned and clever, Ibliss did not recognize the divinity within Adam and it was his ego, expressed through his pride and arrogance, that mislead him.

In a previous chapter, I explained how our soul is essentially on a journey toward perfection. That journey goes from the lower self to the higher self where the soul is at peace. This journey takes countless rebirths and is ongoing for each one of us. It is our journey, and not only are we empowered to make this journey with our eyes open or closed, we also can choose to break our cycle of rebirth and create for ourselves the life we want.

In his book "Care of the Soul" Gary Zukav writes:
>Each human being has a soul. The journey toward
>individual soulhood is what distinguishes the human
>kingdom from the animal kingdom and the mineral
>kingdom. Only the human kingdom has the experi-
>ence of the individual soulhood. That is why its
>power of creation is great.

It is ironic that we see so much power outside of ourselves in things like wealth, influence, luxuries, domination and ownership. In this illusion, we are imprisoned until, of course, we experience the power within, which makes all that is outside of us pale in comparison.

Taking a close look at our higher self, the soul center, we can see from our earlier discussion that it is eternal and made of the same substance as the creator. In other words, in its perfect state, it is divine and so are its qualities. Obviously, this is a penultimate state of existence because the soul has dominion. Being centered in the Soul Center would make that individual enlightened.

"The qualities of truth, goodness, beauty, generosity, nobility and love do not occupy a remote place in their lives, but is the substance with which they nourish their spiritual being. They enjoy the light emanating from the universal soul, and while their hands are in society, their heads are cool in solitude and in their presence, our own souls are nourished."

The great prophets, messengers and wise man and woman were all soul-centered. The soul is fully awakened and conscious of itself and consequently, all its divine qualities are expressed in their actions. The ego has absolutely no sway. It is subjudicated and obedient to the voice within. This is the apex of the state Buddha referred to when he expressed the imperative, "awaken." Similarly, Ali said, "He who knows himself, knows God." We also find the same theme in a saying from Shakespeare's *Hamlet*, "Know thyself."

Buddha was fully awakened, and so was Jesus, Moses, Abraham, Mohamed, Shri Krishna, Shri Ram, and countless others who have graced our world. It is written that no civilization at any time is ever without such advanced souls in their midst. They exist in our time and provide the necessary balance when, through our own ignorance, we upset the equilibrium of the physical and spiritual creation and put our world at risk. Just think about how many narrow escapes there have been in the past 50 years alone, when human actions could have destroyed our whole civilization and the numerous occasions when we have been on the brink of a nuclear holocaust.

Firoz was an advanced soul who passed away many years ago. I received a letter one day from a stranger in Red Deer, some time in 1985. In the letter, the stranger told me that Firoz, who had stayed in Red Deer, Alberta with him, was looking for me. He gave me a phone number for Firoz, who had moved to the States. One day I phoned him. I was flabbergasted to learn that Firoz knew everything about me. He said that he did not know why he had to contact me, but in time, he would. A year later, Firoz returned to Calgary. I was expecting to see some successful and dashing young man at our first meeting. As it turned out, he was a parking lot attendant at a city parking lot just behind my office. He was an overweight, unassuming person with very little knowledge of English and no formal educational background to his name. During the next few years, I met him frequently, during which time he told me many things that absolutely amazed me, things he said I needed to know. I remember him telling me that the earth was suffering from convulsions and the consequences would mean wars, suffering, disease and natural disasters inflicting untold suffering. How right he had been!

There are other cataclysmic events he told me may happen, though I cannot mention them in this book, but the thought of these events often keeps me up at night. However, he made it very clear that we are the co-creators of our future, and through our choices, we can change our destiny. It all starts by shifting our balance, and that means moving away from the domination of the ego center toward the middle. He also explained that in every age, there was a minimum of 313 advanced souls in our midst, and that their highly developed spirituality was instrumental in moderating the consequences of the imbalances, which were pushing our civilization to the edge. There are angels in our midst, and just like Jesus, who appeared to the Romans as a penniless hobo, such souls as Firoz, perhaps not quite as advanced, exist among us and are found in the unlikeliest places and families. I miss him and am so glad that he recognized me and enriched me because like most people, I would not have recognized him.

Balance, however, was his key message. We have allowed ours to shift internally, and the consequent internal conflict has transposed itself into our physical world. Restoring that equilibrium starts with us. The root of all our problems lies in our overwhelming and sometimes obsessive attachments to worldly things, because they have anchored us into the material world of repossession.

Nowhere is this material obsession more noticeable than in the way individuals handle their money. As a financial advisor with more than 20 years of experience, I can tell you exactly which clients made a good return on their investments over long periods and which ones did not. The clients who had a good balance between equity and income investments got the good return. This is because their equity assets were diversified in the ownership of well-run, profitable companies. Similarly their income assets were diversified in debt instruments of good grade maturing at staggered intervals. This balance between asset classes enabled them to survive all the distortions that were occurring in the financial markets, including the stock market crash, economic recessions, gyrating interest rates, inflation, wars and energy crisis.

The clients who did not do as well were those who would speculate, continually trying to outfox the market, jumping from one investment to the next in the hope of catching the big wave. Sometimes they did, but they never made much money because what goes up, comes down and many of them lost their life savings. It is difficult to get someone who has ridden the market up to take the chips off the table, because they think it will keep going up. It is the greed factor. The phrase, "Do not fall in love with an investment," goes unheeded. The same investor will be panicking to sell when investment values are collapsing and decreasing in value, and it is hard to get them to buy good, under-valued assets because of the fear factor. It is a fact that the balance in an investment portfolio, the asset allocation, will provide better returns in the longer run with less risk. Unfortunately, people lose sight of proven principles because we have become so attached to our money that we have to check its value daily. Whenever we identify problems and conflict, whether it is in our personal life, relationships, finances or even in our world, the chances are that the cause is an imbalance within ourselves. Before we can contemplate creating an internal shift, it is wise to understand the cause of our attachments.

We have discussed that we have two centers, and that each one, physical and spiritual, has distinct needs. These needs are constantly being expressed within us. Since our soul center is spiritual, it is from here that our deepest needs emerge. Our soul had an existence prior to this life and will have another one after the death of our current physical personality, because that soul in us, having been separated from its origin, is now on its way back to it. The deepest needs that emanate from the soul are its yearning to return to that origin, the sadness it feels because of its separation from its source, and the soul's longing for unity with the universal soul. Remember, our soul is the main player, and everything that happens has to do with the soul.

Mystic Rumi describes this beautifully in one of my favorite poems.

> Listen to the reed and the tale it tells,
> How it sings of separation.
> Ever since they cut me from the reed bed,
> My wail has caused men and women to weep.
> I want a heart torn open with longing
> To share the pain of this love.
> Whoever has been parted from his source
> Longs to return to that state of union.
> At every gathering, I play my lament.
> I'm a friend to both happy and sad.
> Each befriended me for his own reasons,

Yet none searched out the secrets I contain.
My secret is not different than my lament,
Yet this is not for the senses to perceive
The body is not hidden from the soul
Nor is the soul hidden from the body,

And yet the soul is not for everyone to see.
This flute is played with fire, not with wind,
And without this fire, you would not exist.
It is the fire of love that inspires the flute.
It is the ferment of love that completes the wine
The reed is a comfort to all estranged lovers.
Its music tears our veils away.
Have you ever seen a poison or antidote like the reed?
Have you seen a more intimate companion and lover?
It sings of the path of blood;
It relates the passion of Majnun.

The branch cut from its tree is turned into a flute. The flute, when prompted, plays the music that expresses its longing to return from whence it came. Rumi uses the flute as the metaphor for his soul, which in his deepest contemplations expresses sadness at his separation from the beloved and longs for the ultimate return.

We see, then, that though we are much immersed in our physical life, the expression of our own soul continues. The impulses of love, security, happiness, peace and joy that the soul once enjoyed prior to it becoming separated from its source are the very things the soul remembers and yearns for. All psychologists and psychiatrists will confirm that these are the root of all desires within the human being. However, as these desires, prompted by the soul within, manifest into our lower self and ego center, something very odd happens.

Since we live in a physical world, these impulses emanating from within are given a form and material images. Just as the modern airplane was an idea in someone's head and later expressed as a blueprint resulting in material shapes and pictures, we take these deep abstract emotions within us and turn them into something we can see, hear, touch, smell and taste. Our inner longings of happiness, security, peace, joy and belonging express themselves as happy homes, companionship, wealth and owning items that symbolize those needs. Consider what happens when we are physically sick. Our body tells us we are sick by incurring a fever or fatigue, and it is at that time that we seek medical intervention. Yet when our soul is sick, how do we know and what are the ailments and signs? Furthermore, what is the cure? Well, inner restlessness, pointlessness, the feeling of loneliness, depression and confusion, despite having so much in our worldly life, are the signs that tell us something is up with the soul. Ironically, we attempt to alleviate those ailments by going on vacations, changing our partner or by going on a shopping spree. The next time you have an opportunity, think of the messages heard in advertising. For example, a condo was advertised as a "condo that soothes the soul." A home that was advertised by a builder had a picture of that perfect loving family, secure in their home and relationship. A roadster has a picture of the windstream rubbing against its metallic body and the title read, "Freedom for the soul." The advertising agency understands that, for us to take a second look at their commercial and buy their products, it would have to touch us on the inside, and it does so because, deep inside, we all have the same longings.

I knew a couple who had come to a point in their marriage where all they ever did was argue. Their house was too small, their work was too stressful and both needed a vacation. At least this was their conclusion. Therefore, they decided to build a huge, classy home. For six months, they worked together in getting their dream home built, during which time there were very few problems between them. They moved into their new home, and exactly three months later, the arguments started once again, and soon the two separated. If we are not happy and secure in ourselves, we look to others to do this for us, and when they fall short, we feel let down and disagreements emerge. A dream home is exactly that, a dream. In this particular case, both spouses were unhappy and insecure. Consequentially, neither was able to help the other. Of course, in the final analysis, real and lasting security, happiness and joy can only come when it exists within our spiritual self. As I explained in the chapter on repossession, every dream that we struggle to fulfill will eventually be repossessed. The minute we manifest those deep inner needs of happiness and freedom into worldly and material attachments, we inadvertently close the door to reality and open the door to suffering.

We are spiritual beings and our needs are spiritual. So how is a vacation in Mexico or a new roadster going to satisfy that spiritual need? We are constantly ignoring the signals that are coming from the soul prompting us to do those things that nurture and care for the soul. Becoming overly materialistic simply binds us to the physical world under the complete influence of our ego center. That is not to suggest that we should renounce all material attachments; on the contrary, taken in their proper context, our physical and material comforts can be used as tools in satisfying our inner need. For instance, if we did well for ourselves and decided to help others, invariably we would always feel good. Something inside of us is touched every time we act selflessly because there is an equalizing process at play. When we do something meaningful and satisfying in one area of our life, other areas of our life will automatically benefit. Similarly, negative things occurring in one area of our life—say, work for instance—will show up elsewhere in our life. Everything we do is connected to everything else. For instance, when we pull on one end of a long string, eventually we will feel a tug at the other end. What we do in our physical life will undoubtedly affect us spiritually sooner or later, because it is a matter of our balance equalizing itself. "Help thy neighbor" and "desire for your neighbor what you desire for yourself" is timeless wisdom that has been resonating from the lips of the great teachers for ions. We are, after all, empowered to make a difference and touch the lives of others. This means that the wealth and comfort with which we are blessed should be a means to an end rather an end in itself. The minute we gauge our success or failure in life by what we have been able to accumulate or own, we have lost the plot.

The King's Birthday—King Wagt had amassed wealth beyond imagination and a huge kingdom. The day before his birthday, the king decided that the first person he saw on his birthday would be offered the gift of their choice.

The king awoke early the next morning, went for his usual walk, and saw a man sitting under a tree. Keeping the promise he had made to himself, he offered the stranger any gift that he chose. The stranger thought about it and remembered how all his friends had a house and a horse. Therefore, the stranger asked the king for the same gift for himself.

The king granted him his gift and than exclaimed, "O fool, I offered you any gift of your choosing, and you asked for a house and horse!" In our lives, we are indeed offered the greatest treasure of all and instead, settle for trinkets that will eventually be repossessed.

Our two centers are interdependent. It is our physical body governed by the ego of the lower self that enables our souls to experience, feel, have fulfillment and grow. Our attachments have a purpose. Human love, for example, is a stepping-stone to the experience and attainment of the greater divine love. The choices we constantly have to make are often difficult, yet it is the friction from those decisions that enables us to develop. However, balance is the key. It is the way we were meant to be; therefore, our endeavors should focus on moving our inner self back to the center, the point of balance. Here the selfish nature of the lower self is equally balanced by the selflessness of the higher self. It is the place where our need to own and possess is offset by the joy we feel when we share a part of it with others. There is inner harmony, and we do not have the constant conflict between the two grinding against each other. The practices of the Invisible Way will enable us to move our balance back into the center and beyond.

The Two Wolves—One day a sage sat down with his disciples and shared some esoteric knowledge. "How can we enter our sacred space?" a student asked. The sage explained, "Within each of us are two wolves. One is aggressive, ruthless, selfish and assertive. The other is kind, clever, intelligent and very wise. They are fighting with one another. Who do you think wins?"

The students thought about it and seemed divided in their response. The sage answered, "It is the one you feed."

The two wolves represent our two centers. When we feed our lower self and ego, we move to strengthen the ruthless wolf. However, when we nourish our higher self and care for the soul, we move toward our sacred space.

Shifting back into the center, the point of balance is only the starting point. Admittedly, it eliminates our inner turmoil and restores our harmony, but the real essence of the Invisible Way is to shift us from our center toward the soul at peace, the higher self into our sacred space. When Prophet Moses climbed Mount Sinai to meet God, he found him in an open space where God spoke from the fire in the bush. God said, "Remove your shoes and come closer." I have always found this encounter a very powerful allegory and imperative. When we get closer to the divine, it requires us to leave the world of the profane behind. Removing shoes in this parable is a symbol of exiting the world of the profane and entry into the sacred space that surrounds the divine.

Similarly, our soul's journey from the center toward the higher self is our entry into that sacred space. This is when the real awakening of our consciousness occurs. We begin to develop new sensibilities, discover inner faculties and begin to see the blinds and shutters from concealed windows withdrawn to reveal to us landscapes, horizons and views that would amaze and startle us. In those moments, we discard all that we ever learned and start form scratch in awe as the echo of the words "come closer" ushers us in.

As the veils are slowly removed, the soul stirs and the third eye opens to give us timeless glimpses into our own divinity. The creaks of the door almost always sounds alike, except one opens the door and the other closes it. Similarly, operating from the lower self, we are closing the door to the divine presence. Operating from the higher self, on the other hand, opens the door and we are able to detect the Invisible Light.

CHAPTER 6

The Fourth Insight

Our Actions Enable Our Soul to Renew and Evolve

Since we are spiritual beings in the middle of a temporary human experience, the real unfolding story is not about our physical identity but that of the ongoing journey of the soul. This essential journey, which is gradually developing our soul to perfection, is continuing, despite the fact most people are totally oblivious to it. Try this simple exercise, and you will see what I mean. Straighten out your elbow and put the palm of your hand against the backdrop of the sky. First, focus on the hand and all you will see is a detail of your fingers and palm and you will hardly notice the sky. Now change your focus to the sky and you will see vastness and infinity, not to mention the beauty of the stars, moon and even the sun. You will not even notice the hand except as an obstacle preventing you a clear view of the majesty beyond. Similarly, most people are focused on the hand, which symbolizes our present human life and physical form, completely unaware of the infinity beyond. However, when we focus on our spirituality, our image changes and so does our perception and context. Our human existence becomes a very pale and insignificant part of the whole picture. Now imagine moving further and further away from your hand and all of a sudden, the hand becomes almost invisible and irrelevant.

I had a friend who wanted to do something special to express the love he had for his wife. Emptying out his bank account, he went to the local municipal airport and hired a small plane with a

pilot to fly a trailing message his wife could see. He phoned his wife
and asked her to watch the sky eastward at noon. Sure enough, a
plane carrying a banner with the message, "I love you" appeared at
noon. Think about the incident for a moment. When the wife
looked at the sky, she could have focused on the plane, the message or both. As it turns out, she focused on the message, felt
blessed and did not even recall what shape or model the plane was.
Applying this analogy to our physical life, we see that when we
become overly attached to it, that is all we see. We are stressed and
traumatized trying to handle all the things going on in our life;
however, without perception and context, everything becomes a
big deal. The purpose for the plane to be in the sky was to relay an
important message to the wife; similarly, our physical body exists
to facilitate and support the development of our soul. That is the
big picture and context for human existence, and when we focus
on our spirituality, all of a sudden the trials and tribulations we
face as human beings become less important. Instead, not only do
we have a greater appreciation of them, we also feel more calm
and blessed.

The mystic Rumi explains this idea of the focus beautifully
thus:

> "Beware! Do not run in pursuit of the crow like
>   freshly soul,
> For it carries thee to the graveyard, not toward
>   the orchard."

In the previous chapter, I explained that we have two centers:
the lower self, represented by the ego, and the higher self, represented by the soul. Our soul's journey is gradually shifting us from
the lower self to the higher self, and it is a process that is happening right now, even though it may not be in our focus. This movement toward perfection is an indomitable law of creation. Physical
life is not static. Everything in creation, from the seeds, plants, and
animals to humans, are constantly evolving toward a higher state.
The journey of the soul is really the journey of everything, and all
that happens in our life serves this end. Reflect on our natural
world and you will notice that everything is in a state of flux. The

stars in our celestial system are dying each day as new ones are being born. The same goes for plants, animals and even mountains. Everything in every moment is dying and regenerating itself, aspiring toward the higher end. Within our own bodies, cells are dying and new ones are coming into being.

Rumi describes the depth with which this process is occurring:

The mountains bleed
and again become solid
But you do not see them bleed
You are blind and reprobate.

Our blindness is a consequence of our focus. When something is not in our focus, it is not in our perception; therefore, we are blind to it. However, when we see ourselves as a part of creation rather than something separate and superior, we realize our place within it. Ancient wisdom tells us that nature is a mirror that reflects the divine and by studying it, we can learn how these divine laws bind us all.

I have always found beauty and awe in nature, as do so many people; Yasmin and I get away to the mountains as often as we can, where we indulge ourselves with walking meditations. Somehow, nature brings out the fact that we are kindred spirits and allows us to recalibrate our focus upon the creator whose handiwork we call nature. It is not a coincidence that some of the greatest inspirations experienced by the prophets of old took place in mountains and other natural places.

The mystic Shantideva writes:

To the eye of the seer
Every leaf of the tree is a page of the holy book
That contains divine revelation
And is inspired every moment of his life
By constantly reading the holy scripture of nature.

There are four principles very evident in our natural world, and everything, including the human being, is bound by this natural order. First, when we look at nature, we have to accept that the way things are is not the beginning or end, but rather work in progress. This progress occurs as a result of cause and effect. Many of the ancient teachings refer to this as the law of Karma. Second, in our natural world, destruction always precedes construction. Things break and fragment to evolve, and progress occurs because of renewal and revitalization. Third, there is a plan, a law, that determines the progression. Nature may be work in progress, but there was a beginning and there is an end. Therefore, nothing is random. Last, there is a subtle interconnectedness at work; everything effects everything else.

Although we are spiritual beings, our manifestation in a physical body means we are bound by these natural laws. Let us now look at the fourth insight of the Invisible Way, which states:

"Our actions enable our soul to renew and evolve."

A reminder: The real story is the soul, which is manifested in everything within natural creation. All that happens has just one purpose. Let us look at how these four principles operating in the natural realm affect us physically and spiritually. First, we are work in progress. Our soul existed prior to the current form in which we find ourselves, and undoubtedly it will continue to exist after the death of this physical personality. Since our soul had a before and will have an after, our life on earth now is but one of many encounters in our ultimate destination to a higher consciousness. Our soul has a history in this physical world of time and space; as a result, we are all bound by the laws of cause and effect, as is everything else. The Bhagavad Gita states:

Nature is the law which generates cause and effect.

God is the first cause and creation is an effect. Time, as Einstein said, is simply the distance between cause and effect, separating actions from reactions.

The law of cause and effect governs all things because everything that happens in the natural world has a cause. As Sir Isaac Newton would say, every action has an equal and opposite reaction. Eastern mysticism uses the term Karma. Karma means action. In other words, our actions are the cause. Therefore, our present life and circumstance is a consequence of our past actions. Hence, what we did in the past, which includes a past beyond this current life, is the cause of who we are and where we are today. This occurs because all that the soul experiences in its previous physical encounters is stored and etched upon the soul, which it takes with it in subsequent rebirths. The recollection of past lives is now a frequently discussed subject by psychologists and writers alike, and the taboo label it once had has been shed.

I also am aware of some of my past rebirths, but rather than dwelling on them and allowing them to become a distraction along the Invisible Way, I simply use them as a stepping-stone, validating our real spiritual nature. My belief is that spending too much time looking backward takes away the focus on the journey ahead, making what appears to be an exciting discovery yet another prison.

The Bhagavad Gita states:

> As a man discards his threadbare robes
> And puts on new
> So the spirit throws out
> Its worn out bodies and takes fresh ones.

Our actions in past rebirths stay with the soul and therefore our present life is a direct consequence. As a result, our present life circumstance is exactly where we need to be, and the script for it was written by us a long time ago. Therefore, we cannot change our present. It is what it is because we wrote the script. Our life at this moment represents a complete cycle of cause and effect that encompasses a sum of all our actions, creating our present life situation.

The Dalai Lama writes:

> Countless rebirths lie ahead, both good and bad.
> The effect of Karma (actions) are inevitable, and in
> previous lifetimes, we have accumulated negative
> Karma which will inevitably have its fruition in this
> or future lives.

Jesus put it more simply when he said:

> A person reaps what he sows.

Here is how the process works. The universal laws operating in the ether decode what we put out through our thoughts, intentions and actions. This process validates our spiritual status, and what comes back in life circumstances is a direct consequence of that.

Whatever emerges into our life is a carefully measured response that is designed to move our soul along its spiritual journey.

Let me give you an example. My mother has a heart condition, and to minimize the likelihood of blood clotting, which would prove fatal given her situation, she goes to the medical clinic every Monday for a blood test. The laboratory analyzes her blood and phones her back Tuesday, at which time they tell her how may tablets of Warefarin to take each day that week. The blood analysis indicates to the specialists the exact nature of my mother's blood, and the medication is than prescribed accordingly.

Similarly, the spiritual laws that govern the multitude of dimensions evaluate the thoughts, intentions and actions we put out, and the prescription that comes back is there to aid us. The dosage of life's blessings and burdens given to us do not discriminate; they are based entirely on what we need and not what we want or wish for.

Sometimes, we are overwhelmed with the adversities that come into our life, and it is easy at that time to be discouraged. Often people will blame themselves and think that either they are paying for their sins or God is unfairly meting out all this punishment. The circumstances that enter into our life that sometimes make us suffer are not supposed to be punishment or retribution for some wrongdoing we may have done in the past. The dosage of medicine was given to my mother as a result of a blood test; the sum of all our actions in response to what comes into our life is analogous to that test. We have all heard the cliché, "Life is testing us." Whatever enters our life is based on our "score," which is determined by the actions we have put out. It is futile to compare our lives to the lives of friends and family. The measure of pain and happiness that does come into everybody's life balances itself out. If we miss our share of happiness, it is not that we did not receive any; rather, it is more than likely that we allowed it to pass through our life unnoticed. Just as friction creates movement, life's circumstances are designed for only one purpose: to move us forward. Since we are all at a different point in our spiritual journey, the situations that come into our life are personalized because our actions are evaluated, tested and decoded by the natural laws. Ultimately, whatever comes into our life increases our capacity to love, care and evolve as spiritual beings. Life's struggles are the fuel that shifts the soul, and the experiences we encounter along the way are the stuff out of which our spirituality is nurtured. This makes every moment of our life important because within each moment are concealed intentions and actions that affect our future.

The second principal of nature that affects us equally is that, since everything is moving toward a higher state, there is constant renewal in our natural world. We see this happening at two levels. Physically, as we go through the aging process, our cells are constantly dying as new ones are being formed. Of course, this is similar to what is going on in the natural world. The corn needs to be crushed to evolve into oil; the egg has to break to allow life to emerge. The laws of nature clearly demonstrate that destruction precedes construction. A seed, for example, has to fragment if it wants to become a tree. Unless the seed experiences the pain of its own destruction, how will it ever enjoy the pleasure of being a tree? What of the caterpillar, which, also experiences its own destruction to become a beautiful butterfly able to ride the wind?

As the mystic Hafiz wrote:

> The abode of pleasure is never reached except
> through pain.

Spiritually, it all works in a similar fashion. Our soul is progressively evolving from the lower self to the higher self, and this necessitates the gradual destruction of the ego. This leads us to the consciousness, which occurs naturally as we move closer to the Invisible Light. Happiness and suffering, therefore, are really a byproduct of the transformation we are all going through.

As Rumi writes:

> The spiritual way ruins the body
> And after having ruined it
> Restores it to prosperity.

A farmer ploughs and toils on his land to transform it and, in the process, the soil feels the pain of destruction as it journeys toward richness and fertility. Similarly, life's trials, tribulations and adversity transform our soul and, in the process, we experience the destruction of our ego as we journey toward purity and perfection.

The third principal in nature that we also conform to is that life and creation are not accidents. It is fashionable to bring up the Big Bang theory by the antagonist who sees that as the accidental cause of creation. Once again, it is really a matter of focus, because by broadening our perspective, we can see that the galaxy within which this Big Bang theory occurred is now considered by the scientist to be a small part of the outer world.

In fact, there are likely to be innumerable galaxies and Milky Ways beyond the ones we can see, and we still don't have the scientific advancement to discover them. As the story of the worm in the apple narrated in the chapter on reflection went, white surrounded the worm, and therefore he thought the world was white until, of course, his munching brought him outside the apple. In other words, even the Big Bang had a cause! As I explained earlier in this chapter, the first cause is God, and creation is an effect. In between, there is a chain reaction of subsequent affects and causes. Every cause has a reaction, and it is time that separates cause and effect. Many scientists explain creation as a random event. However, the exactness and precision with which everything in our universe fits, sustains itself and survives is not random. Creation has a prime cause, a creative intelligence that is God, and it is good to see that many modern scientists are beginning to accept this.

As in the natural world, every life, death, moment, and circumstance that we find ourselves in spiritually is part of the great plan. We are blind to it because it is beyond our perception and focus. Yet the plan unfolds, sequestering the natural laws of cause and effect to allow our soul to evolve toward perfection, a state of God consciousness, and that is when we "get it." This process culminates when the awakening leads to union, the subject merges with the object, and all duality seizes to exist.

The Awakening—A nameless man had pursued the Invisible Way for two years since he had been introduced to it by his spiritual master. He continued to progress and gained much insight into his past lives. By chance, he arrived at that final door and knocked for it to be opened to him. The door remained shut but there came a voice asking, "Who is it?" "It is me," said he. At this, the door remained shut. He continued to seek progress and indeed was fortunate to get the glimpse of the light. In this companionship, he formed an intimate relationship with the divine. Having strived in time that could not be measured, he was fortunate once again to approach the final door. Once again, he knocked, wishing for it to open, and the words were heard, "Who is it?" "It is me, your friend and companion," the man answered. Once again, the door stayed shut. Undeterred, the man returned to the practice of the Invisible Way and for lifetimes that cannot be measured, he struggled and contemplated for yet one more opportunity to enter that final sacred door. One day, he was granted that grace and the final door emerged in his vision. Once again, the voice behind the door was heard. "Who is it?" This time the man answered, "It is you." The sacred door opened and allowed the man in.

As the raindrop merges with the ocean and loses its "I" ness, our soul merges in the divine, and there is no longer "I" and "him."

The mystic Arabi describes this experience beautifully thus:

When my beloved appears, with what eye do I
   see him?
With his eye, not mine,
For none sees him except himself

We must trust the plan because everything in the perceptible and imperceptible world conforms to an order. The same water that nourishes the smallest plant and largest mammal nurtures us, too. As much as we struggle to subjudicate and adapt the natural world for our use, we are still bound by the same laws. All of them exist for one goal: to develop and awaken the latent divinity in mankind. As a result, there are no coincidences; Everything happens for a reason. It is the plan unfolding exactly the way it should. That means our own life right now is exactly as it should be. We cannot change it because it is the effect of causes that have a history. Furthermore, all the circumstances within it at this time, good and bad, exist to illicit a reaction from us and influence our future. Therefore, the place, country and family we are born into, not to mention our life circumstances regardless of how difficult or adverse they may be, all serve a purpose.

When we are in the midst of a personal crisis or the throes of suffering and helplessness, self-pity often overwhelms us. Trusting the plan is a hard pill to swallow during such times because it means we have to accept the adversity. It is always easier to find something or someone else to blame, yet in the larger context, these are the experiences from which we grow. As Jesus said, "My power shows best in weak people." Saint Paul elaborated from his personal experiences when he said, "I delight in weakness, in insults, in hardships, in persecutions, in difficulties, for when I am weak, I am strong."

Weakness is something all of us face at some time in our life, and it spares no one. In my own life, I have watched my wife go through a life-threatening illness and my children struggle with never-ending obstacles. I had become a bystander when my grand-daughter's physical safety was at risk, not through choice, but circumstance. It is hard to hold a family together in the face of such adversity, let alone accept that whatever occurs has a reason. In addition, when everything is happening all at once and your family is fragmenting and sinking right before your eyes, it is tough to trust the plan. However, trust we must, because we cannot change the present. Our reactions during these troubled times are the substance from which our future is shaped, one that transforms us into stronger spiritual beings.

Shantideva the monk wrote:

I do not desire suffering
Yet fool I am,
I desire the cause of suffering.

Of course, it is easy to look around at friends and family to compare. It is particularly easy to ask why this is happening to your wife, daughter, or granddaughter. "Why me?" is an easy question to ask, but spiritual laws determine how these things work, and just because we do not understand them does not negate the way in which these laws operate. For example, giving always precedes receiving; we see how our nurturing of land results in a rich harvest. We see how giving back part of the harvest as seed enables the prosperity to continue. A child may ask how giving away a part of what we have can bring prosperity, yet it does. Similarly, in our weakness lies our enduring nobility and power.

As Rumi writes:

> He who gave waters to the rivers and fountains,
> Hath opened a fountain within me.

It takes the tracks of our tears to open up these concealed treasures. They do not exist outside of ourself; rather, they are hidden deep inside. My wife is perhaps the most humble person I know. When you are forced to undress before countless doctors and specialists and lose all concept of privacy, it's hard for the ego to exist under those circumstances, and the scars on your body always remind you of that. Yet in her humility was the emergence of her nobility, and the family is blessed as a result.

The Bhagavad Gita states:

> Look upon pleasure and pain
> Victory and defeat
> With an equal eye.

Nothing that is happening in our lives is random. There is a concealed plan. For example, when we are standing at the shore and watching the waves break, it almost seems chaotic. Yet, when we step back, we see a vast and beautiful ocean moving to a gentle rhythm. Similarly, when we are in the face of tough trials, things appear chaotic, just like at the shore, where the waves are breaking violently. However, when we see ourselves as spiritual beings, there is a calm and natural rhythm.

The mystic Rumi writes:

> In tears there are laughters concealed
> Seek treasure amidst the ruins.

Waves of turmoil break onto our shores for a reason, and they serve the purpose of teaching us. Ultimately, it is in these lessons that we find enlightenment and transformation.

It was 1988 when I ran as a candidate in a federal election. It was a period when life was asking me some tough questions. During the election, I had received mail threatening the death of my chil-

dren, and our campaign signs were defaced with hateful slogans.
On one occasion, a man in a truck deliberately tried to run me over
while I was campaigning. It is not easy to ignore death threats
aimed at one's children. Still, I took all that in stride, believing that
we must all stand up and contribute if we are going to make our
world better. The greater disappointment was the election defeat
and the huge debt that I had accumulated to finance the campaign.
No one ever remembers a runner-up, irrespective of the sacrifices
he has made. With Yasmin's support, I sold our family home, paid
all the debts and moved our family into a small rental. For four
years, we diligently saved our pennies and finally, in 1993, we put
down a deposit to build our own home. Two months prior to us
moving, the builder went bankrupt. It seemed that no matter what
plans I made, there was a bigger plan at work, that wanted me to
continue staying in the basement of a rental home with a wife and
three children. Eventually, our spring did arrive and we moved into
our own home on a lake. Ironically, my children look back at the
time we lived in the basement as the happiest years. It was a period
when we developed the love and friendships that we take for
granted today. However, when I reflect on that time, especially the
past few years that have been so difficult and trying for our family,
I know that, had we not developed such strong bonds back in that
basement, we could not have survived the storms that came into
our life. We may never get what we wish for, but we all get what we
deserve. I cannot say that there exists a way to avoid our share of
suffering and pain, but by doing things right, inwardly we will
always have the strength to surmount our outward problems.

I remember watching Lance Armstrong competing in his final
race, the Tour de France (recognized as perhaps the most grueling
bicycle race in the world). If you stood Lance up head to head
against his competitors, you would see athletes with better phy-
siques and outwardly stronger personalities. This was understandable because Lance Armstrong returned to bicycling after battling
cancer. Yet, what Lance lacked in stature, he more than compen-
sated for with his inner qualities. Ultimately, the strength we have
in our spirit overwhelms all that is outside of us. When we are

strong on the inside, we cannot be beaten by the problems life gives us. Lance Armstrong won seven Tour de France races after cancer had threatened to end his life.

In 2000, Yasmin was afflicted with a life-threatening illness. The doctors did not give her great odds for survival. My two younger children, Alqaim and Aziza, were in high school. It was a time of great soul searching because not only did they have to pay attention in school, but they also had to be there for their mom. They were faced with a crisis and the possible loss of their mother; for a child, I am sure, that is about as bad as it gets. Especially because we were a close family, our years together in a basement suite had given us all a special connection with each other. What my children did astonished me. Not only did they dedicate their time to nurturing and caring for their mother, they excelled in their education and received their diplomas. Astonishingly, it did not stop there because they went out into the world and gave others what they wanted most, hope. On September 3, 2005, Her Excellency, the right Honorable Adrienne Clarkson, Governor General of Canada, came to Calgary, Alberta to award the two of them one of the highest accolades in Canada: "The Governor General's Caring Canadian Award."

They are the only teenage siblings to be granted such an accolade, and the fact that they did this while in the middle of a gigantic crisis makes their achievement inspirational. They really did not have to go out to search for their script, but they did, and in the process, expressed actions that went beyond their natural state. It is easy to cower in self pity and blame when we are in difficulty, but instead, we need to ask ourselves, in the face of this suffering, what it's teaching us, what lesson can we draw from it, and how we can grow from it. I remember a conversation with the governor general at the reception that followed when she congratulated me and said, "You must be the inspiration for your children's achievements." I was proud to say that I was not, and told her that their mentor and inspiration was The Aga Khan. Of course she knew him; his life-long dedication to bringing hope into the lives of those in poverty speaks to all of us seeking a purpose in life. (In my view,

I find that parents are often preoccupied with guiding their children's careers, education and material accomplishment; important as these may be, from the spiritual perspective they are on the periphery). I feel a parent's first responsibility is to guide his children toward finding their Invisible Light. Unless our children are centered and their success rooted in that wellspring, their achievements will be mostly self-serving. If we are endowed with the opportunity of a good education, I feel that it should also be used in the service of humanity.

Life's circumstances are here to transform us, and we always need to keep in mind that this transformation happens inward because of how we behave outward. As physical beings, we see things within our realm of time and space, seeing yesterday, today and tomorrow. However, what if we could see yesterday, today and tomorrow now? In this case, everything would make sense because we would see the beginning and the end simultaneously. Is that not how the wise prophets lived their lives? The practice of the Invisible Way transforms us into spiritual beings operating outside the boundaries of time and space. This is how they were able to trust the plan.

The fourth principal of nature is the inter-connectedness of everything in our creation. There is a natural balance and hierarchy that sustains our world. It is written in the ancient texts that man is the best of the best in creation, both in the seen and unseen world. The parables from the sacred writings tell of the primordial time when God created the first man. He then asked all the angels to prostrate themselves before Adam. Though Ibliss, commonly known as Satan, rebelled against this command from God, the rest of the angels understood that the divine essence was manifest within Adam. Man therefore stands at the apex within creation, and what separates him from all the other species in creation is that only man has choice. Animals and other lower species act according to their nature and are not endowed with this faculty, which limits their ability to exceed the boundaries of their nature.

A lion will always act as a lion, and he will always express his natural state, as will all species within creation. Animals tend to be selfish and self-preserving, and it is their natural state to be this way. The human being endowed with this faculty of freewill and choice enables him to go beyond the borders of his natural state.

The Bhagavad Gita states:

> Even the wise man acts in character with his nature;
> Indeed all creatures act according to their natures.
> What is the use of compulsion then?

Having looked at the four principals of nature, we see that, though we are bound by these laws, to some degree we can transcend them through our ability of choice. This is particularly important because, although we have to trust and accept our circumstance, it does not mean that we should resign ourselves to and accept our fate. On the contrary, our gift to choose empowers us to change our destiny and create for ourselves the life we want, because it enables us to see beyond the visible world of our five senses.

Let us take a closer look at how we can do this. We understand that our actions express our natural state at any given point in time. Our expressions of that natural state through our thoughts, intentions and actions are wired into the universal laboratory, and the exact circumstances that would move us forward emerge into our life, challenging us toward that purpose.

Let us look at this diagram:

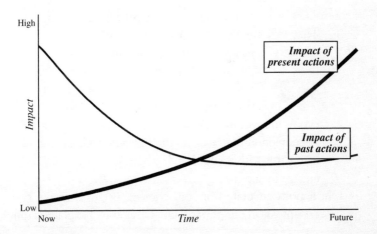

We can see that the impact of our past actions and choices dominate our present circumstance. This means that what we do right now, the choices we make, have a marginal effect on our life today. It is for this reason that we need to accept our present circumstance. The wheels of our today were set in motion a long time ago because these accumulated past actions were imprinted on our soul and carried into our present physical rebirth. However, as time evolves, our present actions become our past, and they will have a gradually increasing influence on our future.

This might explain to us the virtue of patience. In our microwave world, we have become accustomed to instant results; spiritually however, the instant formula just does not work. We can see that the law of cause and effect is at work; our actions are being decoded and attracting back into our lives situations that solicit further action. Therefore, we struggle from test to test and in the process, move toward a higher consciousness. It is a slow and gradual journey, and in a sense, we are passengers in a car.

However, the Invisible Way teaches us that we do not need to resign ourselves to being passengers in this journey of our soul. Our latent potential as divine beings empowers us to move into the driver's seat, travel at our speed, and co-create our destiny. The key to this lies in the way we use our gift of choice and freewill with respect to the opportunities life offers us.

The Dalai Lama writes:

> Some people misunderstand the concept of karma. They take the Buddha's doctrine of the law of causality to mean that all is predetermined, that there is nothing the individual can do. This is a total misunderstanding. The very term karma or action is a term of active force, which indicates that future events are within your own hands. Since action is a phenomenon that is committed by a person, a living being, it is within your hands whether or not you engage in action.

Our actions emanate from our choices. Let us examine how this process unfolds in our physical life. Previously, I explained that at each moment, everyday abundances are either entering or leaving our life. Different situations and predicaments approach us; sometimes they come and go quickly, other times they stay longer. Some of them bring us happiness and joy; others cause us grief and suffering. We call these experiences abundances because they conceal opportunities for our spiritual development. Therefore, in a way, they are similar to the scripts of plays and films that producers send famous actors in Hollywood. These actors receive countless numbers of these scripts each month. Some require the actors to be the main character; others may require a supporting role or even a cameo appearance. Actors have the ability to choose which script to accept and which ones to reject; their ultimate choice will depend on what they consider to be in their best interest.

In many of the ancient mystical texts, physical life is compared to a game, theatre, or drama. Since our physical life is temporary, it is easy to understand this analogy. Similarly, as in the case of the Hollywood actors, scripts arrive into our life for approval or rejection. We get to choose if we want to be the main character, a supporting character, or make a cameo appearance. Look at your life right now and observe the scripts you have already accepted. If you are married, you accepted the role of spouse; if you have children, you accepted the script of a parent. If you are a student, you took on that part. One could take this idea to the smallest level of detail. For instance, tomorrow morning you might see an acquaintance at a bus stop and offer him a ride. Similarly, every day some scripts that you take a role in are ending. For example, if you are divorced, you are ending the marriage script. You might just have left work, ended a relationship, or decided to move cities, and your role in these scripts is concluding. The key thing to remember is that, whether we accept or reject a script, we do so through our choice. We are in control and we get to choose what we do, how we live, and with whom.

I knew a nice couple that appeared to have a loving marriage. One day, the wife was diagnosed with cancer and soon after, the husband moved in with another woman. Without being judgmental we could say that a new script entered into the husband's life.

The script had him playing the part of a devoted and caring husband, and it was his choice whether to accept or reject it. Similarly, the wife also had the choice to accept the role of the cancer-stricken wife who is hopelessly wounded by the infidelity of her husband, or that of a woman who had the courage and faith to move on. At the same time, the children had scripts offered to them to accept the role of filling the void left by their dad or to ignore it.

Our physical life has us involved in many different soap operas, plays, and movies at any given time. We are all very important actors within creation. The scripts and roles that come into our life are ours to accept or reject. However, make no mistake, these scripts are personalized and they have our name written on them. In other words, they come for a reason. They are opportunities in disguise that come to teach us and help us evolve.

However, when we are imprisoned in the world of repossession dominated by our ego, our sensibilities are so dulled that we miss 90 percent of the roles presented to us for acceptance or rejection. The roles that come calling solicit just one thing: action. Since action is the active force that enables us to change our karma, we are unfortunately destined to be the passengers until we sensitize ourselves to all the roles offered to us and select only those that would aid us spiritually.

I was watching television recently and a breaking news story interrupted the program. The news showed a passenger jet in the air and as the story went, the jet's front tires were jammed. The plane was going to land soon and there was a real fear that an accident would occur with potential casualties. As I was sitting in Calgary watching this developing story in the United States, it was obvious that there was little I could do. In fact, I would have been helpless to lend a hand even if I was in the same city. However, I still wanted to do something, so I said a short prayer for the safety of the passengers. Since I am empowered to accept or reject any script I wished, I wrote in a cameo appearance in this one.

Yet how many such scripts flash by us every day and go unnoticed? You are driving to work and an ambulance rushes by you!

Later you see a fire brigade overtake you on the way to put out a fire. There is a car with a flat tire on the side of the road, a stray dog wandering onto the boulevard, or an old woman attempting to cross the road. Countless scripts designed to extract the best in us are offered in the hope we will grasp the opportunities they conceal. The Boy Scout who knocks on the door to ask for some pop cans, a sick friend who could use a visit, a neighbor who lost her husband and our children who seek our loving attention—all cry out for us to act. Thousands of these seemingly unimportant scripts arrive into our lives daily and most of them leave unnoticed.

As Buddha said:
> Do not think a small virtue will not return in your
> future lives. Just as falling drops of water will fill a
> large container, the little virtues that steadfastly
> accumulate will completely overwhelm you.

We are empowered to write ourselves into any script we feel will assist us. Those roles that draw out the love and virtue within us are the ones that move us forward. First, we must sensitize ourselves to the idea that the trials and tribulations that knock on our door hide something important for us.

The Bhagavad Gita states:
> What is action and what is inaction?
> It is a question which has bewildered the wise
> But I will declare unto thee
> The philosophy of action
> He who sees inaction in action
> And action in inaction is the wisest among men.

It is our actions that enable our soul to grow and evolve, and it is up to us to pick the roles that enable us to perform actions that can change our destiny.

I remember the summer of 2002 quite clearly. My oldest son, Alkarim, came home and introduced us to his girlfriend with, "She is pregnant." Parents always wish for these things to happen as a consequence of responsible behavior, and even though we were disappointed with the news, Yasmin and I offered our full support. The girlfriend had been advised by her family to have an abortion, but we pleaded with her to give life a chance.

Serena, my granddaughter, was born on January 18, 2003. Approximately eight months after her birth, my son came home with the baby and did what I consider the most courageous thing he has ever done. He asked us to look after the baby because of circumstances that are just too complicated to explain. Yasmin was still weak and recovering from the life-threatening illness and, as a family, we were trying to pick up the pieces, still unsure that the worst was behind us. Yet a script approached us for a response, and asking our son to seek an alternative solution would have been easy and reasonable given our situation. Who could have faulted that decision, as we were still struggling to make it ourselves? In addition, Yasmin and I were not getting younger. Saying yes, on the other hand, would have meant uncertainty and huge sacrifices for the whole family, but we never really had to think twice.

Yasmin immediately pulled out a brand new baby blanket a stranger had once left for her and welcomed Serena into our life. We chose the script and everything that it entailed. That meant changing hundreds of diapers, running to the doctor's office and spending nights at the children's hospital, nighttime vigils when she had a fever, spoonfuls of Pedialyte to keep her hydrated when she could not keep anything down, and countless specialists' appointments. We made these sacrifices effortlessly and in return, we received joy beyond description in helping her crawl, teaching her how to walk, feeling her warm embrace when picking her up from preschool and most of all, accepting her unconditional love and trust. There can be no giving without receiving: This is a spiritual law.

Serena will soon turn 4 and in hindsight, we realize that, had we turned down the script of giving her our unconditional love and care, there was a high probability that she would have been hurt or maimed. More than that, we learned that our sacrifices were an expression of love, and this helped us discover something we had forgotten. The question is, did we arrive to take care of her, or did

she come into our life to help us? The answer is both. Every script
we accept has two sides. People who look after their disabled children or tend to their sick parents may think that they are making
a great sacrifice, which indeed they are. However, these sick children and parents are angels who have come into our lives to help
us. Everything happens for a reason, and within these scripts, especially the difficult ones, treasures are concealed. Things are rarely
what they appear.

We saw from the chart that our past actions influence our
present circumstances and that our current actions, at least in the
near term, have a marginal effect on our life today. The question
is, can we do anything to increase the influence of our current
actions? The answer is yes! There are ways in which today's
actions can have a far greater impact on our near future, ways in
which we can move from the passenger's seat to the driver's seat
in determining what comes into our life, but like anything else, it
is not easy.

The Monk and the Scorpion—Two monks sat by the river,
cleaning the dirty dishes from their monastery. One of the monks
noticed a small scorpion fall from a pebble into the water. He
picked up the scorpion and pulled him to safety, at which time the
scorpion stung him. Regardless, he continued to wash the dishes
and some time later, the same scorpion fell back into the water.
Once again, the monk moved the scorpion to safety and once
again, he was stung.

At this, the second monk inquired, "Why did you not let him
die in the water when he stung you the first time?" The first monk
responded, "To let the scorpion die is not in my nature. I do not
wish to act below my nature."

All of us at any given time act out of our natural state.

The Bhagavad Gita states:

Even the wise man acts in character with his nature.

All our thoughts, intentions and actions emanate from our
natural state, and these signals, as explained, are decoded in the
ether. What comes back to us is based on this. Therefore, as
difficult as the scripts and roles that come into our life may be, they

already reflect our level of spiritual attainment. The burdens carried by the prophets of old were huge in our eyes, but in the context of how spiritually evolved these prophets were, they were not.

Noah witnessed his own son drown in the flood. Jesus experienced betrayal. Mohamed faced ridicule and was chased by dogs. Abraham turned his back on his own parents and offered his son in sacrifice. Lot suffered sickness and loss of his family. The closer we get toward the Invisible Light, the more blurred the distinction between the past, present and future becomes. When we are "awakened," we can see yesterday and tomorrow, today. Similarly, as we move toward our higher self, we are able to see past the pain, problems and suffering of today. If we are able to see what others cannot, what we achieve appears impossible to them.

Everyone is at a different level in his or her natural state. The divine knows this, and therefore we need to accept that what life is teaching you is different than what it is teaching me, even though our problems may have certain similarities.

I remember Mother Teresa's comment when asked which of all the burdens she carried was the greatest. "God burdens most those he trusts. I wish he would not trust me so much."

As human beings, if we find life's exams hard, then remember they are supposed to be. How else can they transform us? If I have a kind disposition toward others and I continue being kind, how is my behavior likely to change anything? If I am being me, then my actions are simply maintaining the status quo. Being and acting out of our natural state, therefore, has a neutral effect on my karma and soul journey. In other words, my evolution will continue at the slow pace it is naturally taking, and I am not going to influence the near future.

Our present actions can meaningfully influence our present and diminish the influence of past actions in two ways. The first way requires our actions to go beyond our natural state. Anytime the sum of our response to life's challenges goes beyond what we would have done naturally, this increases its effect on our current circumstances. The second way requires our actions to fall short of our natural state.

This line chart shows the impact of our actions:

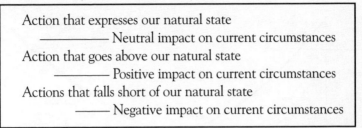

Actions that express our natural state represent our effortless and natural reaction to whatever circumstances or situations life introduces to us. For instance, you are driving on a cold day and you see an elderly woman with a flat tire on the side of the road. What would your natural response be? For argument's sake, let us say your natural response would be to stop and offer whatever help you could. If you did that in this particular circumstance, it is called an "action that expressed your natural state." You did what you do; you were being you. This action would have zero or neutral impact on our present circumstances because it expresses our current level of attainment.

Let us look at the same situation again. Although our natural response may have been to stop and offer help on this particular day, you just could not be bothered, so you ignored the whole circumstance and rejected the script. Most likely, you felt a little guilt, but it was soon forgotten. We can see that your action fell short of your natural state. In this case, your action would have a negative effect on your present circumstances because your actions fell short of your own standard.

Finally, let us assume that your response was to stop to offer help and, on this particular day, you decided to either roll up your sleeves and change the tire for the old woman or wait with her until the auto club arrived and left only when she was well on her way. In this case, you expressed action that went beyond what you would naturally do. This action would have a positive effect on our present circumstance because we acted beyond what we normally do. Let us look at the chart again.

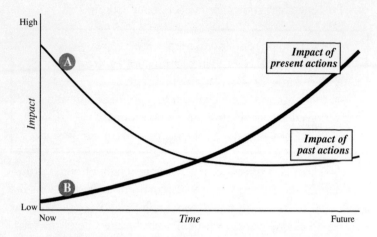

IMPACT OF PRESENT ACTIONS ON OUR LIFE INCREASES
WHEN WE ACT ABOVE OR BELOW OUR NATURAL STATE

As we can see, line B represents the impact of our present actions on our current life. What the chart shows is that our present actions have a marginal effect on our life today. This is because of the large influence of our past actions accumulated through previous rebirths. Therefore, when we act in a manner that reflects our natural state, we are simply expressing the status quo. In this case, there is no effect on the trajectory of line B.

However, when we express actions beyond or below our natural state, line B is pushed up; thereby the influence of these actions on our present life is increased. Our choices that fall below our normal state increase the negative elements in line B disproportionately, and this will change our current life correspondingly. Similarly, when our actions go above our normal state, this increases the positive elements in line B disproportionately, and our current life will be impacted accordingly. By using our freedom to choose wisely, we are able to affect our lives to a greater or lesser degree in a negative or positive way.

The Angry Man—A Sufi master was walking in the market with his student. Suddenly, an angry man rushing by bumped into the Sufi. Offended by this, the angry man pushed the Sufi master to the floor. The Sufi regained his balance as if nothing had happened. The student was visibly agitated and asked why, having been pushed to the ground needlessly by the angry man, he had not responded in kind. The master said, "The man was acting from the ego of his lower self, and he had a choice to react from his lower self and respond with anger or from his higher self with calm." "But he pushed you," the student said. "Yes," the master said, "and what he puts out through his actions and intentions will attract his just reward."

We are all wired into the creative process and everything we do, think, and intend is synthesized and the effect is returned. Allowing others to push us into acting below our natural way empowers them to control our destiny.

The process of cause and effect are very misunderstood. The idea of our past actions as a cause of our present problems leads many to think that perhaps our suffering is a consequence of mistakes we have made. This is far from the truth. This karmic doctrine is a spiritual principle, and therefore, it is rooted in our spiritual lives. Thus, the causes for any suffering we have today have their origins before this birth. Second, cause and effect is not a punitive law. Everything needs to balance out; this idea is programmed into the creative process. In the same way that a pull on one side of a string will create a tug on the other, if we have weakness in one leg, the other leg will automatically compensate. God does not sit on a throne dishing out suffering because we may have fallen short on occasion. Everything we do is wired into the creative law, and it maintains an equilibrium. When our actions shift that balance, instinctively a process occurs to restore that parity.

Because we do not see the whole picture, we are shocked and surprised when problems or tribulations enter our life. "Suddenly" is a term we use too often. *Suddenly* I became sick, *suddenly* my business went under, or *suddenly* we are overwhelmed with problems. There is no such thing as suddenly; everything is evolving toward its perfect state, and only when we broaden our perception do we realize that the causes are hidden. For instance, we see a tree but not the seed; we see a child but not the sperm. The causes are always concealed before and after manifestation; there are no sudden or random acts within the creative process. The seeds to our present life were planted a long time ago, even as our personal evolution to perfection continues today. That does not mean that we accept our fate as discussed, because through our actions today, we are empowered to co-create the life we want. When Jesus was slapped, he turned the other cheek. Some people see this as a sign of weakness of character. Yet he did not allow one person's anger to make him feed his ego. He had a choice to accept a script where his part involved being angry, or one that enabled him to feed his higher self. He chose the latter, and in the process, his outward weakness became his inward strength.

As simple as it sounds, expressing actions that go beyond our natural state are difficult to sustain. We can all bring ourselves to rise above our own natural standard some of the time. Unfortunately, to do this consistently and all the time, though not impossible, is at least extremely difficult. Of course, we are human, and often we fall short of our expectations. This happens because we are conditioned by the world of repossession, which influences us to be selfish and self-centered.

The Sacred Stone—There was a man who, upon his journey, discovered the sacred stone of the ancient tribe. It was an ordinary looking stone but it concealed some magical powers. As the man was returning home, he dropped the stone. He realized what had happened and frantically began looking for it. Since he was walking along the river's edge, this task became extremely difficult because the riverbank was lined with thousands of similar looking pebbles. He quickly started picking up the stones from the floor and, after a quick glance, threw them into the river. As time passed, he became desperate and worked at a faster and faster pace. In his haste, he picked up the stone he was searching for and, through force of habit, threw it in the river. As soon as the stone left his hand, he realized what had happened and rushed into the water to look for it.

We are conditioned by the material world to behave in a certain way. Scripts and roles enter into our lives, hiding opportunities, important lessons, and treasures, and sadly, most of them go by unnoticed. We are discarding the precious experiences that can help us transform and awaken. We can change our life, and it all begins with choice, for it is the cause that will manifest the effect. Once we expand our awareness to all the scripts that are floating by, we are empowered to pick those that affect us positively and walk away from those that have a negative effect on us. Now we can begin to act in a manner beyond our natural state and hasten our transformation.

The Boy and the Ants—There once was an enlightened Sufi master whose youngest pupil was a 10-year-old boy. He looked at his young student's face and saw that a terrible accident would befall him, causing him to lose his legs. When it was time for the student to return home, he asked the boy not to return for one full year. The master felt that, at the time of his suffering, he should be with his family. The boy obliged and returned home. Exactly one year later, he saw the young boy arrive for more teaching. The master was surprised, as he did not expect to see him and asked the student everything he had done in the last year. The boy explained his long journey back to his home and then explained a particular incident. He was crossing a stream and he noticed a whole colony of ants stranded in the middle because the stream had split in two and had carved a new path. As the stream gathered speed, slowly the ants were being washed away. Therefore, he picked up a long branch and held it over the median so that all the ants could cross to safety. Once each one had escaped death, he went on his way. The master realized immediately that the boy had acted in a manner far beyond his natural way and, as a result, his destiny had changed.

When we go beyond what is our common nature, we are having a positive effect on our karma. However, it can work in reverse, as we see in the parable of Moses. God had promised Moses that he would attend his feast of thanksgiving. Moses sat about, preparing a kingly affair, tending to the minor details himself. The feast was ready and Moses waited for God. Just then, a hungry beggar approached Moses, asking him for food. Moses was preoccupied waiting for his Lord to arrive and was rather upset that the beggar was intruding on his most important day, so he told the beggar to leave at once. Moses waited, but God never arrived. Later, a very disappointed Moses asked God in his vision why he had not kept his word and attended the thanksgiving feast. "I did come," God said, "but you turned me away." Moses fell short of his naturally high state of being when he ignored the hungry beggar, and in the process, missed God's grace at his table. Destiny is shaped by our actions and, when we go beyond, a positive effect is felt in our life immediately. Similarly, when we fall short, the effect is negative.

Actions that go beyond our natural state are difficult to sustain. To live a life the way Gandhi or Mother Teresa lived involves great sacrifices and discipline. There is a second way in which our actions can have a huge influence on our life today. It is easier, sustainable, more powerful, and we will look at it in the next chapter.

CHAPTER 7

The Fifth Insight

'Lasting Change Happens From the Inside Out'

The world we live in appears as though it is filled with conflict and chaos, yet when we are introspective, we see that everything within creation, from the smallest plant to the human being, is evolving toward a higher state through the process of death, renewal and rebirth. There is a connectedness between everything, and changes in one thing create an effect on the other things. This process of transformation is the unfolding history that makes our life today what it is. Who we are and the circumstances into which we are born are not accidents, rather the outcome whose causes lie in this history, and these experiences are etched on the soul. This is one of the universal laws of creation, and like any other law it works all the time. Day in and day out, while we are asleep and even before our birth, these laws are the foundation of everything within creation. We see in nature the law of gravity and how it affects everything. Children fall and cars go off cliffs, yet these laws do not discriminate, they just work. It is like electricity; when we turn on the switch, the light comes on, irrespective of how or why it works. The laws of cyclical rebirth are part of the universal laws of creation; they exist because they have always existed. We cannot change these laws, yet when we understand them, we can harness their potential and progress spiritually.

The Master and his Son—The wise master was traveling on a small boat with his beloved son. Soon, the weather changed and the sea became very rough. The son was afraid and very distressed. The conditions worsened and a thick fog enveloped their boat as it tossed from side to side. Fearing for his death, the son approached his father and sought comfort. The father smiled, but did not say a word. "Why do you smile at such a critical time? Do you not fear death?" the son asked. The father picked up his son and, holding him over the water's edge, asked, "Do you think I will throw you into the water?" The son smiled and said, "No, I know you love me and I trust you." The father replied, "I was smiling for the same reason; I trust the divine will because he has our best interest at heart."

We must begin by an unflinching acceptance that our personal situation today is exactly what it should be and to trust that it is a part of a carefully designed personal plan. Our abilities to reason, hard earned through the cycle of rebirth, give us an intellect and with it the power to change our fate. Our next level of development is in our hands, and we can co-write the scripts and become the architects of our future.

As human beings, we have been very successful at doing this in our physical and material life. Just in the last 100 years, our civilization has gone from one whose members lived in villages with a horizon that spanned a few hundred miles to one that goes beyond our planet itself. Knowledge has transformed the way in which we live. As human beings, we were able to harness our resources and abilities to control time, and this was instrumental in the rapid increases in our progress and standard of living. The concept of accelerated productivity, for instance, encourages more production in less time, not just in our factories but also on our farms where we have learned to shorten the time it takes plants to grow and chickens to lay eggs. In the area of healthcare, the focus of research has been to reduce the time in the development of vaccines and medicines. Our transportation system is geared toward delivering passengers and goods between two points in the shortest time. Finally, we see how we have pushed our communication technologies to provide us with real-time information on what may be happening in any part of our world and even beyond. By focusing all our efforts on getting things done faster, we have reduced the time between cause and effect. In other words, the more we have reduced the distance between cause and effect, the more progress we have made.

Similarly, to progress the soul toward the Invisible Light, we face similar challenges, because the same universal laws bind us. We can see from the previous chapter that our present actions have a marginal affect on our life today, essentially because there is a large lag between these actions and their consequent reactions. However, when we take a closer look, we can see that it is really a matter of context. The soul's existence is infinite, and therefore 20 and 30 years are mere seconds. Yet human life is limited, and the same period represents almost one third of life. Hence, what we do today is having an effect, but it is invisible because of its conversion to spiritual time.

It is a natural tendency to be attracted to our material life because here our actions illicit almost immediate reactions, ones that can be tested and measured. We see this in the way we approach weight loss. The dietician will recommend a healthy lifestyle incorporating good eating and exercise habits. The results are slow but sure. Yet, in our search for fast results, we are attracted to the instant results promised by the myriad of commercial diet programs. It is this attraction to instant results that continues to anchor us to our lower self under the domination of an ego driven by tangibles.

The mystic Rumi writes:

O son, burst thy chains and be free!
How long wilt thou be a bondsman to silver
and gold?

Like a child captivated by a new toy, we feel a sense of power when we are able to initiate an act and see immediate results in our material world. Consequently, we put little conviction in efforts that would enable the soul to progress, because results and rewards are intangible and take much longer. To move into the world of intangible reality, as Rumi advises, we must let go of the tangibles to which we have become enslaved. I am not suggesting that one gives up material attachments, but rather the significance we give them. As the saying goes, "It is all right to have possessions as long as we are not possessed by these possessions."

Although our actions today appear to have a marginal effect on our soul's progress, we need to remind ourselves that the life of our soul is not measured in years and human lifetimes. In fact, our actions today have a far greater effect on our soul life than we realize because their impact lasts beyond our current human life. However, the most fascinating wisdom from the ancient scribes tells us of a way in which our actions can be so powerful that their effects show up on the radar screens of our life today. We can witness this change not in decades and lifetimes, but now.

The mere fact that we have an intellect empowers us to shape our destiny and change our fate. The way to reduce the time between cause and effect in spiritual matters does exist, and this is exactly what the wise sages of the old did. The real miracle that Moses performed at the Red Sea was the melting away of time between his prayers, hopes and aspirations and the subsequent parting of the Red Sea. This may seem like an extreme example, but the lives of the prophets were replete with such impossible happenings. When Jesus brought the dead to life, he did the same thing, condensing the time between death and rebirth. Similarly, Mohamed was able to converse with the angel Gabriel by transcending physical time. All of them were silently practicing the Invisible Way, which enabled them to reduce the time between cause and effect, but with one big difference. They effected spiritual time.

Since our soul's existence is a measurement of spiritual moments, the only way to affect its course meaningfully is to ensure that our actions transcend physical time. This is how we are able to reduce the time between cause and effect and progress the soul beyond its nature. Knowledge of these spiritual practices, however, is not learned at our schools and universities. This is because there are two types of knowledge: learned knowledge and revealed knowledge. Learned knowledge is the know-how of the physical and material realm, and this is learned in schools, universities and from studying books. As man discovers and understands his physical environment, this knowledge is preserved and learned by subsequent generations. Revealed knowledge, on the other hand, is knowledge of the spiritual realm, revealed to man through divinely inspired messengers. In total, there have been 124,000 such wise souls, and it is written that no generation in any epoch of time is ever left without the presence of a sage of this caliber in their midst. Revealed knowledge, by its very nature, is a higher knowledge because it emanates from the ether, the realm of the infinite, and is a grace from the divine. Since revealed knowledge encompasses the know-how of the spiritual laws, it is in the wisdom of the prophets and messengers that we find the methods by which we can go beyond the barriers of physical time. By understanding and emulating their silent practices, we are able to condense the time between cause and effect in spiritual matters, thereby achieving what appears impossible. It was Jesus who said that man would one day do greater works than his.

If we can understand that our worldly circumstance is the outcome of a series of decisions we have made over a period of time that precedes our current life, then it is easy to understand that our present condition is the effect, the cause of which stems not from our physical life, but from our spiritual life. The cause of our present life remains an imprint within the soul, and any change we wish to create in our life has to begin with the soul, the cause. We can now look at the fifth and final insight: "Lasting change happens from the inside out." Appreciating that the foundation of our physical life is rooted in our spiritual life, it follows that any change to our physical life must emanate from a change to our spiritual one.

Try this simple exercise. Put the palm of your hand against a wall so that you can see its shadow. We can agree that the hand is real and the shadow is an image. In order to change the shadow on the wall to reflect a hand with a closed fist, we must first form a fist; subsequently, the image on the wall will reflect this. What comes first? The real has to change before its image can. Our physical life is a shadow of our spiritual life; we discussed this at length earlier in the book. Unlike the chicken and egg debate, our soul did precede the physical body and will remain, even though our physical body will not. To create a change in our physical life, we must first make a change in the real, spiritual one because the soul exists in the unseen world of cause, and the physical body in the seen world of effect.

One of the biggest myths that exists today is the notion that, if we identify the habits of successful and wise people and incorporate them into our life, we will become successful and enlightened also. Consequently, people spend millions of dollars each year buying into this illusion. I remember reading about the Titanic. Despite the serious damage the ship had suffered during its collision with the iceberg, the band played on it as if everything was fine. This, of course, did not stop the Titanic from sinking. Similarly, our physical life today is really an expression of where we are on the inside. We can mimic the habits of the wise and successful all we want in our external life, but if the soul within is sinking, our ship is going down! Unless our outer habits can substantially change our inner essence, these habits will only make us feel good temporarily. Considering that the self-help genre has huge shelf space in our bookstores, you would think that by now, with the introduction of all the successful habits and spiritual insights, we would have a correspondingly enlightened populace. I am not suggesting that the habits and secrets of the authors are flawed or inaccurate in any way; I am stating a fundamental spiritual principle that is at work. This principle states very clearly that unless our outer behavior changes and transforms our real spiritual self, these external changes are just a temporary illusion. We may know someone who has purchased courses and materials offering sound advice that they tried to incorporate into their daily life in the hope of finding success and happiness. Well-intentioned as these attempts may be, invariably their lifestyles always seem to revert to the old, deep-seated ways. I have a friend who has a shelf full of books and courses from renowned public speakers and authors in nicely packaged boxes dating back to the year 1975. He has tried them all, but his life has really not changed that much. In fact, he tells me that trying to ingrain these wise ideas and ways into his personal life was always like trying to fit a square peg into a round hole. That just about sums up the dilemma, because trying to fix a problem from the outside in is like transplanting something. We all know the law of transplantation; it works but only for a short time. Lasting change needs to happen on the inside within our soul first, and this effortlessly expresses itself permanently in our physical life. Needless to say, my friend has given up listening to the tapes and is happy to lend them out. Interested?

I was reading an article in the newspaper recently and the headline caught my eye. It read "Soil is the Soul of the Garden." How true, I thought; it provided a good analogy to the fifth insight. To achieve success with the plants and flowers that we plant in our garden, the key element we use is the soil. The microorganisms in the soil help convert the nutrient into a chemical form that the plants use. However, If the soil was unhealthy, the plants will not receive adequate nutrients, which would stifle their growth. Similarly, as human beings, if we desire to have a fulfilling life, it all depends on the health of the human soul, which is the heart of the spiritual beings that we are. If our soul is weak and distant, it could be comparable to an unhealthy soil. The consequences will be felt in our outward form, meaning our physical life. For instance, by changing and nurturing the soil to health, we would eventually see a change in the quality of flowers and plants in the garden, because the change needs to occur on the inside before results are visible in the garden. Similarly, to change our external life and circumstances, we must first nourish and strengthen the soul within us.

Suppose we decided not to change the unhealthy soil, but instead, proceeded to transplant fully-grown plants. What can we assume the outcome would be? If we have planted healthy plants, then the garden will look good for a time, but slowly the new plants will be stifled and starved of nutrition and in time, these plants will start to wither.

Perhaps this may further explain why much of the advice from self-help authors does not work. Let me elaborate. By taking the habits and principles suggested by authors, no matter how wise and sound they are, and simply incorporating them into our daily lives, we are putting new plants into unhealthy soil. You might feel good and notice a change for a while, but the unhealthy soul will soon choke and stifle them.

We see ample evidence of this in our own life. How often, after an uncomfortable incident, have we told ourselves that we will change behavior in the future? We tell ourselves that in the future, we will be more loving and more kind, or we will not become angry and upset. Yet we are caught up behaving in a similar fashion; it seems there is often a disconnect between what we intend to do and how we act. We are always trying to manage, control and police our outward actions, which is a constant struggle because we are transplanting these ideals into our life instead of allowing them to emerge from the inside. The fifth insight of the Invisible Way tells us very clearly that we first need to make a change on the inside, and we will succeed only to the degree that the advice helps us do this.

The Lost Key—A man was shuffling outside his home, clearly looking for something on the street. He seemed to be frantically searching. A wise sage was passing by and, in a gesture of goodwill, he walked up to him and asked, "Can I help you?" The man replied, "Yes, you can help, I have lost my key." The sage asked, "Do you know where you lost it?" The man answered, "I don't know where I lost it." The sage then asked, "Why do you keep looking in this place?" The man replied, "It is the only place that is bright and lit up."

This is really the paradox of the visible world. We are in the world of repossession, searching for the valuable keys to joy, enlightenment, love and peace of mind. We seek these profound, abstract inner needs in our external world because it is bright, visible and tangible and the only place we know to look. Unfortunately, the keys are not outside but inside. The way inwards appears dark but is not, because the Invisible Light illuminates the path. Similarly, the outward appears bright, but is really a dark shadow of realty.

Nelson Mandela, who spent decades in a prison cell, once said:

> Our deepest fear is not that we are inadequate.
> Our deepest fear is that we are powerful beyond
> measure. It is our light not our darkness that most
> frightens us.

Let us go back to our exercise, holding the hand up against the wall and creating a shadow. How can we change and move the shadow? There are two ways. First, we can allow the sun to move as it does, and this will automatically change the shape of the shadow and move it. The movement of the the shadow in this case happens in its own course and time. The second way to change and move the shadow is by moving our hand, which will have the same effect, with one big difference. We can regulate the time. Therefore, by acting out of our natural state, we are passively allowing our soul to develop and move toward its higher self in its own course and time. However, by acting above or below our natural state, we are initiating movement and thereby affecting the timing. In other words, we are moving our hand and speeding up the process of change.

We find this idea expressed clearly in one of the oldest stories told, the parable of Adam's paradox. The story goes that Adam was happy and content with Eve in the Garden of Eden. God had instructed him, however, not to approach the forbidden tree. Adam had the freedom to obey or disobey what God had revealed to him. The developing circumstances influenced Adam to approach the forbidden tree and in the process, he lost his place in Eden.

> O Adam! Dwell thou and thy wife in the garden
> And eat of the bountiful things therein as ye will.
> But approach not the tree or ye run into harm
> and transgression.

Such parables are allegories that hide timeless wisdom. The tree represented learned knowledge. The real choice Adam had was that either he could stick with the knowledge revealed to him from God or become enamored by the worldly knowledge he was discovering. Adam was distracted and fascinated by material knowledge, unaware that he had let go of the revealed knowledge and, in the process, acted below his natural state. This speeded up his fall and, in essence, he moved from his higher self and surrendered to the ego of the lower self. The journey of Adam back to paradise, then, is the journey of all of us, from the lower self dominated by the ego, to the higher self where we are divine in potential. This is our journey, the journey of the soul. The most revealing aspect of this story is actually what happens next, because God does not forsake Adam, nor does he abandon him. Rather, he tells Adam of the Invisible Way by which he could regain his divine status. In essence, Adam is asked to turn inward.

> Then learned Adam from his lord
> Words of inspiration and his lord Turned toward him
> For he is oft returning most merciful."

By deconstructing this wise parable, we learn so much about the Invisible Way because the paradox we find ourselves in is no different than the one Adam found himself in. As human beings, we have an inner faculty that is divine in potential and is our soul in perfection. We also have an external faculty that is dominated by our ego, and is instinctively selfish and ruthless in potential. We exist in balance, and when the fulcrum shifts, it creates ripples in our life positively or negatively depending on the direction of the shift. It is like a string on a bow: If it is too tight, the cord will snap, and if it is too loose, the arrow will not fly.

In the context of our potential, when we are centered in the higher self, connected to our divine qualities, we find the peace and joy Adam found in Eden. However, because we exist in the physical world, which is constantly conditioning and influencing us, there are loud external impulses affecting the decisions we make. Think about it. We are surrounded by video lottery terminals and great cities built for gambling. We have 500 channels on our television and neon messages that speak to us the moment we leave home.

A friend sent me a joke, and the irony is so noticeable that it made me laugh: Last night, my wife and I were sitting in the living room and I said to her, "I never want to live in a vegetative state, dependent on some machine and fluids from a bottle. If that ever happens, just pull the plug." She got up, unplugged the TV and then threw out my beer.

It is good to see ourselves in the mirror of reality because it can be quite sobering. The fact is that we are glued to external impulses, especially the television. How often have we been in a conversation and someone justifies their point of view by suggesting, "I heard or saw it on TV," as if it is a truth box! The power to influence our lives is wielded by the scriptwriters and journalists who impose their views on an unsuspecting public, who appear more interested in the lives of fictitious characters on television than their own. We are relentlessly bombarded by the messages that tell us how to live our lives and even what clothes to wear. To complicate things, we anesthetize ourselves with drugs and alcohol, adding an extra veil to reality. These external voices come to us in the home, on vacation and even when traveling to work in a car or bus, creating a gradual internal shift disconnecting us from the insight of the within. The external noise becomes louder and more prominent, just as those original internal impulses slowly fade into the distance. Over time, and in the absence of an awareness of what is happening, we are drawn closer and closer to the mythical fruits of the forbidden tree, and the disconnection to our spiritual and real self is complete. This happens very gradually, day-by-day, unnoticed, until one day we find that our life is a wreck, as Adam did. Moreover, we have counted down our precious breaths, bringing us closer to the end of this physical encounter. If you are reading this book, then you still have time to pick up the keys.

The King and the Servant—King Wagt lived in a large palace that contained great treasures. The king loved his possessions, but he was always troubled and found it very hard to get a good night sleep. He was constantly worried that the rulers from the neighboring states would come to plunder his wealth. In the mornings, he used to gaze at the gardener with envy. He saw him perform his duties diligently and always seemed to be happy and at peace with himself; he wished he, too, had that. He did not know that, after the gardener finished his work each day, he lay awake at night in his small cottage. He used to gaze at the palace and be envious of the king, thinking how peaceful life would be if he had so much wealth.

In the world of repossession, everyone looks outward for happiness and meaning; the grass is always greener on the other side. This, indeed, is a prison that steals our time.

Our way out of this quagmire is no different than Adam's. To change our lives externally, we need to create an internal change first. Lasting change comes from the inside out; this was the message for Adam and it is as valid today. This spiritual insight shows us that, for our actions to dramatically influence our life at present, they have to effect us at the core of our essence, in the soul. Any act that we engage in that affects our soul will substantially contribute to changing our worldly circumstance. The greater and more profound the impact on our soul, the more pronounced will be the reaction in our physical life. This means that the only things that can create a lasting change in our current life are those that can induce a core transformation in our essential self. By making changes in the soul, we can change our physical lives.

The internal solution is the only way to create lasting and meaningful changes to our physical life, because the imprints of our past actions are etched onto our soul, binding us to the karmic laws. The Invisible Way enables us to erase the negative imprints on our soul, empowering us to rewrite our future.

The Mystic Rumi writes:

> I have lived on the lip of insanity
>
> Wanting to know reasons.
>
> Knocking on a door. It opens.
>
> I have been knocking from inside!

Our negative acts from the past clothe the soul; they leave barriers and keep it distant from its source.

The sacred texts tell us:

> Ask and it shall be given.
>
> Knock—The door is opened.

But always from the inside! However, our positive actions also cloth the soul and in this case, it becomes a shield. By finding a means to remove the negative imprints on our soul, the proportionate value of the positive imprints increase, and this moves the fulcrum of our center toward the higher self. In the process, we rediscover that which we had lost: peace, love and joy.

Since the foundations of our physical life are rooted into our spiritual life, it follows that changes to our outward life can only come by first changing the inward.

I remember talking to a gardener about turning the weed-laden dirt patch on the side of my house into a healthy flowerbed. He told me that the basis of strength and potency of a plant runs from the seed to the root, then to the leaf. The flower, as it turns out, has little potency. This made me realize that since we are a part of this physical creation, we are bound by the same laws. Our potency lies in our seed, the soul, which is the blueprint. This is a concept all of us can embrace, because to build anything physical we need a blueprint. Before a house is built, for instance, a blueprint is constructed, and any changes we wish to make to its design must first be made on the blueprint.

Our advances in science, for example, have led us to discover the human genome, the blueprint of the human body. Since many illnesses are hereditary, the likelihood of their manifestation in our life is prewritten in our genes. Yet in the discovery of our physical blueprint, we may soon have the ability to erase the sickness from our genes before it manifests in our physical life. Imagine if we understood and discovered the blueprint of our real self. We could identify all the negative prewritten attachments and erase them, thereby changing our past, which would automatically change our life today. Also by selectively removing those dark imprints, we would progressively bring light into our life immediately.

Joe (not his real name) and I have known each other most of our life. I know everything about him and we have shared a trusting relationship. He is someone who is, in his own way, enlightened. He used to care for his wheelchair-bound father, with whom he shared a deep spiritual bond. One day, in a vision, his father came and told him of his impending death. Joe felt the pain he would have in that event, so he asked his father's soul to postpone his death! When the day and the date of the father's prophesied death arrived, it went without incident. Joe was deeply relieved. Over the course of the next three months, he began to regret what he had done. His father's health took a turn for the worse. Though he was still the same disabled father, he was tormented with unknown pains that the doctors could not identify. One day, the father looked at Joe and said that God was unjust and merciless for keeping him alive in the suffering of his pain. Joe realized at that time that his father, in his "self," had postponed his death to please his son who had cared for him and was suffering. Joe was in extreme regret when he came to talk to me. He had been thinking of himself when he had asked his father to postpone death. His father knew the torment that lay ahead, but acted selflessly to please the son who cared for him.

Joe and I talked for a while and, at the end of the conversation, I did not need to advise him on his next step. Joe spent the next two weeks paralyzed and unable to work, eat or converse with his wife and children. He was absorbed within himself, seeking forgiveness and waiting for an opportunity to right a wrong. This he got, and in the spiritual conversation his soul had with that of this father, he let go and gave back that decision to the divine will. Three months later, his father passed away peacefully in his sleep.

Earlier in the book, I had suggested that we can postpone death. Yes, this is how it is done. If we are able to go into our soul and change the blueprint, then we can change everything! Our death is programmed into the soul, based on the number of spiritual breaths it is allocated on the day it is given a physical form. The promise of the return the soul made at birth in a human body is based on all that soul has accomplished in its previous life and what it needs to accomplish in this particular life. By changing the mix of accomplishments from the previous life, we can change what remains to be completed in our present life. However, we need to be cautious of empowering ourselves to prolong or shorten our life. Because physical life is part of an intricate matrix connected to the ether, changes to any part will have a ripple effect. Think about Joe's situation. In prolonging his father's death, there were ripples in the physical and spiritual dimensions. In the physical world, the father was in torment while the son, because of his selfishness, created negative attachments to his own soul, which would affect the lives of his wife and the children who were not yet born to him. In the spiritual dimension, the father's entry into the higher dimension was postponed, and this had consequences on his spiritual journey. In other words, by tampering with the death of one human being, we create ripples that become a wave in the universe. It is best to leave the decisions of life and death to the Divine, which is constantly altering the destiny of the human being in response to our actions. However, by trusting and allowing the divine will to prevail, our well-intentioned acts will not unwittingly create negative imprints on our souls.

At about the time I was writing this chapter, rather coincidently (or not) a friend emailed me this fascinating story. One day, while a poor Scottish farmer was going about his labor, he heard a cry for help from a distant swamp. Having been to Scotland, I knew that the bogs in the Highlands could be very dangerous. The farmer ran toward the swamp and there he found a terrified boy up to his waist in the mire. Farmer Fleming risked his own life and rescued the little boy from what would have been certain death. The next day, a nobleman's carriage pulled up to his small cottage, and the well-dressed gentleman thanked Farmer Fleming for saving his son's life. He offered Fleming a reward, but the farmer refused it, for he felt that his deed was reward enough. Just then, his young son came out and the nobleman asked if he could at least provide his young boy the same level of education he would provide his own. To this, the farmer agreed. The son of Farmer Fleming attended the very best schools and graduated from St. Mary's Hospital Medical School. He became famous all over the world as the renowned Sir Alexander Fleming, who discovered penicillin. Years later, the same nobleman's son became sick and his life was saved by penicillin. The name of the nobleman was Lord Randolph Churchill.

I found this story particularly revealing. When the farmer saved a little boy by risking his own life, he went beyond his natural state. The ancient scripts tell us, "He who saves one life is as if he has saved the whole of humanity." In doing this, the farmer dramatically changed his own karma, which we see in the way his son's destiny changed. However, the ripple of these kinds of outstanding acts creates waves, and in this case, the boy whose father saved a life discovered the medicine that has saved the lives of millions. All our intentions, thoughts and actions leave a mark on our soul, which is wired into the natural creative process, and the degree to which they affect the soul is proportionate to the changes that manifest in our physical life. Little mistakes we make may appear small but they accumulate, and at some point, the equations have to balance out. It is like a log that is easy to pull in the water but much more difficult to pull on land. We need to be very cautious of all our acts because they will need to find closure in our life eventually. Decisions that relate to matters of life and death, such as abortion, euthanasia and the justification for war and terrorism, are extremely serious for the individuals making them, as well as humanity. We may be able to rationalize our choices, but it is important to ask whether the wellspring from which we draw when making such decisions is outward or inward. Wrong choices will exact a heavy price when the rebalancing occurs! Therefore, if in doubt, choose actions that preserve life.

Our outward practices, unless they are way beyond our natural state, which is impossible to sustain consistently, have little affect on our soul. Consequently, our external habits cannot be relied upon to accomplish an internal change. We cannot alter our inner state from the outside in. Broken water mains cannot be fixed by patching up the hole from which the water gushes on the ground. You must go in and repair it at the point of break. Similarly, to alter our inner state, we have to go inward to the essential self. The sacred books tell us that we have charge of our own souls. Therefore, our past actions may have already set the sails of our present life, but, by altering our inner state, we can reset the sails.

However, there is one important thing to keep in mind. We may be able to change our karma to the degree that we exercise our powers of freewill and choice, but this does not make us exempt from them. In other words, we cannot stop circumstances coming into our lives that might give us some pain and unhappiness if those circumstances were closing out unfinished equations. Everything we have done needs to balance out in the end, and since our life today has many unfulfilled lessons, broken promises and incomplete equations attached to our soul, these need to find closure. However, there is one significant change that does occur, and that is that our experiences of these circumstances are at a very high and enlightened stage. Hence, even though we may feel and encounter the difficulties and suffering, we do so from an illumined context.

This reminds me of a story that explains this idea quite well.

The Squirrel and the Chipmunk—There were two friends, a squirrel and a chipmunk, that often played together in the woods. One day as they were chasing each other around, the chipmunk suggested a new game. "Why don't we climb the tree and tell what we see in our woods?" So the chipmunk went up the tree first although he was not accustomed to climbing trees. He returned rather abruptly and seemed very scared. "What is the matter?" the squirrel asked. "It is chaotic and very unsafe in this jungle; I saw snakes and monkeys and many other creatures fighting each other on the branches and trees, so I rushed back down," the chipmunk said. It was now the squirrel's turn to go up the tree and tell what he saw. He did not return for quite some time and when he did, he appeared very calm. "I did not see what you saw," said the squirrel. "I saw the tops of the trees and way beyond I saw a beautiful lake where we could go and play." The squirrel had climbed much higher, and his view of the forest was very different.

As we become illumined, our view of the world and the circumstances existing in our life change. We are now seeing a different movie, and our role in that script is different. The enlightened perspective that I am referring to comes to us from an expanded consciousness. It is not that we are able to avoid painful events emerging into our personal lives; rather, our role and script within it changes. Let me give you an example. When we throw a pebble into a small pond, we can see the large ripples spreading outward to the edge. Now, if we turned the pond into an ocean, the pebble we throw into it would hardly create a ripple. Similarly, when we are like a pond, problems are huge ripples that throw us into waves of turmoil. However, when our consciousness expands, the same pebble hardly creates a ripple in our life. Compare the situation Jesus faced when Judas betrayed him. An ordinary person would have been devastated by a close friend's betrayal, yet Jesus was an ocean and his enlightened perspective allowed him to see a way beyond that one act of betrayal. To have an expanded consciousness, we have to change our inner state. As Jesus explained, "A good man brings good out the treasure of good things in his heart."

We live in a perishable world in which we seek a security that, in reality, does not exist. We are surrounded by turmoil and deconstruction, and holding onto anything for an extended period is almost impossible. Everything we need to overcome—all that this physical life inflicts on us—exists within us, for it is the only constant. What the soul knows is unknown to most of us who have a soul, but when we shift our balance to the higher self, it is from the sacred space that we get glimpses of what the soul knows. The blueprints of our present life, therefore, are in the soul, and the map of our past, present and future exists therein, as does the genome of the divine creator. We have charge of our souls, and we can change our life today, but this is only possible from the inside out.

CHAPTER 8

The Primary Practice of the Invisible Way

The five insights we looked at in Chapter One represent time-less spiritual wisdom brought to us by the enlightened souls who also tell us of a way out of the paradox we find ourselves in. We are spiritual beings mired in the mist of our own ignorance and impris-oned like a bird in a cage. We are reminded by the ancient scribes that our destiny is exalted and it is up to us to reach for it. We have wings and we can soar into the sky, they tell us. The doors of the cages are open, and we are free to fulfill our calling and create for ourselves a life of meaning, purpose and happiness. Listen to the lament from within; it sings the tunes of sadness and anguish, call-ing us to discover the Invisible Light whose radiance melts away the ignorance and releases the captive. That quest, my friend, is inward and the path is invisible.

There is just one way in which we can journey within and that is through meditation. This is the primary practice of the Invisible Way. All the great divinely inspired messengers, saints, and sages, and the inspired mystics who came subsequently, incorporated this one basic practice that was so welded into their being that it became a wellspring from which all their thoughts and actions emanated.

Much is written about meditation in this day and age. Sadly, in the rush to commercialize it, the essence of this ancient and sacred practice has been lost. Today, meditation is packaged, marketed and sold in stores. Newspapers write 200-word editorials on the merit of meditation and include it in the New Year's resolution list, while television stations give us 60-second sound bites. We have taken what is fundamentally a sacred practice that empowers us to transform ourselves from terrestrial to celestial beings, and consequently the destiny of our world, and have reduced it to yet one more product we can own in the world of repossession.

In the days before the birth of science, the wise sages of the time practiced the art of alchemy, through which they hoped to transform base metals into gold. However, where this search took a stronghold was in their quest to transform the soul from imperfection to perfection, to progress the soul from the lower self, where it has animal passions and instincts, to the higher self, where it is free of impurities and thus divine. The philosopher's stone was the mythical substance that enabled this transformation to occur. As a consequence, the lifelong aspiration of all the learned and the wise was to find the philosopher's stone, for it had the magical powers to change anything that was base and impure into something perfect and pure.

When we examine the lives of the ennobled souls, we can see that all of them had the philosopher's stone, and it gave them the power to affect the soul, the every essence of our being. By transforming the core, they were able to reduce the time between cause and effect and, in the process, change the lives of human beings and the destinies of mankind. What was the philosopher's stone? It was the Invisible Light! It turns base metals to gold, darkness to light, and seeds into flowers, and gives life to the human clay. Its breath sustains the multitude of dimensions within creation and its fragrance has the touch of Midas.

The Invisible Light is the philosopher's stone; it can do anything because it is everything. The secrets of the ages, past and present, reside in it, as does the power to change it. We cannot own it, yet it is in us and we are its trustees. The ancient scribes tell us that God offered the trusteeship of this light to the mountains, which declined to accept it because the burden was too onerous. The trusteeship was then offered to mankind, who accepted, but has been foolish. They sought to discover all that is outside of them but neglected the wellspring of the tangible and intangible realities, the Invisible Light, with which it was entrusted.

There are four stages to our inward journey.

Stage One: *Waking stage*—This represents us fully awake in our physical state as we go about our daily lives as physical beings.

Stage Two: *Dream stage*—This is the stage when we are asleep and dreaming. All of us dream each night.

Stage Three: *Dreamless stage*—This is the stage beyond the dreams. It is dark and very little is known about this stage except that it is the place before we reach point c, which is the outer boundary to the sacred space. This is the stillness where our meditation should occur. It is said that only when it is dark can we see the stars. Similarly, to be physically asleep and inwardly awake in this stillness makes it possible for us to gradually glimpse the distant light emanating from the sacred space toward which we journey.

The unknown mystic who penned "The Cloud of Unknowing" writes:

> And therefore shape thee to bide in the darkness as
> long as thou mayest
> Ever more crying after him that thou lovest.
> For if ever thou shalt feel him or see him as it may
> be here,
> It behoveth always to be in this cloud in this darkness.

Most people are in deep sleep in this darkness, yet some of the deepest and most sacred meditations happen in this dark stillness.

Stage Four: *Sacred space*—The darkness dissolves into the sacred space that is the realm of timelessness and spiritual experience. This is the realm of the Invisible Light, and when graced and beckoned, we are blessed with a momentary glimpse of the Invisible Light.

The author of "The Cloud of Unknowing" writes:
  Then will he sometimes peradventure
  Send out a beam of ghostly light
  piercing this cloud of unknowing that is betwixt
      thee and him
  and shew thee some of his privity
  The which man may not, nor cannot speak.

The darkness is pierced by the radiant light during meditation; here the divine self reveals itself in a splendor of glory that words cannot describe. For in these rare timeless moments of grace, whole lifetimes are concealed.

Here is another passage from "The Cloud of Unknowing:"
  And therefore take good heed into time
  How that thou dependest it
  For nothing is more precious than time
  In one little time as little as it is
  May heaven be won and lost."

The Invisible Light, the philosopher's stone, which mankind sought because it gave people the power to do anything and be anything, is within us. The only way to attain it is through meditation. Meditation, of course, can reduce your stress, give you clarity and bring calm in your life, and if that is the limit of your vision, then this is your cue to close the book and practice the five-minute version. However, if you wish to use the ancient practice of meditation to seek the Invisible Light and empower yourself, read on. For in the pages that follow, I will outline the rigorous and demanding practices of the Invisible Way that enables the third eye to see that which was invisible. The journey to the sacred space within us where the Invisible Light resides will require discipline and sacrifice. For this is the treasure and knowledge of creation entrusted to man from the beginning of time. It is everything, and in order to approach it, we must first give our all and nothing less.

Meditation affects our real self in five profound ways: First: Meditation is the vehicle that empowers us to shift our center from our lower nature to our higher nature. Second: Meditation is the only way in which we can permanently remove the negative

attachments from our soul. Third: Meditation is the only moment
when we are truly alive. Fourth: Meditation opens the third eye
and awakens the soul. Fifth: Meditation makes us receptive to the
experience of the divine.

FIRST: **MEDITATION is the vehicle that empowers us to
shift our center from the lower self to the higher self.**

Our soul, as we discussed previously, is evolving toward a
higher state, as is everything within creation. Since we are
anchored to our lower self dominated by our ego, this journey continues, though we are unaware of it. We see evidence of this all
around us. A tree does not remember itself as a seed, nor does the
butterfly flying on high see its origin in the caterpillar below. When
we are ego centered, we are imprisoned in the world of repossession,
and here, we are like all the other lower species that are unaware of
the divine essence within. Our ego has a very limited perceptory
range of the other sensualities and dimensions within, yet feels the
need to express an over-inflated image of its self importance. Our
feelings of pride, arrogance and anger all emanate from the ego.

The Lesson—The master sat with his pupils, teaching them
about the nature of things. "How important is our ego?" asked a
student. "It is extremely important," responded the master. "Our
ego is very valuable, then," added another pupil. The master interjected, "No." The pupils sat rather confused as to how something
could be important, yet without value. The master provided a
demonstration. He took a bucket of water and asked one of the
students to insert his two hands clasped together into the bucket.
As the student did that, it created a big splash, displacing the
water. Then the student was asked to remove his hands, and once
again there was a splash, and then the water filled in, returning to
its previous state.

The master explained. "The water represents our real self, the
soul. The hands represented our physical self and ego. The hands
entered the water, creating movement of water for a short time, but
soon the water filled the void left by the withdrawing hands until

there was no trace that the hands had been in the water. Similarly, our soul is the water and our physical life enters into it momentarily and soon vanishes without a trace. All the activity, accomplishments and possessions we idealize soon disappear, when the physical body disappears after death. The soul is very valuable because it is the essence, but the ego is important because its entry creates friction and movement, enabling the soul to evolve.

Our choices in this physical body empower us to move the soul toward a higher state; however, human life is limited in time, and it leaves without a trace. I remember visiting the grave of my father on each anniversary to offer prayers. As the years rolled by, it became difficult to go each year; life was so busy. I went recently and looked at the stone that read 1922-1982. I thought a while about his life, the 60 years he had lived and how quickly they had gone. Today, the 60 years were symbolized by a dash between 1922 and 1982. A dash is what comes of our life—about the time it takes to enter this world, create a splash and leave. Yet, this dash we call life conceals the only opportunity to make choices that will care for the soul and nurture its development to realization.

What is the purpose of life? is common cliché. Yet, if the presence of our soul makes our body alive and full of life, and its absence makes us limp and dead, what can be the purpose of life if not to ennoble the soul? This is possible when we move away from the strong impulses of the ego toward the awakening of the higher self, because like animals, the ego is grounded to our lower instincts and ingrained conditioning.

We used to own a house cat named Raja who had been declawed. He was trained to stay indoors and for the longest time he was happy and content. One time, however, he was looking out of the screen door and caught sight of a bird that had ventured near to it. Soon, he did what was forbidden and sneaked out. Raja got a taste of the wonder of outdoors and from that day on, it was a struggle to keep him indoors. He used to be happy and content, but now he sought every opportunity to rush outside, even though it was dangerous for a domesticated, de-clawed cat.

All animals have ingrained instincts from which their actions emanate, and although they have the faculty of sensuality, they do not possess a developed intellect. Angels, on the other hand, have a developed intellect but do not have sensuality. Human beings have both sensuality and intellect that enables them to choose and reason. When our sensuality overcomes our intellect, we can be worse than beasts, and when our intellect overwhelms our sensuality, we are considered higher than angels. This power to reason enables us to shape our destiny either toward the lower instincts or higher, toward exaltedness.

The question that may come to mind is that, if our soul is already on a journey evolving toward a higher state, why do anything? If we go back to the example in Chapter Seven, we see that there were two ways in which the shadow of our fist on the wall moved. One was a passive act on our part, because as the sun moved, the shadow moved. The other was a proactive method, where we moved our hand and thereby moved the shadow. In other words, we can accept our fate passively and do nothing, thus allowing our soul to evolve according to the prewritten plan. Alternatively, we can change our fate and create for ourselves the life we want because our reason and intellect empowers us to do this. How then is this possible? It is through meditation, serious meditation. Let me give you an example. Most of us have ridden in a car as a driver or passenger at night time. I remember driving from Calgary to visit my brother in Red Deer at night. It was pitch black, and the only light we saw was the full beam of the car illuminating the road some 30 yards ahead. To the left, right and rear, however, all was an envelope of darkness, and it seemed that we were really not moving. The next morning, as we were returning, I looked at the black spaces of the previous night and found a view vibrant and full of life. There were farm animals and deer, not to mention rabbits and gophers. I realized that they were all there the night before, yet they did not exist in my perception during the night journey.

Similarly, when we are mired in the lower self, our spiritual journey continues in the dark, and we are oblivious to everything because we cannot see or realize our movement. Meditation opens our perceptions to landscapes, views and vibrancy that exist all around us, and the difference is darkness or light. However, going from our lower self to the higher self represents our transformation from physical beings that occasionally have spiritual experiences to spiritual beings that are in the midst of a temporary human encounter. This type of shift, in which we move from asking to be loved and understood to giving and seeking understanding, cannot happen because we flicked a light switch, even though it's a remedy most people look for in our microwave world. There is a painstaking process that needs to be followed, using vehicles that include concentration and meditation. In fact, this internal journey can be broken down into three phases.

The first phase is that of concentration. The second phase combines concentration and meditation, and the third phase combines meditation and divine grace.

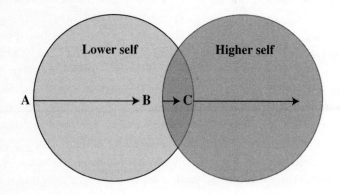

Phase 1 is from A to B

This journey from the lower self to the edge of the inner circle requires concentration, since it is the domain of the ego and lower instincts.

Phase 2 is from B to C

This journey between the two edges of the inner circle requires concentration and meditation, as this space is occupied by both the ego and the illumination of the Invisible Light.

Phase 3 is from C and beyond

Entry into the sacred space requires meditation and divine grace, as this is the holy space illuminated by the Invisible Light.

I will be looking at the techniques and understanding of concentration, meditation and divine grace when I outline the methods and practices.

Since our ego is anchored in the world of repossession, it is the gateway to all illusions. When we subdue it, much of these illusions will vanish, just as a child imagines all sorts of monsters in a dark room until the light is turned on and the fear disappears. Just think about it. If our real self is divine, what stops us from becoming awakened to this? The barrier is the ego, and it functions within the laws of creation. There is an old saying which tells us:

> Those who are controlled by the lower self must
> serve it;
> Those who control the lower self serve others

There is the ego of the lower self, and there is our soul, the essence of our higher self; we need to choose who is in charge, because we cannot serve two masters. It is in this choice that our destiny is shaped, either lower into the animal world or higher into the spiritual one. The great design aims to evolve us upward, and therefore the ego has to be subdued, which is possible when we use an aspect of itself. Think about some of the diseases we have overcome in recent times, from yellow fever and polio to cholera. These serious obstacles to our physical well-being were overcome by the development of vaccines that contained a trace of the disease itself. In other words, the disease was used against itself to beat it. Similarly, the only way to overcome the ego is to use our mind, which is a part of the ego, and this we can do with the practice of concentration. However, the ego is not one to relinquish its control easily.

The Mystic Rumi explains:

> Whatever possessions and objects of its desires the
> lower self may obtain,
> it hangs on to them, refusing to let them go out of
> greed for more or out of fear of poverty and need.

Using the mind against itself, we are able to conquer the lower self, and the only known process to achieve this is concentration, which is the twin sister of meditation. I will elaborate on the methods of both later in the book.

The Hunter—There was a hunter well known for seeking and catching his prey. One day, he set out to hunt deer in the forest. He glimpsed a deer standing by the lake and aimed his arrow. Carefully, he pulled his bow and let the arrow fly, but he missed. It was not often that he missed a target twice, so he aimed once again and let the arrow fly. Again he missed his target and felt very agitated. Frantically, he started to pull out more arrows and shot them at his target. The more he missed, the more frustrated and angry he became until there was just one arrow left. Just then, the deer, which had finished drinking the water, moved, and the realization dawned upon the hunter that he had been shooting his arrows at the deer's reflection in the water.

When we live in the world of repossession, we are dominated by the ego, which is continually agitated and frustrated because it is not able to possess and own what appears real to it. We see evidence of this in human behavior in this example. When the batteries of our television remote are weak or dead, what is our first reaction? We just push the buttons even harder, thinking this will bring the dead batteries to life! When our arrows don't hit the mark, we become ruthless and frustrated, and when we can't deal with our disappointments, we often turn to anger or alcohol and drugs. It never occurs to us that the remote will not work by pushing the buttons harder, but by changing the battery. Nor do we realize that, in the world of repossession, we can use the abundances that we seek, but can never own them.

Tosun Bayrak writes:

> The lower self is like a thief who sneaks into your
> house at night to steal whatever is valuable and
> worthwhile. You cannot fight this thief directly
> because it will mirror whatever force you bring
> against it. If you have a gun, the thief also will have
> a gun. If you have a knife, the thief will have a knife
> as well. To struggle with the thief is to invite disaster.

So what can you do? The only practical solution is
to turn on the light. The thief, who is a coward at
heart, will then run out. How do we turn on the
light? Through the practice of remembrance, awareness and heedfulness.

We have two centers, and by reining in the influence of the
ego, we shift toward the higher self, a realm illumined by the
Invisible Light and one that is our real and permanent self. The
process to achieving this is meditation, preceded by concentration.
We have the inherent choice to adapt the wisdom and practices of
the wise souls of old or condemn ourselves to a lifetime of night
journeys when we are surrounded by a dark envelope that blinds
us to the multitude of dimensions around us.

SECOND: **MEDITATION is the only way in which we can
permanently erase the negative attachments from
our soul.**

We note from chapter six that the script for our present circumstances was pre-coded into our soul at birth. However, we do
not have to accept our fate and passively surrender to our designed
cycle of births and life circumstances. The ancient texts tell us that
we have "charge of our own souls," and this represents a fundamental imperative and call to action. Therefore, not only are we
given the means to change our destiny, we also are challenged to
take the keys and get into the driver's seat. This means we must
make changes to our blueprint, the soul, and this is possible only
when our endeavors affect it. We have learned that there are two
ways in which we can do this.

First, when we outwardly act beyond our nature and second,
when we go inward and actually adjust the designs on the blueprint. The ability to behave beyond our basic natural state consistently is obviously very difficult. The prophets and the enlightened
souls have been able to do that at great personal sacrifice. In our
case, we have moments when we are able to rise to those lofty
heights sporadically, but similarly, there are times when we fall

short. In other words, this balancing out ensures that we have limitations on the degree to which we are able to profoundly affect the soul through this approach. The second approach, however, is much more direct and powerful, putting the charge and ownership squarely in our hands by using the penetrating qualities of meditation. Meditation is an inward practice that the wise people of old preceded us used because it is the only approach that directly touches the soul; since our negative attachments are imprinted on the soul, only meditation can remove them. The mystics have continually reminded us that, "There is a polish for everything, and the polish for the soul is meditation."

As the mystic Rumi writes:

Dost thou know why

The mirror of the soul reflects nothing?

Because the rust is not cleared from its face.

Our soul, hindered by our lower nature, has layers of curtains around it, and only meditation can slowly remove them.

Rumi the mystic explains this wisdom in a story. The Chinese said to the king, "We are the better painters," and the Greeks rejoined, "We have more skill than you and a greater sense of beauty." The king gave each a room, with doors opposite each other. The Chinese asked the king for 150 different colors, gold, silver and gems. The Greeks asked only for polish and polishing cloths and shut themselves in and polished continuously. When the Chinese finished their work, the king entered and looked at the pictures they had painted. He was awestruck by their beauty. Then, the Greeks raised the curtain that was between the rooms. The reflection of the paintings fell upon the polished walls, and all that the king had seen before seemed even lovelier there. The Greeks are the Sufis who have purified their hearts. The pure heart is a spotless mirror that receives innumerable images. The pure have left behind fragrance and color; each moment they see beauty without hindrance.

The ancient scribes tell us that there are 70,000 veils between Man and God; however there are no veils between God and Man. We are empowered to remove these veils through meditation because the soul cannot act on its own accord.

Al-Antaki writes:

> True knowledge comes through the light of cer-
> tainty, by which God enlightens the heart. Then you
> will behold the things of the spiritual world and by
> the power of that light all the veils between you and
> that world will be removed.

I remember watching the movie "Back to the Future" featur-
ing Michael J. Fox, released in 1985. In this movie, Marty McFly,
a teenager, goes back into the past to right a wrong that affected
his life in the future. Ironically, this movie was released just three
years after the incident in which Joe, the enlightened sage, had
been able to do something similar in a spiritual context. The background to this particular story can be found in chapter seven; in
essence, it involved the way in which Joe had been able to postpone his father's death. I thought a lot about this after I had
watched the movie and discussed it with Joe. The idea that we
could change human destiny so fundamentally was obviously very
fascinating. He had explained that our physical life was a shadow
rooted in our spiritual life, whose fulcrum was the soul. Our physical life was bound by time and space and the laws of cause and
affect. The soul, however, is beyond boundaries and timeless.
Meditation, he explained, was the process through which we could
transcend the physical constraints of time and space and connect
with the soul directly. Nothing else could do this, he stressed. The
conversations he spoke of took place in the meditative state,
whereby the soul was not bound by the past. Therefore, with meditation, we are able to cleanse and remove the impurities and do
what the sages advised, purify the soul. Just as coal is slowly
cleaned to ultimately reveal a shining precious diamond, by polishing our soul with meditation, we are removing the veils and
attachments, a process that will ultimately reveal the precious
Invisible Light.

Imagine an old car in the garage, covered in dust and cobwebs,
and you will get a picture of the state of our soul in its lower ego
nature. Only when we clean up the car and remove all the dust are
we able to create a spark that will start it. Similarly, meditation

cleanses the soul, removing the ignorance and attachments, ultimately to reveal the spark of the Invisible Light.

Ghazzali the mystic wrote:

> Dear friend,
> Your heart is a polished mirror.
> You must wipe it clean of the veils of dust that has
> gathered upon it,
> Because it is destined to reflect the light of divine secrets.

This type of cleansing is achieved through meditation, which
requires patience and discipline, as the impurities have accumulated over a long time. In the same way that a dirty coffee mug is
harder to clean the longer we put off cleaning it, our soul has layers of illusion upon it. The longer we wait, the harder it becomes
to cleanse it, and for this reason, constancy of practice is important. By removing these negative imprints, we are proportionately
increasing the value of the positive attachments. By redesigning
the imprints on our soul, we are creating a core transformation that
will manifest itself in a substantially changed physical life.

The Boulder—One day, an earthquake dislodged a very large
boulder from a mountain, and the boulder crashed right into the
middle of a small town. Time passed and the boulder became a nui-
sance for the townsfolk, but it was too large to break or move. One
day, a local merchant took it upon himself to break the boulder and
remove it from the town center. Every day, he would spend countless hours pounding the boulder with a large hammer. At first, you
would hardly notice a chip on the large rock, and the town people
laughed at him for taking on an impossible undertaking. For two
years, he kept at his task with unwavering conviction until one day,
he hit the boulder with a single swing and it cracked and fragmented.
The townsfolk were overjoyed and built a legend around the merchant who, with a single swing, had broken the giant boulder.

The rewards of breaking the boulder were significant for the
merchant, who became a legend, but what was forgotten was that
it was not a single swing of the hammer that made this feat possible. Rather, it was his determination to be disciplined in the practice of grinding down the rock's resistance. Similarly, the adherents

of the Invisible Way will penetrate into the sacred space and experience the great spiritual awakening, allowing them that union with the Invisible Light. However, it is the practice of meditation with constancy and the painstaking polishing of the soul that makes this possible.

Often I am asked if prayers work. Yes is a simple answer, but this is a subject perhaps for another book. Let me share a couple of insights on this subject. Prayers can be exoteric (outward) or esoteric (inward). The degree to which our outward prayers affect the soul is the degree of their value. Rituals and prayers that do not touch us where it matters, in the soul, have little relative value. The esoteric (inward) prayer has often been referred to as meditation by the greatest prophets and saints, and this was a part of their daily practice at the deepest of levels. After all, at that level, what indeed is prayer if not communication between Man and God, and is there another way to achieve this besides meditation? Let me just say that our outward prayers represent man worshipping and asking God, whereas our deepest meditative prayer goes beyond because it empowers man to fulfill his divine potential.

In the Master's Chamber—A former student visited his master, and the master learned that the student had stopped his practice of meditation. The master inquired the reason from his student. The former pupil explained that he had meditated for five years and thus has cleansed his soul. Now he could pursue other endeavors. The master brought out a mirror and asked the student to polish it until it was spotless, which he did in earnest. He then gave the student the keys to his chamber and asked him to hide the mirror wherever he wished so that it remained polished. The student found a perfect spot to conceal the mirror and returned to the master after locking the door behind him. "Keep the key and return in seven days," said the master. "Until then, the chamber shall remain closed." In seven days, the former student returned and fetched the polished mirror. The master ran his finger over the mirror, revealing how a film of dust had settled on it despite the fact that it had been concealed to prevent just such an occurrence.

The student looked and understood that, living in a physical world, it is impossible to avoid negative attachments to the soul, even one that was clean and resigned. The soul must be polished constantly, because surely it would slowly become veiled, and the task to clean it later would be much more difficult.

Our meditation cleanses our soul, but there must be constancy of practice or the hard won gains are soon erased.

The mystic Rumi writes:

> If you could get rid of yourself just once,
> The secret of secrets would open to you.
> The face of the unknown
> Hidden beyond the universe would appear on the
>   mirror of your perception.

Meditation enables us to remove the mist surrounding our soul and, in the process, reveals the most sought-after treasure, the Invisible Light.

THIRD: **MEDITATION is the only moment when we are truly alive.**

In the matter of spirituality, there is one irrefutable fact: Our physical body encompassing all our organs and mind is alive when the soul is present, and dead in its absence. The essence of human life that makes us alive is the soul, which is the life energy that sustains our physical existence. Therefore, any time we are connected to this life source, we are considered alive, and when we are disconnected from it, we are considered dead.

We learned that we have two centers: the lower self, where the ego reigns supreme, and our higher self, where our soul is at peace. We also understand that the closer we are to the lower self, the greater the veil that exists between us and our soul. In other words, the more we are dominated by the ego of our lower nature, the more disconnected we are from our soul.

> People in this world are like travelers whose journey
> is going on though they are asleep. Your life is a
> dream, and this dream will not stay long. Awaken
> now and perform meditation.

Imagine for a moment what happens when we are in sleeping mode. At that time, we are oblivious to everything that is going on because we are unable to feel, see or hear anything, and during that sleep, we are dead to the world existing in another state. Similarly, when we are engrossed in our material life and engulfed by the tentacles of the ego center, we are unaware of our spirituality and unconscious of the reality of the soul. In that state, we are unable to feel the spiritual impulses from within; hence we would be termed soulless. The mystics tell us that in this state, our world is an illusion and we are spiritually dead.

When we examine human life, we can see how true this is. Our ego dictates and dominates everything we do, and its priority is very evident. It is either preoccupied with the past, from which it draws its identity, or the future, where it seeks security. We can see signs of this in our personal lives. We are either dealing with the baggage of hurts and regrets from the past or we are busy planning for the future.

The past haunts us, and the future is so vital that all our attention is focused on getting there. But the "there" never arrives. The cliché "tomorrow never comes" is the paradox of our imprisonment because, when tomorrow becomes today, just as when there becomes here, we have recalibrated ourselves and are waiting for tomorrow again. In the process, we lose the most precious thing we have—here and now.

The King's Advisor—A wise man lived at the court of King Wagt to advise him on important matters. One day, the king summoned the advisor and asked, "I am constantly meeting with kings, princes, generals, the wise men and even the workers in my kingdom. Who is the most important person to be with?"

The advisor answered, "Whoever you are with at any given moment is the most important."

"Why?" the king questioned.

"Because that is the only time you are alive," the wise advisor responded.

Now, the present is the most important time, yet it is also the shortest. It is a string of moments that contain within it the only opportunity to seize our destiny, for now is the only time when we can actually do something. This is because the past and the future are simply realms of thought. Now is the realm of action and, in the final analysis, it is our actions that shape our fate. In the spiritual realm, time is not broken into compartments because it is indivisible. Both, alpha and omega, the beginning and end, the past and future exist in this period we call now. Time exists only in our physical creation as the distance between cause and effect. Since we are essentially spiritual beings, we can only operate in the now. To do otherwise would mean that we are binding ourself to the lower realm of time and space, and in the process we constrain our evolution to the higher realms.

The soul cannot exist in the past, nor can it exist in the future; it is infinite and beyond time and can only exist here and now. Similarly, our connection to the soul cannot occur in the future nor in the past, but only in the present moment. The way to become alive is to connect with our life source, the soul, and that can only happen now. There is just one way to connect to the soul and that is meditation.

The mystic Rumi writes:

The past and future veil God from our sight.

Burn up both of them with fire.

When we take our aliveness and segment it into the past, present and future, we imprison ourselves in the physical world where time exists.

Meister Eckhart, the spiritualist, writes:

Time is what keeps the light from reaching us.

There is no greater obstacle to God than time.

We cannot find our divine essence in the past or in the future, but we can discover it in the only moment we are alive, which is now. An old mystical saying states, "Be wary, my friend. The angel of death can come while you are only chalking out programs of meditation. Whatever you can do to make initiation and spiritual progress, do it today."

The Jewel—There was a wise old man who, in his travels, found a precious stone. As he continued his journey, he came across a fellow traveler who was extremely thirsty. The traveler asked the wise old man for some water. The wise man opened his bag to give the traveler the water. Just then, the traveler noticed the shining stone. He forgot about his thirst for a while and asked the old man if he could have the precious stone instead. The wise man obliged and gave the stranger the stone. The traveler went on his way thinking, "Now I have wealth, I will be happy." Two days later, the wise old man came upon a dead man lying on the ground. He looked closely and saw that it was the traveler he had met two days ago. It seemed that he had died of thirst!

This moment is the only one that has any value, for only now can satisfy the thirst that exists within. Waiting for the future is meaningless; it holds nothing but death and lost opportunities.

Try this simple exercise any time during the day. Just stop yourself and reflect where your thoughts were at that time. Chances are that either you were recollecting some past experience or thinking about something concerning the future. Since neither the past nor the future exists at this time, where were you? "Zombie" is a word often associated with something technically dead, a robot or something which is lifeless. Because we are imprisoned by time, either in the future or past, we have become soulless. However, the only moment we are alive is now.

Remember, thinking of the car that has not arrived does not get us to our destination, nor will reminiscing of the car we missed. The car that sits in front of us this moment can get us to our destination.

The mystic poet Hafiz writes:

> Now, now while the rose is with us, sing her praise,
> Now while we are here to listen, minstrel,
> Strike the lute!
> For the burden of all thy songs has been that the
>   present is all too far short,
> And already the unknown future is upon us.

The Sunflower—The Sufi teacher, wishing to teach his student an important lesson, took him out to a huge valley filled with sunflowers. "I would like you to find me the most beautiful sunflower you can," he instructed his student.

The student set off with enthusiasm, determined to find the prettiest flower. Hours passed and he had not returned. The teacher went to the valley where he found the student still searching for the most beautiful flower. "What is the matter?" asked the teacher. "You could not find me that flower?" The student was tired and a little discouraged. "Every time I found what I thought was the most beautiful flower, I found yet another one that looked better, and so I am still looking."

The Sufi teacher smiled. This is the paradox indeed. People are seeking to find happiness and joy in the material world of repossession, yet they never do. They always believe that the thing they do not have will give them more. They spend their lives looking for it in the way your day was spent today.

"Pick a flower, any one," instructed the teacher. The student obliged. "Do not be distracted by the beautiful flowers you never found, nor by the other beautiful flowers you may have discovered. Instead, sit and admire the beauty of the flower in your hand; contemplate its journey from a seed to the uniqueness it has attained."

As the student did that, his mood became calm and he discovered a peacefulness that had eluded him all day while he was searching for that perfect flower. The teacher said, "Remember, we cannot find happiness by living in the past and thinking about our regrets. Nor can we find joy by constantly looking into the future. The only moment we are alive is now, and this is where happiness and joy exist, in the moments now."

Since the past and future do not exist, our connection to the divine self within happens in the present because it is the only moment that is real. However, there is one monumental barrier in this endeavor, and that is the ego of our lower nature. It is the obstacle unleashing a barrage of thoughts that quickly distracts us into the illusions of the past and future, imprisoning us in the lower realm. To be alive to the present, we have to stop the myriad thoughts that emanate from our lower physical nature, and the mystics of old confirm meditation as the process for achieving this. Meditation is the realm of the unthought and therefore, a meditating person transcends time and enters the consciousness of the moment, not externally in the tangible, finite and illusive world, but in the infinite intangible reality that is within. This sacred space, where we are awake to the life-sustaining energy of the divine, can only be arrived at by meditation, which penetrates the world of thought, transcends time and connects us to the Invisible Light. Here in this eternal realm exists the sublime bliss in which lifetimes are experienced in moments. The portal to these higher dimensions exists in the now and the vehicle is meditation.

The Mystic Rumi writes:

> When the rose is gone
> And the garden faded
> Thou wilt hear no more the nightingales.

FOURTH: **MEDITATION opens the third eye and awakens the soul**

We have discussed that everything within creation is evolving toward a higher state, from the mineral state to the vegetative state and then the animal and human state. The soul as an embryonic elemental state evolves toward self consciousness through all the experiences we see as strife, struggle and suffering. Furthermore, creation itself has many planes, and vibration forms the basis of everything in these planes.

The physical plane is the lowest one, and here, the vibrations are the slowest. As we evolve upward toward the higher spiritual realms, the vibrations speed up. Our journey, as defined earlier, as one from the lower self to the higher self, also can be seen as one from physical beings where our vibrations are slow to spiritual beings where these vibrations are much faster.

The Bhagavad Gita states:

> Those who with the eye of wisdom
> Thus see the difference between matter and spirit
> And know how to liberate life from the law of nature
> They attain the supreme

When we look at our five senses, in particular our sense of vision through the two physical eyes, our sight is limited by the vibrations of the object. Any object that vibrates faster than the speed of sound would not be visible to us. This is easily understood because, when a plane in the sky breaks the sound barrier, it automatically becomes invisible to us. Our five physical senses have limitations, and there are many things that we cannot see, hear, feel, taste or smell. For instance, we cannot see air or the smallest particles, nor can we hear certain sounds that animals can.

Our soul is spiritual and, since all objects and entities within the spiritual planes vibrate at a faster rate, we are not able to see entities like Jinns and angels, who exist in the higher realms where the vibrations are greater. As human beings, we all have within us a developed, self-conscious soul, which has latent sensibilities and faculties waiting to be actualized.

The mystic Grant Sahib writes:

> In the deep silence of the soul
> There is a perpetual light
> With no sunrise and no sunset

How then do we actualize the latent and dormant senses of the soul? This is possible only through meditation that enables us to subdue the ego and rise above the limitations of our five senses, which simply do not possess the capacity to let us see and understand everything. In the same way that we cannot use a screwdriver to pull out a nail, our physical eyes cannot see the reality that exists beyond the physical plane. For that celestial sight, we are all endowed with inner vision, often referred to as the third eye, which is located between our two physical eyes at the root of the nose near the pineal gland. This is also the juncture where the breath enters our body and thus becomes the focus during our meditation.

The holy text explains:

> The light of the body is the eye
> If therefore thine eyes be single
> Then the whole body shall be full of light.

In our physical world, the greatest power a human being possesses is the power of choice and reason. Yet within the soul are existent faculties that would make these worldly powers pale in comparison. Since the soul is the microcosm of the macrocosm, it is made of the divine substance, and when our third eye opens and the soul awakens, we are filled with the Invisible Light. However, the way within is from without, and it is here in this physical world that we are empowered through reason and choice to make the efforts that will lead us to the treasures.

The poet Khusraw writes:

> O young man! Arise from sleep of negligence
> And look up the world with the keen eye of the intellect.
> What you need is a new eye and a fresh ear
> So that you may experience the great kingdom of God.
> To be sure, he will not grant you an audience there,
> If you do not take with you an eye and ear from here.

Like a seed that lies dormant for many years before a chance rainfall brings it to life, our souls remain silent within us, waiting for the time we sacrifice our attachments to the physical world and nurture our souls through meditation.

The Darkness—The student, having practiced the beginner's meditation, approached his teacher. "I see only darkness, master," he said. The master answered, "The deep sea conceals hidden treasure, and the diver who searches sees only the darkness, too. Yet the diver is surrounded by creatures that see because for them, the darkness is light. Similarly, the inward journey is dark when seen with the physical eye, yet within the soul is a third eye, and for it, that inward darkness is light. Patiently persevere, for the soul will awaken and the inner eye will open, revealing to you the treasures you seek.

The Mystic Hafiz writes:

> Knowest thou not
> That parting goes before all meeting
> And from darkness comes light.

There are five levels of the third eye's vision, and each one has countless gradations within it. The list below falls short because the number of higher states and the levels of soul experiences within each are incalculable; however, the levels are designed to give us a perspective of the great potential. Meditation will develop our inner faculties, and these will express themselves in our enlightened perception influencing the way we contextualize our physical and spiritual life.

LEVEL ONE: *Feeling things beyond our physical nature*

At this level, we have an emergence of deep and profound feelings of love and compassion. Sometimes these are sporadic and intuitive, while at a higher level of awareness, we may dedicate our lives to the upliftment of those who are less fortunate or express that love toward others like spouses, parents and children. A good example of this would be the manner in which Mother Teresa dedicated her life to the poor. In doing this, she was merely manifesting her inner love in outward action.

LEVEL TWO: *Seeing things beyond our physical nature*

With our inner eye we can see our past lives and future, because it is the eye of the soul that has an imprint of its past and future journey. Once again, they can be elementary, like clairvoyance, or more developed, like that of the visions of Nostradamus. However, at the apex are the prophetic visions, which have depth and clarity.

LEVEL THREE: *Hearing things beyond our physical nature*

There is a language that exists beyond words that are spoken, and our inner ear has these sensibilities. Great artists and musicians, including those who have made great discoveries, have all, to some degree, relied on the music from within. We also note that Saint Francis talked to birds and Mohamed was able to converse with the Angel Gabriel. Similarly, Moses and Abraham conversed with God.

LEVEL FOUR: *Knowing things beyond our physical nature*

This involves the insights of the spiritual realm and knowledge of the divine. Once again, there are intuitive impulses we often hear from within, but at higher, more advanced levels the nature of that knowledge can be mind-boggling. Jesus knew that Judas would betray him and understood the purpose of that act, and Mohamed knew beforehand that an assassination attempt would be made on his life, knowing full well that his escape to Medina would mark the Hijra, an event that would commence the Muslim calendar.

LEVEL FIVE: *Experience of the spiritual reality*

This is the grace and experience one receives during meditation that jolts the soul and bathes it in the Invisible Light. These experiences have many levels and correspond to the higher spiritual realms however, in each case, they are personalized to your own soul history often in metaphors related to your sensibilities. For this reason, discussing them may be misleading to others and indeed may harm you since the feelings of pride and self importance may awaken the subdued ego drawing you back into your lower nature. At the pinnacle of this experience is the union, a moment when the subject merges with the object, this is when our soul, the microcosm, comes together with the macrocosm which is the universal soul, the way a rain drop unites with the ocean and loses itself. A moment so precious that it contains within it the mystery of all mysteries.

When we look at the great prophets and wisemen of old, we see that they were able to do what in a physical sense seemed impossible. Abraham conversed with God as did Moses, who also parted the Red Sea. Mohamed ascended to the highest spiritual realm at the point of Sidra and experienced the glory of God. Jesus brought the dead to life and healed the sick, while Buddha experienced the union. All these souls and many others who were divinely sent were fully awakened and consequently operated at a much higher frequency of vibration. Much more important, however, is the recognition that all of them meditated; in fact, it was the foundation of their being.

The mystic Araby writes:

> Were it not for the excess of your talking
> and the turmoil in your heart
> you would see what I see
> and hear what I hear.

Meditation allows us to withdraw from the outer world of conflict where the apparent chaos reigns to the inner world of harmony and reality. It is said that only when it is dark enough can we see the stars, which were always there. Similarly, it is meditation that allows us to gradually awaken the soul and gain sight of our existent celestial reality.

The Awakened—After a discourse on awakening, the student asked his master how one knows when he or she is awakened. The master responded, "Humans learn habits, but so can animals, when taught. The animals in a circus are a good example of this. Similarly, as humans can memorize knowledge, so can birds, like the parrot, who are taught to speak. Finally, humans can look in the mirror and recognize themselves, but so can monkeys. The awakened is one who can look into the mirror of their own souls and say, 'That's me.'"

This is a gradual process. Just as the cataract on our physical eye distorts the image, our physical vision is a distorted manifestation of the real. It is meditation that slowly awakens the inward eye. Through each anguish and hurt, through our sighs of pain and sickness, the veils of our lower desires are slowly peeled away. Only through meditation are we able to transcend the cycle of birth and rebirth and create the environment for our awakening.

As the Buddha taught:

> My teaching is not a philosophy
> It is the result of direct experience…
> My teaching is a means of practice
> Not something to hold onto or worship
> My teaching is like a raft used to cross the river
> Only a fool would carry the raft around after he had
>   already reached the other shore of liberation.

Buddha is often referred to as "The Awakened One," and we are all aware that meditation was instrumental in helping him achieve that state. However, it is not the knowledge, understanding or importance of meditation that enables us to become awakened. It is the practice of it, for meditation is the raft that we can use to cross the river and reach the shore of liberation. To hold onto the knowledge without practice would be like carrying the raft on land while the river that could carry us in the raft flows by.

These souls who are full awakened are referred to as "the perfect man." Their souls were illuminated by the divine Invisible Light at all times, and those who came in their presence were touched and their souls illuminated. It is not a coincidence that all prophets of old had very faithful disciples; they understood the degree to which they were enriched. It is written that such fully awakened souls exist in every age and time, It is my conviction that back in the year 1979, when I was outwardly rich but inwardly destitute, I was touched by such a one and, in the process, not only was my impoverished soul illumined but my physical destiny changed. However, the one thing the masters of old have told us is that, through our reason and effort in meditation, we can change our fate, enlighten our souls, open our third eye and awaken to divine reality. We have charge of our own soul, and only through meditation can we can discover the philosopher's stone and transform.

As the mystic Rumi writes:
> He opened the inward eye
> and gazed on the ideal form of that
> which he had only read in books.

FIFTH: MEDITATION makes us receptive to the experience of the divine

In the early formative years of civilization, mankind needed the ego and relied upon it for existence. By harnessing the creative and survival instincts of the ego mind, we emerged from caves into a civilization that is advanced beyond words. Yet all this time, unknown to us, another journey existed, the journey of our soul, which was returning to the source from which it originated.

The holy texts state:
> We are from God and unto God is our return.

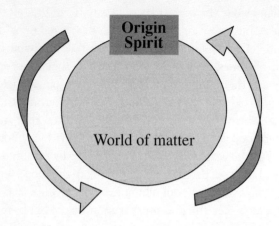

Our primordial existence was spirit, and our journey is one of spirit to matter and back to spirit. We emerged into the realm of matter from our primordial spiritual existence in an embryonic state, and our current phase is our gradual evolution from matter to spirit.

The Mystic Rumi writes:

> Every form that you see has its original in the divine
> world. If the form passes away, it is of no conse-
> quence because its original was from eternity. When
> you came into the world of created beings, a ladder
> was set before you, so that you might pass out of it.
> At first you were inanimate, then you became a
> plant; afterward you were changed into an animal.
> At last you became human possessed of knowledge,
> intelligence and faith.

It is this intelligence that enabled us to progress in the way that we have. However we cannot call ourselves an advanced race sim-ply because we have made progress in science and physics. We can only call ourselves advanced when we discover the primordial source that created and continues to sustain us, enabling us to see and discover the wonder of creation and all the manifest laws in it.

The holy texts confirm that we are made of the same substance as that of the source that originates us.

> And the lord God formed man
> of the dust of the ground and breathed into his
>> nostril the breath of life and the man became a
>> living soul.
> "Behold!" thy god said to the angels
> "I am about to create man from sounding clay
> From mud molded into shape
> When I have fashioned him and breathed
> Into him of my spirit."

We are now in the final phase of our journey from matter to spirit, and only meditation enables us to take this concluding step toward our complete transformation, which occurs from the sacred space within. Our outer eye allows us sight of solid matter, but it is the inner eye that brings us closer to the first cause and the experience of the divine source to which we are all bound.

The Humbled Master—A Sufi master sat with his students and constantly reminded them that the doors to the divine remained closed and that it was man's destiny to open them. One day, the mystic Rabia asked the master, "You keep referring to the doors of the divine as being closed; could you tell me when they were closed?"

The master understood his error and felt humbled.

Rabia the mystic writes:

> How long will you keep pounding on an open door,
>> begging for someone to open it?

Everything within the seen and unseen creation is continuously sustained. Our physical world is supported by the energy of the sun; our human body with energy and air. Similarly, our soul is sustained by the divine light at all times. If obstacles and barriers exist to our experience of it, it is because we have constructed them and allowed them to impair our connection to the divine source.

The mystical wisdom tells us:

> There are 70,000 veils between Man and God.
> There are no veils between God and Man.

The mystic Yohananda adds:

> You do not have to struggle to reach God
> But you do have to struggle
> To tear away the self-created veils
> That hide him from you.

Since the veils that surround our vision of the divine are self-created, they also can be removed by us. It is darkness that clouds us, and it is light that removes it, for darkness is simply the absence of light. Meditation polishes and cleanses the soul and awakens the inward eye to the Invisible Light that annihilates the ignorance and manifests consciousness.

We have learned that the greatest barrier to our experience of the high is the ego of the lower self. Once vital to our survival, this ego today is the barrier to our transcendence from physical beings to spiritual and from matter to spirit.

The Bear—Once a poor man without a shirt was fishing on the banks of a river. Some bystanders observed a seemingly dead bear floating in the river. Thinking that it must have died from a fall, they shouted to the shirtless man to pull the dead bear out of the water, since it could provide a nice fur for a coat. The shirtless man jumped in to get the dead bear. No sooner had he done that than the bear awoke and grabbed the shirtless man. The bystanders, realizing that the bear was alive, screamed at the shirtless man to let go of the bear. The shirtless man shouted back, "I have let go but he will not release me!"

We used the ego mind when we needed it and in the process empowered it. Today, it is the master and, though we wish to reduce its influence in our lives, it is like a bear that won't let go. This is the struggle, for, in order to move from the lower self to the higher self, we must extradite ourselves from the bear hug of the ego, which considers itself master.

We see in this chart that our journey can be viewed in three phases.

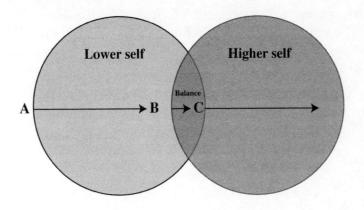

Phase One: From A to B

Here we are at the mercy of our lower nature. The only way to navigate this zone is to use the ego mind against itself, as discussed earlier. Therefore, the major tool of progressing in this phase is concentration.

Phase Two: From B to C

This is the realm of balance, and it is assumed that the subdued ego cooperates with our real self in our endeavor to progress and transform into spirit. The main tool in this phase is meditation, because it allows us to detach from our physical identity and merge with our consciousness and awaken.

Phase Three: From C and Beyond

This phase brings us to point C, which is the edge of our sacred space. Progress into the sacred space is by invitation of the Invisible Light, and that invitation arrives only when we are receptive.

We see such an "invitation" in the story of Moses, when he saw God speak to him from the burning bush. God invited Moses to come into the sacred space where there is no trace of the ego, and in this respect, Moses was approachable. A good analogy would be the radio stations. These stations broadcast continuously, and if we are driving in the car and unable to hear a particular station, it is because we have not tuned our radio to that broadband frequency. We could not hear the station because it was up to us to set the dial, which we were empowered to do. Similarly, we need to set the inner dial so that we are able to experience grace when it arrives, and it is meditation that moves us into the receiving frequency.

I was inspired by these words from Paul Brunton in his book, *Perspective: The Timeless Way of Wisdom.*

> In that sacred moment when an awed silence grips
> the soul, we are undone. The small and narrow
> bricks with which we have built our house of
> personal life collapse and tumble to the ground. The
> things we worked and hungered for slip into the limp
> of undesired and undesirable relics. The world of
> achievement, flickering with activities of ambition,
> pales away into the pettiness of a third-rate play.

When we meditate, we cleanse the soul, slowly removing the veils, making it receptive and worthy of the divine call. First, however, we have to empty ourselves and discover the silence of stillness in deep meditation.

As the mystic Hafiz writes:

> When stillness unbroken around me lies
> The vision of her
> Makes my solitude sweet.

The mystics tell us these words of God:

> I who cannot fit into the universe upon universes
>   that I have created
> Fit into the heart of the sincere believer.

The pure heart is the temple of God, and our meditations free it from the lower self and empty our attachment to the physical world, allowing the divine presence to manifest itself.

When we reach the edge of our sacred space, our meditations melt away, and in that sanctuary of stillness, where the Invisible Light eternally illumines the heart, love emerges of its own accord, because it is the fragrance that appears wherever the divine reality is contemplated.

The mystic Attar writes:

> From each love demands a mystic silence
> What do all seek earnestly?
> Tis' love,
> Love is the subject of their inmost thoughts
> In love no longer thou and I exist
> For self has passed away I the beloved
> Now will I draw aside the veil from love
> And in the temple of mine inmost soul
> Behold the friend, incomparable love
> He who would know the secret of both worlds
> Will find that the secret of them both is love.

It is at this furthest point that the transformation occurs. For here in the silence is a quiet waiting unlike anything we have known. Not the impatient wait of the physical being, but the lovers yearning in the garden where the songs of separation sing from the heart, and the memories of the past union intoxicates us. Here, in the stillness, we are alive in the timeless state, knowing of the inevitability of that reunion when the sun will rise and the Invisible Light will usher us into the arms of that we have sought since the beginning of time. This is Point C; getting to it requires a lot of patient inner work which often competes with our worldly responsibilities. I was very fortunate to have a very supportive wife, who not only encouraged me, but also tried to find me time so that I could pursue my inner quest. For instance, when the children were young, she was okay with me taking them for the afternoon nap so that I could meditate at the same time, or when we went on vacations, she planned the children's outdoor activities during times I could steal away to my sanctuary and sit in stillness and quiet contemplation. Once the children were older, my birthday present tended to be a four-or-five day getaway into the mountains alone, where I could fill my days with walking meditation and at night feeling the coolness of my eye as I waited patiently at the sacred place. There is just something about the Rockies, which are a short one hour drive from our home, that are replete with profound messages which are discernible when we are able to switch off and disconnect ourselves from our material world and gaze at the signature of the creator.

The mystic Hafiz describes this moment thus:

> Though the wind of discord shake the two worlds
> mine eyes are fixed upon the road
> from whence cometh my friend.

And Jesus explained it thus:

> Be like a servant
> Waiting for the return of the master.

It is in these moments that the invitation arrives and the Invisible Light manifests itself. Our heart is illuminated in an rapture of effervescence, and the soul is awakened by the ecstasy of the sublime bliss, for which there are no explanations.

The Buddha writes:

> By comparison, with the hundred year long life of
> the one who does not see the path to immortality,
> one day of a man who does is greater.

Beyond words and thought, past the barriers one and all, that which we have longed and yearned for a thousand years becomes manifest as an epiphany of light energy that takes the nothingness within and transforms it into a divine state. Our emptiness is filled with the Invisible Light, and the thirst we have forever carried is finally quenched.

As Saint Paul wrote:

> Everything is shown up by being exposed to the light
> and what is exposed to the light, becomes light.

This is the grace; it is given but cannot be taken, but in order to even be considered, first we must be receptive. As the holy texts tell,

> God guides to his light whom he pleases.

Everyone will one day die and face the divine. Alas for some, they are restless for that experience now. These are the real seekers and mystics, and for them, meditation is not something that is fitted into their busy lives; rather it the highlight around which a whole lifestyle is planned.

The mystic Junnaid writes:

> Those who walk on the path
> have no longing after fine palaces and fair gardens.
> In their hearts is nothing but the
> Pain of yearning love for God.

Conclusion—I recently came across a photograph taken by Kevin Carter in 1994. The picture depicts a small famine-stricken child, exhausted and completely dehydrated, trying desperately to crawl to a United Nations food camp located a kilometer away. Standing and waiting beside the child was a vulture. This photograph won the Pulitzer in 1994, and I am told it was a picture that shocked the world. I guess it did not shock the world enough because millions of children continue to die each year of causes that can be prevented. The image of the helplessness of the forgotten child, its struggle for life and the vigilance of the vulture haunts me, and I remember the word of God from the Holy texts when he admonishes the human being:

> I offered the trust to the mountains
> And they declined.
> I offered the trust to Man
> He accepted, and how he was negligent.

The whole world and all its resources are entrusted to humanity, enough to ensure no one dies from hunger, yet people do by the millions. We call ourselves an advanced civilization but are constantly agitated and anxious, torn apart by the desires of the world that ground us in our animal nature. Endlessly impatient for something or someone to complete us, we are like a salmon forever struggling to reach upstream.

We have taken our world and our life in it for granted, assuming that when we go to sleep tonight, we will awake in the morning. We have taken it for granted that, when we say goodbye to our children or family in the morning on our way to work, we will see them at the end of the day. We are busy dealing with the faults of yesterday and planning the life of tomorrow, unaware that our death is concealed in a moment called now.

It is written in the sacred text:
> In the moment of death, the dying person
> shall say that his stay on earth was just like a dream
>   or possibly it was shorter.

The King's Legacy—The aging King Wagt summoned his trusted spiritual advisor and informed him that, after a long and fulfilling life, his days were now numbered. The King, who had grown wise and had ruled his kingdom with compassion and generosity, wanted to leave behind a lasting legacy. King Wagt asked his advisor to come up with an enduring legacy of wisdom that he could leave behind for his subjects. The advisor went away to consider the king's request and, after a few days, advised the king that wise words would last through time. Thus the advisor gave the king the following wise words: "This, too, shall pass." King Wagt took these words and spread them all over his kingdom. To this day, it is remembered in every calamity that befalls upon us, in days of blessings as well as suffering, and indeed in all the possessions that we became attached to, wisdom emerges when we speak these words, "This, too, shall pass." Such was the legacy left for us by King Wagt, whose name meant time.

In the same way that a dream vanishes upon awakening, our life will disappear at death. Any footprints we wish to leave can be imprinted, not on the limp carcass we call our physical body, but the essence, the soul, whose journey continues.

The Mystic Hafiz writes:
> I have estimated the influence of reason upon love
> and found that it is like that of a rain drop upon the
> ocean, which makes one little mark upon the water's
> face and disappears.

Such is our life that, in our death, our real self just slips out of the body and in the process, everything we believe to be so important and vital, our belongings, family, possessions and personality, will fade away, just as a dream does when we awaken.

As the mystic Rumi writes:
> This world is a rotten walnut.
> O man of trust, do not make trial of it,
> But behold it from afar.

We could spend a whole life struggling and striving for our passions to achieve the things of the world, only to discover that, in making this pursuit exclusive, we have indeed gained the world and lost our soul. A rotten walnut, as Rumi put it, would hardly be a fitting epitaph of a life of struggle.

I remember when I was 12 years old living in Staines, England with my two brothers. Every day I would pass the toy store and admire the magic set which was displayed in the window. Somehow, the magical powers of doing something extraordinary always resonated with me as a kid. When my birthday came, I informed my brothers that it was the magic set I wanted for my birthday. On my birthday, I opened the present with great anticipation only to find that it was not the magic set, and I was devastated. I had my heart set on it; a day had not gone by that I did not see it in the window on my way to school. My disappointment turned to tantrums and finally, my brothers went and got me the magic set. It was not in my perception to think that my brothers, both students on a meager allowance my dad sent from Africa, could not afford the set. The magic set also was never what I imagined it to be. In fact, I don't even remember playing with it.

When we get older, nothing much changes except the things we set our hearts on are found in car showrooms, malls and show homes. We are all engrossed in our little world, getting attached to things, having created some conception in our minds about their value and importance. The world of repossession is harsh, and we feel the wrath of constant let-downs and disappointment. But, like ants, we just continue doing the same things and walking down the same road.

Alas, where is our compass? When do we get it that the happiness we yearn for does not exist just around the corner? We live in the world of repossession and there are no happy endings here, just endings. And it is in this state of ignorance that our life is slowly unraveling. Like a cat that innocently pulls at the sweater and ends up turning it into a pile of yarn on the floor, we slowly take apart our life, quietly and silently. But just like a truck that hurtles off a cliff, there is a long silence before the inevitable crash; our lives are unraveling and coming apart and, at some point, we will hear the sound of its torment.

The clouds are free to roam the skys, and the birds are free to fly and soar; the rain and snow are free to fall, yet where is man's freedom? Is it in owning and possessing? Is it found in those vacations in the sun? Is it in our relationships? If so, how come they are all sooner or later repossessed? Remember the words of King Wagt, "This, too, shall pass." How can a civilization so filled with inner conflict and outer chaos call itself advanced? That state can only be reached when we transform ourselves from the physical beings that we see ourselves as to the spiritual beings that we are. That conscious realization is the final frontier of human development.

The ancient prophets state:

Be still and know I am God.

An imperative to meditate, it is as simple or as hard as that. Meditation is the foundation of our being, and in that context should be our central activity. It is the sacred place where we can be who we are, a place where we cannot be hurt or stressed, criticized or talked about. This is the sanctuary where we are not judged, compared or measured for our size and the color of our skin. This place is free of harshness, depression and regrets and yes, even free of sickness and disease. For in the garden of the soul, we are all unique, beautiful and special without conditions, and it is here that we discover our freedom.

Vongoethe writes:

My greatest wealth is the deep stillness in which I
strive and grow and win what the world cannot take
from me with fire and sword.

When we have lived in this world and drunk everything there is to drink and still find an unquenchable thirst within, it is the divine nectar emanating from our meditation that finally quenches our thirst. This is when we get it. It is here that our mind slowly unravels, where the barriers are torn down brick by brick until our thoughts and attachments melt away. It is a slow process, as the layers of our past hurts and anger are dismantled, where the noise from without is silenced so that the attributes of forgiveness, joy and love are allowed to emerge, until all that is left is the divine self.

Light was the first manifestation of the creator, and this life force that emanated from the primal light is the Invisible Light within each of us. To realize it, we have to go inward and empty out all that our physical world has put into it, so that the Invisible Light can fill it with its divine essence.

The holy texts tell us:

When twisted, you will be upright

When hollowed out, you will be full.

Meditation is not the beginning of the quest for our real self, for that started a long time ago. Meditation is the end of our journey, for once on this path, it becomes a river that carries us to our destination.

CHAPTER 9

The Secondary Practice of the Invisible Way

We have learned that meditation is the first and foremost practice of the Invisible Way, one that was incorporated into the lifestyles of all the ascended masters. Furthermore, upon close examination, we discover that their inner meditation always expressed itself outwardly in their physical life. It is evident that all of the divinely inspired messengers are remembered by the things they did rather than what made it possible. In the same way that we admire the beautiful flower but are unaware of the seed that made it all possible, the Olympian accomplishments of these sages was rooted in meditation.

The Two Wells—The student asked his master how his life could be more fulfilling and free of stress. The teacher answered, "Imagine a farmer's house under which there are two water wells. One is polluted and the other is pure. If the farmer draws water from the toxic well, it will affect the health of everyone in his family. By switching wells and drawing from the clean water, he nurtures the health of his family."

Similarly, all human beings have two sources within them from which to draw wisdom and inspiration, the lower animal nature and the higher divine nature.

As long as man continues to draw his direction and thinking from the impulses of the lower ego center, he will continue to be misguided. Consequently, this will express itself in his physical world as agitation, confusion, personal unhappiness and stress, and he who is unhappy and confused with himself will find unhappiness and chaos in everything. He who sees chaos and confusion in everything will fill the world with conflict.

"So how do we draw from the clean well of the divine self?" the student inquired. The teacher explained, "We have to close one well before we can open another one because things have to follow an order. When a man is drowning, you have to pull him out of the water first before you can get the water out of him. Concentration, then, is the first step, because it enables us to close our connections to the well of the lower nature, and meditation follows because it alone opens our connection to the higher self. The man who draws his thoughts and actions from his real self will be wise, fulfilled and happy. He who is happy and content with himself will see the order in creation, and he who sees the invisible can do the impossible."

This is a simple concept, and we see it working in our material world. For instance, at will, we can close the cold water tap and turn on the hot water tap. Living in Alberta, Canada we have countless oil wells, and when these oil companies are drilling for oil and gas, frequently they will hit sour gas wells. Since this is a toxic gas, these wells are capped and sealed. However when they hit oil, this is immediately connected to the transmission lines and put to use. Similarly, the impulses of the lower self are sour and therefore hold us back, imprisoning us in the world of repossession.

The Bhagavad Gita states:

> A fire is shrouded in smoke, a mirror by dust.
> And a child by the womb, so is the universe is
>   enveloped in desire.
> It is the wise man's constant enemy. It tarnishes
>   the face of wisdom.
> It is as insatiable as a flame of fire. It works through
>   the senses, the mind and reason;
> And with their help destroys wisdom and confounds
>   the soul.

The only way we can close the tap of the ego center and seal it is with the powers of concentration. Once we have accomplished this, we can use meditation to dip into the well of our higher self and draw from it the wisdom and inspiration that will bring into our lives understanding, love and fulfillment.

However, in the same way that the oil gushing from the ground upward falls back on the ground, rendering the oil useless until it is harnessed to a transmission line, our meditation connects us to the whispers and impulses of the awakening soul, and these emanating spiritual fruits must be similarly harnessed. The essence of the radiating divine self must be given form through our intentions and actions. In this regard, there were two simple things the wise of the old did to harness the gushing life energy from within. First: They expressed their higher self. Second: They practiced detached observation.

Let us look at these in detail because, once we commence meditation, the emerging impulses need to be harnessed and expressed in our actions. In doing this, we are caring for our soul.

FIRST: Express your higher self

Our essential higher self is divine in potential. As our meditation polishes our soul, the divine attributes begin to shine like stars. The internal vibrations start to change, and we find ourselves needing to give form to these attributes in our physical life. This requires a significant change in the way we live and express ourselves. Generally, we tend to decipher impulses from our physical environment, ranging from the things we are taught, our past experiences, and what we read. People say and allow these to influence our responses to the circumstances we find ourselves in. We are always acting from the outside in, and our reactions to any situation conceal ingrained prejudices, resentments and conditioning. Since these are the impulses from the toxic well of the lower nature, we must cap them; it is here that concentration plays a vital role. As we shall see in the next chapter, subduing the influence of our lower ego will require us to tame the mind and make it obedient to our real purpose. Concentration is the tool through which we can accomplish this. It is not an easy process, but with practice and some willpower, it can be done. An obedient mind is a vital ally in our journey from A to B because it is a journey that takes place predominantly in our lower self; therefore as explained previously, we have to use our mind to aid us in our quest.

The Bhagavad Gita writes:

> To him who has conquered his lower nature by its help,
> The self is a friend.
> But to him who has not done so, it is an enemy.

The shift I was referring to is the necessity of thinking and acting inside out. Of course, we are not used to responding and reacting to life in this manner; however, as meditation uncover the veils over the soul, its divine nature is slowly revealed. We need to allow this personality to inform, guide and influence the way we live our lives and confront circumstances. Living inside out allows the divine attributes of the awakening soul to express themselves in our actions and this, in turn, pulls us further into the soul. We have discussed at length that change always occurs from the inside out and, since meditation is making a fundamental change within, by thinking and acting inside out, we are really giving expression to the transformation that is taking place inside. It is hard at first, but by being consciously alert, we can form the habit of checking inward before reacting to the situations that approach us. The more we meditate, the deeper is our connection to our soul, making its whisper more perceptible and easier to follow. In time the ego becomes very subdued, and the awakening self makes this process effortless and natural.

When we examine these divine attributes of the soul, we find that all of them are rooted in love. Love is the glue that holds together the whole of creation, encompassing all realms. Love is the wellspring that nurtures the natural beauty and balance in our cosmos and is the essence that sustains and supports everything, including our real self. This is why it is often said that God is love because it is difficult to separate them through our limited perception. Love is the heart of everything, and the language of the divine and its pulse rhymes in every seed, on every mountain top, in every tree. It sings in the beat of every heart, as it does in the very breath that makes creation alive, because it is indeed the cause of creation.

I came across this beautiful quote from an unknown author:

> Love is an end onto itself.
> Everything else raises the question "why"
> In our mind, and we require a reason for it,
> But when we say "I love" then there is no room for
> the "why," it is the final
> Answer in itself.

Since our soul is fashioned from the substance of God, love is the power that is manifest in the soul. The more we polish the soul and awaken it, the more love we feel, and when we act inside out, it is this love that comes out. All of the higher qualities like forgiveness, generosity, compassion, tolerance, kindness, integrity, and ethics are rooted in expressions of love. Therefore, when we express these higher ideals emanating from within, we are in fact being God-like.

The Beggar's Lesson—A blind man sat on the street corner, awaiting the passersby who might throw him some change. A man passing by reached into his pocket and put some coins in the beggar's bowl. The beggar responded, "Thank you, God." The man seemed a little puzzled at this response. "Why did you thank God?" he asked the blind man. "It was not God who gave you assistance; I did." The beggar spoke, "I cannot see you; therefore, I identify you by your act, and I can feel your love, and it was this love in you that assisted me, and this love is God!"

The mystics tell us these words of God:

> When I love a servant, I, God, am his ear so that he
> hears by me. I am his eye, so that he sees by me, and
> I am his tongue so that he speaks by me, and I am
> his hand, so that he takes and gives by me.

When we express our love through service to others, in those expressions of the higher self, we are a mirror reflecting God's essence. We see this in the lives of the great prophets and saints. All of them were selfless-living exemplars. They were forgiving, compassionate, humble, tolerant to the old and generous at all times because they lived their lives inside out. They expressed their higher self and allowed the essence of the divine attributes within to reflect in their physical life. In this way, they were constantly connected with their divine self. This unity between body, mind and spirit occurs when we control our lower ego impulses with concentration and tap into the wellspring of the higher self with meditation.

Bowl of Water—The teacher sat down with his students to explain the laws of abundance. He took a large bowl of water and asked a student to pour water in it. The student obliged, and as the bowl filled up, it began overflowing. The teacher explained that the bowl needs only so much, and what it does not require, it surrenders. Similarly, you will see evidence of this in nature. The clouds take from the sea only the water they require, and the bird takes for its baby only the morsels it requires. Similarly, we should take from the world the abundance we require and the excess use to fill up the bowls of others. He then asked the student to go into the garden and pick a rose. The student obliged and brought in a beautiful red rose. The teacher explained that the only way the rose bush could receive abundance was by sacrificing a part of itself. This sacrifice in its giving would allow the abundance to manifest in receiving. The students were still not quite clear about this, so the teacher told his students to be patient for this wisdom. A week later, he took them into the garden where the rose had been plucked, and there in the same branch was a beautiful rosebud. "The way the law of abundance works," the master explained, "is that the rosebush was blessed with another rose when it surrendered its fragrance to others. Similarly, when we wish to receive abundance in our life, we need to remember the wisdom taught to us by the rosebush. You can only give something that you already have within. By giving, we manifest it in our lives. Therefore, we can receive into our lives that which we give away, for these gifts are received by us when we sacrifice and give them to others. In this respect, the human being is a conduit through which God's essence is transferred to his creation. Everything we give away first has to pass through our hands. Like the flowers we may purchase for someone, the fragrance also remains with us."

By expressing our higher self, we are leaving positive imprints on

our soul; therefore, in giving and helping others, we are really helping and ennobling ourselves. However, by acting in a selfish manner
and holding back the divine attributes of forgiveness, kindness and
generosity, we are only harming our own soul along its journey.

The Bhagavad Gita states:

> Consulting only their desires, they construct their
> own heaven
> Devising arduous and complex rites
> To secure their own pleasure and their own power
> And the only result is rebirth.

It is important that our giving and acts of tolerance, forgiveness, and kindness are done unconditionally. Too often we have
expectations when we make sacrifices, and this negates the law of
abundance. For instance, some people want to be thanked or recognized for their acts of kindness, and others expect favors in
return. Living a life inside out requires us to express these higher
divine virtues unconditionally.

It is written in the holy texts:

> Give with your right hand in
> Such a way
> That even your left hand does not know.

When we express our higher self in this manner, we forgive
those who have wronged us and act in kindness, regardless of all
the justifications to the contrary, because ultimately, these acts are
ennobling our own soul. We see Jesus talk about turning the other
cheek; it is tough to do this because our lower instincts tell us that
we should slap the aggressor back. We have all been in situations
where we have faced ridicule, insults and meanness from others,
and our first thought was always to stand up for ourself and
respond in kind. What Jesus teaches us here is that what others do
cannot hurt our soul... but we can! As we learned previously, we
have charge of our own souls.

We see a similar example during the life of Mohamed, when an
old woman went out of her way to abuse him and often resorted to
throwing garbage on him. Not only did he avoid responding in
kind, he also nursed her when she fell sick. We have absolutely no

control over what other people do or say and the decisions they make. Furthermore, our soul growth is not affected by the actions and decisions of others, but by our reactions, thoughts and feelings when responding to them. Therefore, seek out the scripts, even the tough ones, because they provide us the opportunity to express the endless love emanating from the higher self disguised as sacrifice and selflessness and put them forth as seeds that will enrich our lives. Similarly, avoid the impulses of the lower nature that may suggest to us actions of anger, jealousy, pride and arrogance, for these will act to jolt us out of our connection to our higher self.

The Bhagavad Gita states:

> The gift which is given without thought of
> recompense, such a gift is pure.
> That which is given for the sake of results it
> will produce
> Or with the hope of recompense or grudgingly
> That may truly be said to be the outcome of passion.

The fruits of meditation will show themselves in an expanding consciousness and a flowering of love within. If this is not happening, it is a signal that something is not working the way it should. I will explore this in the next chapter. This inner change will sprout in our physical life, challenging the status quo with the introduction of higher thinking and nobler ideals. Certainly, if our meditation is not encouraging us to become more ethical in character and inclining us toward virtuous thinking, then there may be some barriers in our connection to our real self. It could be that concentration has not done a sufficient job in stifling the impulses of the lower self; consequently, our meditation may not be as effective as it should be. It is said that you can tell a tree by its fruit; similarly, a person who has subdued his ego and meditates will have the fruits of good character, integrity and ethical living.

SECOND: Express Detached Observations

It should be apparent that all the great masters had won their inner struggles against the ego of the lower self and had ascended into their higher divine self. Consequently, not only did they see themselves as spiritual beings in the midst of a temporary human existence, but they also lived their lives as such. If there is one struggle they could tell us about today, it would be that each one of us has the latent potential to reach the lofty heights they did, and it is our right and destiny to do this. Being awakened as they were gave them an expanded consciousness and an enlightened perspective to all that was going on in and around their lives, regardless of how difficult or conflicting it may have seemed to others at the time, or indeed to the historians who subsequently wrote about them. Jesus, for instance, did not see the unfolding events surrounding his betrayal by Judas as others did. Even Paul, one of his closest disciples, did not get it. Noah built an ark because he had an enlightened horizon. Most of the people around were ignorant, as was his own son, who drowned in the flood. The landscape and view of those who are conscious are expanded because they are informed by their divine self. In comparison, our view of life and circumstance would be like seeing what they did through a keyhole.

By detaching themselves, even momentarily, from the unfolding circumstances and situations, they were able to observe them in the context of the bigger picture. As we begin to meditate, our consciousness begins to expand, and this heightened awareness needs to be expressed in our physical life. By doing this, we can benefit in two ways. First, by being a detached observer to our own life situation, we can be more effective in dealing with the stresses, pains, hurts and resentment that often accompany the most difficult of situations. Second, our actions and reactions in the face of these troubled periods are likely to be more enlightened, which will have positive implications on our karma. Being a detached observer to our own life situations makes us more effective in dealing with the stresses, hurts and resentments that accompany life's most difficult problems.

We have learned that, at any given time, we are like actors involved in a multitude of scripts that are playing out. In some, we are the main character and in others, we are the supporting cast.

We have chosen these scripts and choose to remain in them, despite the fact that some of them are taxing and difficult. We can walk out of any one of them at any time: Husbands leave their wives and vise-versa; lovers break up; workers quit their jobs. This is happening all the time. Many of the scripts we are involved in may be challenging and the cause of considerable stress and emotional hurt. Unfortunately, when we are doing the right thing, they are a part of the package. However, the scripts we choose to accept reveal much about our character; furthermore, the more difficult the part, the greater the opportunity for soul growth.

The mystic Saint John of the Cross, who had much to endure in his physical life, writes:

> In detachment, the spirit finds quiet and repose for
> coveting nothing.
>
> Nothing worries it by elation and nothing oppresses
> it by dejection because it stands in the center
> of its humility.

By stepping out of ourselves for a moment and observing, in a detached manner, a particular script that is giving us anxiety and stress, our context shifts, and consequently, so does our perception. Earlier in the book, I gave the example of the husband who walked out on his wife for another woman after his wife was diagnosed with cancer. Without spending any time examining the past circumstances, which cannot be reversed, let us look at the two approaches that will determine the actions and reactions of the woman so let down at the time of her personal crisis. The first approach would have her filled with emotions of betrayal, hurt and anger. "How could he do this to me after all the sacrifices I made?" would be a natural response, concealing a deep hurt that would be hard to imagine. Since our thoughts and actions are what we put out into the ether, these negative actions will come back into our life. Since these resentments and thoughts of anger are negative imprints on our soul, the only person who is hurt by them is the person putting them out. The first approach does not change anything today, but puts into motion harmful actions that will affect he woman's soul destiny in a negative way. The second approach would have her momentarily step out of her physical self and into her spiritual one and observe the actors in this particular drama. In doing this, she will observe that the current situation is exactly what it needs to be, since the script for it was written some time ago and what we do presently has little influence on the situation today. Therefore, she needs to trust the plan. However, the only thing under everyone's control is what they do now, for in these decisions is the future hidden.

The husband, on the other hand, also had a choice to remain in this script, and in doing so, he would recognize that the wife needed support and encouragement to overcome her illness, and at this time he could have overlooked any personal differences that may have existed to be there to help her through this. Alternatively, he had the option to simply write himself out of the script and desert her, which is what he did. The woman, in this case, would recognize that she did not need to be judgmental, for he was merely acting out of his natural state. Beyond this, he also was a soul on a journey to redemption, like all of us. Since nothing she could have said would have made a difference, she needed to forgive him and seek solace in prayer and meditation. By doing this, she would not only deal with her own hurt, but she would also have put her actions above her natural state, thereby creating positive imprints on her soul. This in turn would have led to her soul growth and, in the process, she would have used her own suffering as a means to get closer to the divine force who sometimes sends us these difficult scripts.

The mystic Saint John of the Cross writes:

Live in this would as if only God and your soul were
in it, then your heart will never be made captive by
an earthly thing.

As our meditations slowly remove the veils around our soul, our consciousness begins to awaken. Therefore, in detaching ourselves from our physical self, even momentarily, and observing the particular problems and conflicts in our life as spiritual beings, we are able to have an enlightened perspective.

The Buddha writes:

> As a solid rock is not shaken by the wind
> Wise people falter not amidst blame and praise.

The Fruit Tree—The master sat with his students to teach them about the grades of thought. He selected four students and gave them each an unusual fruit. These fruits were from a tree in another town. He sent the four students at different times and they were to bring back an explanation of the source of this beautiful fruit. The first student went in the summer, the second in the winter, the third in the spring and fourth in the fall. Upon returning, the students explained what they saw. The student who went in the summer reported that the tree was lush, beautiful and full of fruit. The second student, who went in the winter, said that he saw a barren and lifeless tree and was unsure how anything could grow on it. The third student, having visited the tree in the spring, said that the tree seemed very young and full of life, but there were no fruits. Finally, the fourth student reported that he also saw a tree laden with fruit and that overripe ones were falling to the ground. Then the master explained that when we think about a specific situation, those thoughts represent only a small view of the whole picture, similar to the different experiences of the fruit tree by the students. However, when we detach from the situation itself and reflect, we can see a bigger picture enabling us to connect our thoughts to the real representation. In our detachment, we are able to see an enlightened horizon and therefore, our actions are informed by our deep awareness of the real. Hence, we need to focus on our actions rather than the outcome, which may be constrained and limited by its vision of the real.

Our actions and reactions during tough times will be more enlightened and therefore, positive for our own soul. Since our future is determined by the thoughts, intentions and actions that we put out into the ether, the problems that come into our life are great opportunities for our soul growth. In the same way that a kite will fly when the wind is against it, our spiritual growth occurs when we withstand the pressure of problems and pain that life brings to us.

The mystic Kheir writes:

Let sorrowful longing dwell in your heart.

Never give up, never lose hope.

The beloved says, "The broken ones are my darlings."

Crush your heart, be broken.

We need to step back from the problems and crisises by detaching from the actors and observing the unfolding drama as spiritual beings. This is when we realize that the only thing we control today is our own intentions and actions, and the choices we make will either help us spiritually or harm us. Therefore, we need to act in ways that will help our soul, and invariably, those are the expression of the divine attributes of forgiveness, patience, tolerance and humility, which we discussed earlier in this chapter. How then do we do this? It is simple. Always focus on the action, not the result.

The Bhagavad Gita states:

Do thy duty perfectly without care for the results

For he who does his duty disinterestedly attains the

supreme.

You see, too often we have already determined in our mind the result we want. Consequently, what we may do or say in any given situation is based on how we want things to be. However, when we detach from the situation, we realize that what is happening now is rooted in the past, and that the outcome we are seeking may be completely disconnected to it. Furthermore, the outcome we are seeking is based on what we think is right, which is very subjective. This obsessive attachment to the result is the cause of all our disappointments, because we predetermine the outcome in our own mind; we are blinded by the fact that our own expectation may have absolutely no connection to the evolving story of the soul. Subsequently when our expectations are not met, we are hurt and resentful. After all, if our actions are free of expectations, then where is the suffering?

There is a bigger plan unfolding and, by stepping out of the script and seeing the picture as the spiritual beings we are, we can observe that.

Khizr and Moses—Khizr had arrived to teach young Moses

about wisdom and enlightenment. They came to a river where a man earned an honest living taking travelers across the river in his small boat. Khizr and Moses crossed the river on his boat and found him to be a God-loving man with a young family. Upon reaching the other side, Khizr paid the man by making a hole in his boat, which shocked Moses. How could Khizr do something so mean? This was an honest man earning a livelihood, and Khizr had put a hole in the boat on purpose. Moses could not understand and was visibly angered by Khizr's actions. "I had told you to be calm if you wished to learn about enlightenment," Khizr informed him. Moses stopped speaking, though his deep inner agitation was apparent. After a time, Khizr explained that the next day, the king would be coming down this river. "Since he is preparing for war," Khizr said, "all boats that are in good repair will be requisitioned. Hence, by making a small hole in the boat, I prevented this man's boat from being confiscated. He can repair his boat and continue to earn his honest living." Moses was humbled and apologized.

When we focus on the small situations and problems that come into our life, we are left stressed and traumatized, particularly when the outcome we conceive does not materialize. To be enlightened is to see the cause in the effect and the effect in the cause. This enlightened perspective is the soul's real nature, and our meditation removes the veils around it so that our real self can provide us with insight.

The Bhagavad Gita states:

> Action is the product of the qualities inherent to nature.
> It is only the ignorant man who, misled by personal
>   egotism, says
> "I am the doer."
> But he, o mighty one
> Who understands correctly the relationship of the
>   qualities of action,
> Is not attached to the act.
> For he perceives that it is merely the action and
>   reaction of the qualities
> Among themselves.

By continually focusing on our actions and not the outcome, we ensure that the qualities of our actions ennoble us. Therefore, we have to step outside of ourselves and, as hard as it may be, avoid attachment to the result. Simply focus on ensuring, as the Buddha would say, "Right Action." This means to do the right thing and express your higher divine qualities, allowing the end result to be what it may. Since it is our attachments to results that create our disappointments, pain and suffering, by following this practice we can exist in an enlightened state free of anger, hurt and resentment, which are a part of the ego holding us to our lower nature in the world of repossession.

The Restless Student—The student approached his master and told him that no matter how hard he tried, he simply was unable to meditate with peace of mind. Furthermore, he found it very difficult to be forgiving, kind and patient. The master looked at his student and said, "I am sorry but I cannot have you as my student any longer." The student was perplexed. The master said, "I have seen your death in 30 days; therefore, it is pointless for you to attend anymore classes." The student went away overcome and in shock at hearing this. Twenty-one days later, the student bumped into his master at the market. The master asked him how things were and how life was treating him. The student said life was wonderful and that he was very happy to still be alive. The master inquired about this, and the student said that he found great peace in his meditation. Furthermore, since he did not have long to live, he was able to express forgiveness, kindness and charity because none of his possessions would follow him at death. The master said, "I do not know how long you will live. When I said that you have only 30 days of life, it is because I was trying to teach you how to find what you were looking for. I am glad that you have found it, and as long as you remember that life lasts only six days, live like five days have passed and you shall always retain the peace you have discovered."

Once we are able to practice detached observation with respect to all the different life circumstances we find ourselves in, we can then go one step further and broaden it. Take a look at everything that comes into your life and vision with detachment. For instance, if you are eating an apple, think about where it came from. The apple is as old as history; both Adam and Eve once grasped an apple such as this. For the apple we hold, someone planted a seed, and others nourished the trees it grew on. However, go deeper. Man is advanced enough in figuring out how many seeds there are in every apple, but only God knows how many apples there are in every seed. Learn to see and observe everything: the flower in your front garden, the bees in your backyard. By detaching ourselves from the physical self and by observing, we are able to discover our own spirituality and create harmony between our body, mind and spirit. This is an important step in our complete transformation, because there is a constant pushing and pulling between the needs of the soul and the physical body. Our inner needs of humility and reflective nurturing are constantly undermined by our outward actions of anger, pride and selfishness, and this causes a clash that holds our soul back. When our outward actions are expressions of our deepest spiritual self, the friction is eliminated and balance restored, thus allowing us to progress.

The Katha Upanishad states:

The self is not born, it does not die.

The ancient one is unborn imperishable.

Though the body be destroyed, it is not killed.

This self forever dwells within the hearts of all.

Meditation is how we became conscious of our unborn self, one that outlives our death and all the possessions we accumulate. That is and always has been the primary practice of all the enlightened and awakened souls who have graced our world since the beginning of time. By expressing our higher self and detached observation in our physical life, we allow the fruits of our meditation to bring wisdom into our actions, and this creates the unity between the mind, body and soul. Friction is what occurs when two objects rub against each other; by creating this unity between the outward and inward, we are eliminating a major obstacle to our spiritual growth and our journey to our sacred space.

The Bhagavad Gita states:

> In all beings undivided, yet living in division
> It is the upholder of all, creator and destroyer alike
> It is the light of lights, beyond the reach of darkness.

It is here in our sacred space that the Invisible Light radiates. This light of lights, the life energy that sustains creation, calls us to our self and empowers us to change our fate and shape our destiny.

The Bhagavad Gita states:

> Meditating on the divine, having faith in the divine
> Concentrating on the divine and losing themselves
>   in the divine
> Their sins dissolve in wisdom
> They go whence there is no return.

The journey, my friend, is inward and the process is meditation.

CHAPTER 10

Meditation: Methods and Approaches

We have learned in the preceding nine chapters that meditation is the primary practice of those wishing to traverse the Invisible Way. I am convinced that the readers will realize the need and necessity of incorporating meditation into their lives, allowing it to become the wellspring that informs and guides what is a brief physical life encounter. In this chapter, we will look at the practical elements of meditation, the methods, approaches and obstacles.

Let us begin by asking what is meditation? My definition is as follows: an effortless, unswerving, free-flowing state of awareness upon a subject or theme we have chosen.

We can see from the above definition that meditation is an effortless and free-flowing state of being, one that is not hindered in any way. Imagine a space craft in the wide expansive space. It has no natural obstacles holding it back from whichever directions it wishes to journey. It floats and stays afloat. As Sir Isaac Newton explained, an object in motion tends to stay in motion, unless acted upon by an opposing force. In space, the craft has no resistance from gravity, therefore, if it sets itself to move in a certain direction, it will keep moving in that direction. However, to get into space, the craft must first travel through the Earth's realm where the laws of gravity will hold it back, which is why booster rockets are attached to the spacecraft. These help power the rocket through the resistance until it reaches space, when the boosters, which are no longer needed are jettisoned.

Similarly, when we talk about being in the meditative state, we are referring to an act that takes place in that place beyond resistance of worldly thoughts and attachments. What should become obvious is that to get to that free-flowing and effortless state of awareness, we have to journey past the resistance of the mind, which provides the opposing force.

Therefore, when we read the often-heard advice that one should meditate, it conceals much ignorance, because it is nonsense to suggest that anyone can meditate without the proper preparation. Can anyone fly a plane without first acquiring the ability to fly? Can we just open and read a Chinese book without first learning Chinese? Similarly, we cannot meditate without first acquiring the ability to concentrate. It is concentration that enables us to get past the resistance of the mind and thoughts so that we can get to the stillness of our inner space. In the same way that a wet cloth cannot be ignited until it has dried, meditation is possible only after we have acquired the ability to concentrate. Therefore, there is more to meditation than just closing our eyes and sitting motionless.

The Bhagavad Gita states:

Without concentration there cannot be meditation;

He who cannot meditate must not expect peace;

And without peace, how can one expect happiness.

The wise souls have taught us that to enter a state of meditation, we must first learn how to concentrate. The operative word here is "learn", because concentration is an ability, and like all abilities, it has to be developed.

Imagine if someone who has never run more than a block decides to run a marathon, a 26.2 mile run. If this individual just shows up to the race, most likely he will collapse after having run just three blocks. However, if he were to practice running every day, building up his strength, muscles, stamina and technique, in time he would develop the ability to run long distances. The individual needed to develop his ability to run before he could seriously consider a marathon. Similarly, before we can meditate, we must develop the ability to concentrate.

The word concentration originates from Latin, meaning something that has a common center and is expressed as one-pointedness. In our everyday experiences, we have observed that anything that is concentrated has more power. For instance, a blunt pencil will not be able to penetrate a piece of cardboard the way a sharpened pencil can. We can also see the power of concentration at work in our society. A lake may have lots of water draining into it from several rivers, yet, despite the vast quantities of water that move, its power is miniscule compared to the power that is generated when a dam is built. In this case, water has to move through a small opening, thereby increasing the force upon the water, which can drive the turbines, creating electric power. All of this happens because there is a simple physical law at work: Force that is applied through a single point acts more effectively and is greater than if applied over many points.

When we apply the law of concentration to inner application, we see that the law applies in a similar fashion. The average mind is filled with countless thoughts and, since there are so many thoughts, each individual one is quite weak. Now, instead of the mental baggage of these countless thoughts, what if there were only one thought? Of course this thought would be strong and very powerful. Especially when we consider that the mind is the most powerful instrument we own; it can think, synthesize and provide solutions to a variety of complex circumstances, yet we use a very small part of it.

Imagine if we could take our mind, that is burdened with innumerable thoughts, and single-mindedly focus it on one thought. This is concentration: the ability to retain awareness on a single subject or object for as long as is desired. This may sound simple, but it is not. I have come across scores of very successful people who have been able to direct their minds to solve complex problems in their vocation; however, when they sat in meditation, they found nothing but frustration. Therefore, it is very important to understand the concept of concentration with respect to its inward application. Failure to do this will only lead to disappointments, which may prejudice the reader from practicing meditation in the future.

The Buddha writes:

> If one man conquers in battle a thousand times a
> thousand men
> And if another conquers himself
> He is the greatest of all conquerors.

Developing the ability to concentrate is not easy because it requires a certain conviction and discipline that requires a sacrifice of our time. We live in a world where things happen instantly, meals are cooked in minutes, and far-away places can be reached in hours. However, developing the ability to concentrate is painstakingly slow. Furthermore, there are no immediate tangible results that we can measure. I once read about a baby who was hidden in an attic for five years during the Nazi regime. Imagine when this young girl emerged from the attic at 6, never having walked or run because she had never had the opportunity to use her legs. Like all of us, she was born with the potential to walk and run, which occurs gradually through the regular use our legs from a young age, yet in her case, all she could do was crawl. However, with physiotherapy and lots of practice, she did develop the abilities, strength and muscles to walk and run. Our situation is not really that different. All of us have the potential to use our mind inward for concentration and meditation, except most people have never used their minds in this manner and therefore have not developed that ability. Then we turn 30 or 40 and even 50, before we decide to meditate, which is an inward practice, and find it difficult. At this time we either quit meditation in frustration or understand that we must develop an ability to concentrate, which will allow us to meditate.

In looking at this whole concept of concentration, we must understand three principles:

1. We are not our minds

Just because our mind acts and behaves in a manner that benefits us, it is often assumed that our mind is us; however, this is far from the truth, and a simple exercise will demonstrate this. Look at your watch and close your eyes. Tell yourself that for the next 15 minutes you do not wish any thoughts at all. Chances are that within two minutes, thoughts will be invading you in complete disobedience! So, who is in control, you or your mind, or are they one and the same?

What is the mind, anyway, except a bundle of thoughts? What happens to the mind if there is no thinking? It is simply a collection of thoughts where solutions are offered, but without the thoughts, there is no mind. The important question is what remains after the thinking stops? That is where meditation begins. Therefore, just because the mind assists us in our careers and in other ways, we should not be deluded into thinking that it will support all our efforts. Our mind's support of our wishes is predicated on whether it recognizes a benefit from them. For instance, if you have a plane to catch at 4 a.m., our mind will fully cooperate in assisting us to awaken when the alarm rings. It can rationalize the benefits of catching the plane because it understands the necessity and also the consequences of missing it. The loss of money in purchasing another ticket, not to mention the added stress, are reason enough for the mind to assist. Yet, tell yourself that 4 a.m. will be the time of your meditation and see what happens. The alarm will ring and the mind will provide countless rational arguments for returning to sleep. It sees no benefit and therefore will provide little support for what is important to us.

We are not our minds; in fact we are very distinct and separate because when the body dies, the mind and all its thoughts die with it. Everything is buried with the body but we will still exist.

2. Only the mind can help us concentrate

We understand that our mind is unruly and disobedient, especially when it comes to the practice of meditation. However, the mind is a paradox; the mind that is obstructing us is the same mind that can assist us.

Ramakrishna writes:

> By the mind is one bound, by the mind is one freed.

The mind can assist us or resist us, and the way out of this conundrum is to make the mind into an ally, a friend who can aid us in our endeavor. Concentration is the ability to control the mind.

The Boat—The disciple sat with the master, a little confused by the master's wisdom. He did not understand how the mind, which presented such resistance to meditation, could also be necessary to its attainment. The master explained. "You have a boat, and the only way a person can travel in it is by placing it on the water. It is the water that allows the boat to move and go from place to place. Yet, if there is a hole in the boat, the same water will cause the boat to sink! The water allows us an opportunity to travel, but it can also capsize the boat. Similarly, an obedient mind allows us to concentrate, making meditation possible, but a disobedient mind will be an obstacle.

We are not the mind, but we need the mind, for it has the ability of onepointedness. The mind can unswervingly focus on one subject at the exclusion of the many other thoughts. If the mind cooperates, we can train it and help it develop that ability. Consider a horse and rider. If we wish to travel on a horse, we must make sure that we are the master and the horse is obedient to our command. In this way, the horse will help us reach our destination. Imagine sitting on a horse and falling asleep, causing us to loosen the reins, which will likely result in the horse wandering off into a meadow to graze. Similarly, our mind is the horse; it can take us to the destination of our choice, but we need to be in charge. When we are not in control, countless thoughts enter our mind and thwart our efforts to meditate.

3. The mind can be controlled by willpower

Since the mind is both the cause of our problems and solution to our freedom, it needs to be harnessed for our service. In the previous chapter, we learned that the first phase of our journey from A to B occurs in our lower self, dominated by the ego. This is where the mind rules, and making progress in this phase means we need to enlist the assistance of the mind. To do this, we need to do a lot of inner work. In the same way as the marathon runner practices running, strengthening and disciplining before he sets out to run a race, we need to engage in concentration exercises that develop our inner faculties before we set out to meditate. The mental exercises will enable us to explore and develop the inner faculties of our mind that have lain dormant. Furthermore, these exercises will help us understand the defenses that are available to us when the mind becomes overly agitated and filled with thoughts.

The most powerful force we have to control the mind is our will, which is the spearhead of self discipline. People often refer to will as "willpower" because it is a powerful conscious mental act that produces physical action. Our will, therefore, is the inner force that is available to us to help us achieve our objectives. By the use of our willpower, we can direct our mind to focus on one thought rather than many, thereby making that one thought concentrated and one-pointed. Using our willpower to assist us in our inner work is easier said than done, because often we suffer from a weak willpower, in which case, little gets accomplished. Many people who try to give up certain habits like drinking, smoking and over-eating are thwarted by a weak willpower.

There are two ways to strengthen our willpower. First, we need to see ourselves as spiritual beings and to see the mind for what it is; some gray organic material that ultimately will get buried. Hence, our attitude toward our real purpose in life is critical, since nothing motivates our willpower more than a purpose. Therefore, by creating a strong purpose within, one that is passionate and vital and attached to our spiritual self, we can motivate ourselves with willpower to perform the necessary inner work. Second, willpower, though a very powerful instrument, can expend considerable amounts of energy for short periods only. To have strong willpower over long periods is difficult. Willpower comes in bursts of dynamic energy that wane; therefore, we need to set up a mental development program that recognizes this. In the same way that we can push a stalled car for a short distance and jump-start it using its own inertia and power, we can use our willpower to get us through the first phase of concentration. Once we have done this, we will have built inward inertia and momentum, and our willpower need only be called upon occasionally. Always remember that our willpower grows in proportion to the effort made; therefore, the greater the sacrifice, the greater the result.

The mental development program that I have set up takes this fact into account. It is important that, if readers are serious about meditation, they complete the program. This is what the program will achieve:

1. It involves inner work, which is vital for a serious student of meditation because it will help expand our understanding of our inner capacity.

2. It makes us aware of the challenges we face when we do commence meditation and provides us with defenses and strategies.

3. It trains the mind to do things it has not done and thus develops its abilities. Like any activity, practice makes perfect.

4. The program is short enough (two to three months) for our willpower to stay motivated and energized. Consequently, when we come to the practice of meditation, which is our objective, we will hit the ground running.

Without the ability to concentrate, our meditation will end in frustration and disappointments, and those who have practiced meditation without having done this inner work will readily admit to this. I find that in most cases, those who have jumped into meditation without cultivating the required inner discipline are actually simply involved in an internal tug of war with their thoughts. It is common knowledge that the harder you try to fight your thoughts, the more difficult it becomes. Ultimately, our purpose weakens and so does the willpower; the mind then reasserts its domination with the "Let's quit this; it's not getting us anywhere" prompting, which is disguised as common sense.

The mental program will systematically develop our ability to concentrate, which we can put to our spiritual benefit when we commence the serious practice of meditation.

The Bhagavad Gita states:

> He who can withdraw his senses from the attraction
> of their objects
> As the tortoise draws his limp with his shell
> Take it that such a one has attained perfection.

The mental development program is designed to help the reader develop the ability to concentrate inward and used as an ally in our meditation. However, developing our concentration will also help us in our material life. Our mental vision is strengthened, as is our capacity to analyze and solve problems. Furthermore, our memory retention is expanded. The program has been set up to be completed in two months, although it can be shortened or lengthened depending on how you progress. Feel free to customize it.

I have estimated that you will spend a minimum of two 15-minute sessions during the weekday and two half-hour sessions during the weekend on the program, but the more time you dedicate to your development, the more you will be rewarded. However, there is one caution. Make a commitment to follow through with the program and, once you begin, be consistent. When we are working inward, it is like digging a hole in the sand at the beach. As we dig, water will continually bring sand into the hole. Therefore, if you stop digging, even for while, the hole will soon be filled with sand. Similarly, as you commence the inner work, avoid taking breaks and missing days, because in no time, the gains you would have made will be lost. In fact, this is true of the inward path generally. I have learned the hard way that gains made in meditation are soon lost if we are distracted from practice for a time. Our physical life unfortunately can be quite demanding, and there is always one crisis or another that forces us away from our spiritual quest. This is true regardless of how advanced an individual is in his meditation.

With respect to this program, missing even one day can be costly for a beginner. Two 15-minute sessions during the weekday and two half-hour sessions during the weekend are a minimum and should be achievable regardless of your vocation and lifestyle. Finally, if at all possible, try and keep the same location and time of the day for these exercises. Performed consistently, these exercises will train our attentiveness and willpower and develop one-pointedness.

BEGINNER

Exercise One

Get a white piece of paper and draw a large black circle on it. Then put a black dot right in the middle of the circle. Place the paper on the wall. Now sit in a relaxed manner on a chair so that the position of the paper does not require you to tilt your neck. Sit comfortably; the only prerequisite is to keep your back reasonably straight. Now, with your eyes open, focus on the dot. Think of nothing else. Our target is to maintain our focus on the dot free of thought for five to 10 minutes. Work your way toward this goal.

Exercise Two

Once again, sit in a comfortable position, either on a chair or floor. Keep your neck and back straight and relax, with eyes closed. Now, gently inhale from the nostrils and slowly count to four. (This inhalation should be performed so that the first two counts fill the lower part of the lungs and abdomen and the subsequent two counts should raise the air upward from the lungs into your head, while the new air is still entering). At four, stop inhaling as your chest is full, and hold the air and breathe to the count of four, then exhale to the count of four. The first two counts transfer air once again into the lower part of your lungs and the subsequent two counts should be air exhaled from the nostrils.

Repeat the cycle. Feel the air enter inward and rise upward. Experience the moment the air is held and the moment after you have exhaled, which is known as the breathless moment. Modify the timing of the breathing so that it is natural and rhythmic. If you have a mantra, you can use it in place of the count. (I will be discussing mantras later in this chapter). If you do not have a mantra, you can replace the number count with "I" in the inhale and "am" in the exhale. Focus on the breathing and avoid all thoughts. Once again, our target is a minimum of five minutes, with an objective of

10. Although this may not be your normal breathing rhythm, beginning a meditation with this exercise will calm and relax you.

Supplementary Exercise

(This can be substituted or added to the beginner exercise).

Take a small pin and hold it close to you, observing it carefully for a minute. Now close your eyes and visualize the pin exactly as you saw it in the black screen inside your forehead between the two outer eyes. The target for this simple concentration exercise is a minimum of five minutes and a maximum of 10.

INTERMEDIATE

Exercise Three

Sit in your usual posture with your eyes closed. Visualize a dark screen in front of you, the way you would sit in a theatre before the movie starts. This screen is positioned centrally in between the two eyebrows at the root of the nose. Now visualize that the whole screen and space is a rose red color. Repeat this exercise and change the space to a different color. The technique to do this exercise is to breathe normally, but imagine that the whole space around your physical body is surrounded by rose red. Now as you breathe in, imagine and visualize this red enter and fill your inner space with red. Repeat this with the other colors. Keep focused on the required color as it enters your inner space; allow your breathing to continue naturally.

Exercise Four

Before you sit for this particular exercise, go into another part of the house. Then slowly walk to the location where you will sit. Along the way, observe everything to the left, right, above and below and make a mental note of everything; do not name the objects, just visualize. When you arrive at the place where you sit, close your eyes and sit in your usual posture. Now visualize the whole walk and all the observations that you had. It is important to be thorough and not to miss anything. This exercise can be simplified by avoiding the walk and simply observing everything in the room, then proceeding to visualize everything with your eyes closed. This exercise can be made more complicated by going outdoors into the garden and walking back to your usual place. Our target for the intermediate exercises is 10 minutes.

Supplementary Exercise

(This can be substituted or added to the intermediate exercise).

Take a pin once again and observe it carefully, this time from all angles. Now close your eyes and visualize the pin, see it hanging in the air. This time, do not just look at it, observe it from all angles, as if you are out in the air where the pin is hanging and you are moving around it to view the angles.

ADVANCED

Exercise Five

Sit in your usual posture, be comfortable, and go into your natural rhythmic breathing. Take a small coin the size of a dime and place it on your forehead in between your two eyebrows. (Moisten it a bit if it won't stay). Now, close your eyes, look at the black screen in the middle of your forehead, and feel the pressure of the coin that sits there. Hold your attention at the spot of the pressure. Now periodically push and expand as if you are trying to dislodge the coin from the inside. This exercise has a target of 15 minutes. In addition, once you move to the next exercise, you should be able to feel the spot of the forehead where the coin was, even when the coin is no longer there. Practice the expansions and hold them in the expanded mode for longer periods until a faint marker appears in your mind. You can focus on this marker at any time.

Exercise Six

Once again sit in your normal posture, relaxed and comfortable. Close your eyes and look at the screen, as if you are in a theatre waiting for the movie to commence. Now allow thoughts to enter. Just watch them float across the screen. Don't get attached to them or be drawn into them. Just observe them float by and dissolve as another one enters. Resist engaging a thought, because once you do, you have to start the exercise over. Simply observe your thoughts sail by. Give momentary attention as each one enters, but don't give it a second moment. Remain as a detached observer to the entering and vanishing thoughts. Our target for this is a minimum of five to 10 minutes.

Supplementary Exercise

(This can be substituted or added to the advanced exercise).

Get a glass of water and fill it close to the top. Take a needle and coat it with some grease or butter and gently let it float on the water. Wait until the movement of the water and the needle stops. Now, concentrate your focus and try to turn the needle. If you have done even a little inner work, you will be quite surprised at the results.

This completes the mental development program. Let us revisit the definition of concentration: The ability to retain awareness on a single subject or object for as long as is desired.

Your inner work will have allowed you to develop at least some ability to concentrate and familiarized you with the nature of the inner obstacles. Consequently, when you commence the practice of meditation, you will be doing so at point B. This is the realm of balance, and our meditation will need the constant support of our concentration abilities.

We have learned that an uncontrolled mind is the biggest obstacle to the practice of meditation. The multitude of thoughts in the form of fears, hopes, resentments and other emotions brings with them a restlessness that prevents meditation. We have understood the definition of meditation as: an effortless, unswerving, free-flowing state of awareness upon a subject or theme we have chosen.'

To achieve this state, it is critical that we tame the rebellious mind, because only it can prevent the outer chaos from entering our real self. The doors to our external thoughts, including work, family or things of the past, need to be closed if our meditation is to become effortless and free-flowing. The idea is to induce outer sleep and inner wakefulness.

This requires us to discipline the mind so that it assists and obeys our will. To do that, as we have learned, we must first develop an ability to concentrate, which enables us to become one-pointed and single-minded. However, like any ability that is latent, it requires work, courage, sacrifice and patience to achieve the fruition of its potential. The mental development program was designed to develop our abilities of concentration and one-pointedness, but how many readers will actually follow through? How many will quit midstream, distracted by the so-called "urgency" of our physical life? All I can say is that the work we put into our meditation and the fruits thereof will outlive our physical life. If that can give you a context of its importance, perhaps it also will provide you with the motivation to develop your concentration abilities so that you can practice meditation with the seriousness that it merits. The inner work you do before commencing meditation will provide you with the ability and motivation to obtain, from meditation, the great spiritual benefits that your real self craves.

The Bhagavad Gita states:

> The wise man who has conquered his mind and is
> absorbed in the self is as a lamp which does not
> flicker since it stands sheltered from every wind.

By developing our concentration, we have been successful in the first phase of our journey. The thoughts and emotions represented the opposing force, just as gravity opposes the flight of the spacecraft. Our concentration powers were similar to the boosters on the rocket, and we now reach the second phase commencing at point B. This journey to C takes place in the realm of balance between the lower self and higher self. Here our meditation practice has to be superimposed upon our concentration. Being the realm of balance, a constant and dynamic pushing and pulling are taking place between the efforts of the ego and the calmness of the soul. Therefore, we use our concentration to subdue the impulses from the ego, which will allow us to feel the impulses from our higher self. Imagine trying to listen to a nice, quiet song, when suddenly someone turns on their boombox with loud rock or rap songs filled with obscenities. The calmness you were getting from your music is drowned out by this noise. So you request for the boombox to be switched off, and suddenly you hear that calm music again.

Similarly, our concentration switches off the thoughts of the profane world, and if you try hard, you will hear the song from within. By blocking out the strong, loud impulses from our physical nature, we are creating emptiness within, which will be filled by the energy from our soul, provided we encourage it. This is what meditation will achieve in the initial phase—a connection to the positive spiritual energy from our interior self. Of course, this will not happen instantly; it requires the continuation of the inner work, this time with the combination of concentration and meditation. Much practice is needed in this quest. Always remember the story about the boulder; it did not crack suddenly, and a lot of time-consuming work preceded its destruction.

Before commencing meditation, do not sit with an attitude of haste nor pressure yourself with time constraints. Sit as if this is the most important moment for you, so prepare not to be disturbed by the family, phone calls and other intrusions. Tell yourself that everything can wait. Remember, many of the obstacles to our practice of meditation are conditioned by our attitude. An attitude of joy, happiness and a sense of meaningful purpose can help us eliminate many of the obstacles. Keep in mind that meditation should take us into that inner space that is free of expectation, judgment, stress and pressure. A place of freedom and aliveness unlike anything we have experienced in our physical life. It is a place that is complete in and of itself; therefore, we need to check all our bags outside and we need absolutely nothing. As mentioned before, constancy of practice is extremely important for two reasons. First, our inner work is like digging a hole on a sandy beach where the water is continually pushing the sand back into the hole. Similarly, the impulses of our lower nature will continually invade the tranquil space we create within. Second, in meditation, we are harnessing the energy emanating from our higher self into a free-flowing harmonious rhythm. It takes time to develop this inner rhythmic wave, and the gains are soon lost if the practice is not sustained.

Once you have completed your mental development program, you will make the following observations from your experiences.

1. You are not your mind. This fact will become very clear, as your real self is not your mind. Observing the mind at work in the program will provide clarity to this understanding.

2. The mind is not obedient. Once again, the myth that the mind is our instrument to use and wield as we feel fit will end. As much as it appears to assist us in our outward endeavors, it does so only when it suits its own purpose. By directing it inward, we soon realize that it is rebellious and disobedient.

3. We have the ability to control the mind, and we can observe that, by the use of our willpower and creating a sense of importance and purpose, we are able to tame the mind. However, we also notice that, like a wild horse, it does not tame easily and offers continual resistance in the hope of deterring us.

Today, there are countless forms of meditations, developed by practitioners through the ages. All of them relate to the inward; however, the methods and approaches are numerous. I have simplified them into two groups because it is not the purpose of this book to educate the reader about all the theories, but rather the practical approaches that work. The method I will outline has come from my personal trials and journey, and I am convinced that, taken seriously, it will work for the reader. I would suggest that, once you are on your way, you adapt the inner work and personalize it in a manner that suits you.

Having mentioned that, in this phase of our inner journey, we will require the use of our concentration and meditation, it should become clear that we will continue to be distracted by the impulses of our lower self. This is natural; we are absorbed in a physical life and constantly dealing with issues of family, work and social life. Therefore, before I introduce the two meditation approaches, let me outline a list of defenses we can use to thwart the distracting thoughts from affecting our mediation. Study them carefully because they are your defenses against the restless and agitated mind. You can use each one depending on the nature of intrusion, and it is not uncommon to vary, adapt and personalize them to fit your inner needs.

DEFENSES

1. *Detachment*—We learned in our exercises that we can detach from the incoming thoughts and allow them to just float and dissolve. There are two aspects to this. First, as the thoughts come in, we may attempt to block them. Wrestling with your thoughts won't work; in fact, it will entrap you in a struggle with the thought. The minute you do that, you will have become distracted from the effortless flow of your meditation. So it is important to let go and allow them safe passage into dissolution. Think about a tug of war; it represents two parties fighting for power, each one exerting great muscle. What happens if one participant in the tug of war lets go? The struggle and fight stops. Similarly, the minute we get involved in a struggle with thoughts, our meditation ends because it is not supposed to be a struggle. So just let go; the battle stops and the thoughts will disappear.

Second, become extremely disinterested in the thoughts. The thoughts that enter our inner space are trying to attract our attention, so don't give in to them. Remember, it is like fishing: if one bait does not seem to work, we will change the bait, and if one spot is not right, we move further down the river. Similarly, when one thought enters and we are able to show disinterest, guess what? Another thought will arrive to bait us! Our mind knows what is important to us, so don't expect any favors. If you have a worry, a problem or fear, this is when they all show up as bait; this much you can count on. But don't take the lure; don't wrestle with the thoughts or show interest. Just detach from them as if they belong to someone else, because they do. Your real self doesn't care about them. Keep telling yourself, "I am not interested" and stand back.

Think of a fierce bull and how it can be calmed and quieted. By restraining it, the bull struggles even more; yet, put it in a large field and it quickly calms down. Similarly, when thoughts enter, expand your consciousness and allow them to fade away in the distance.

2. *Breathing*—Breathing has been used in most practices in one form or another because it allows us to focus on it. By focusing on breathing, we are able to eliminate and ignore other thoughts. Breathing also slows down our mental activity and with this, mental intrusions subside. Therefore, if the thoughts begin to create restlessness, switch the focus of meditation back onto breathing. Center your attention on that breathing rhythm and you can slowly merge back into your meditation rhythm once you have eliminated and quieted the mind. Therefore, creating a harmonious breathing rhythm is important, and some of the meditation time should be devoted to this very important issue. This breathing rhythm is easily merged into our meditation rhythm, making this a very formidable defense during meditation.

3. *Mantra*—In my view, a mantra is one of the most powerful defenses we have. Not only is it a tool to block the thoughts, but it is perhaps an important vehicle for those who wish to enter their deepest sacred space. I will be discussing this matter further when I introduce the second approach to meditation.

4. *Thought Control*—One of the best-kept secrets of the mind is its Achilles heel. Although we can see the unruly mind bombarding us with an endless assault of thoughts at just the time we sit for meditation, the mind can only focus on one thought at a time. Despite the countless thoughts invading our inner space, the mind can only look at them one at a time. Imagine a camera that is loaded with a hundred picture frames, yet it can only take one picture at a time. Similarly, our mind could be filled with countless thoughts but we only see one at a time. This simple known fact provides us with a very powerful defensive strategy against unwanted thoughts. By placing a thought of our choice and holding it there, we will prevent other thoughts from entering! It is as simple as that. Therefore, if we can choose a thought connected to the objective in our meditation, then other thoughts will not enter

as long as we hold on to the thought we inserted. The key, then, is to insert the thoughts of our choice and in doing this, we will eliminate all other thoughts.

5. *Expansion*—We learned the power of expansion in our exercises. By diligently working at expanding your mind into a single point, pushing and expanding it outward right at the middle of our eyebrows, we will eliminate all thoughts. In the exercise, I had asked a reader to place a small coin or button in the middle of the forehead between the two eyes when performing the exercise. By being diligent, we will create a small marker on the inside that we can expand into when we require elimination of incoming thoughts. Expanding our mind in this way has to be done in small episodes. To attempt to create this expansion for too long a period will likely give you a headache. The best way to do it is in small pulses, directing our mental waves gently for small periods of time. Developing this practice is extremely advisable for the serious seeker because it is through one of these expansions that the soul one day will detach from your body, leaving you in complete amazement. Always remember, expansion occurs with our exhale.

6. *Love*—Love is, without question, the most powerful defense we have. Unfortunately, it is one that manifests on its own accordance once the taps to the wellspring of spiritual energy are turned on. I will be discussing this in detail later in this chapter.

7. *Sacred Zone*—Think about some places that you may have visited where you found uninterrupted peace and quiet. It could be a place by a river, a nature walk, a mountain you may have visited, a favorite place you frequent alone, or even a place of worship where you found peace. Before you commence your meditation, visualize yourself going to this place alone and tell yourself, "No one knows I am here, and I don't want anyone or any thoughts coming here." Now make this place your sacred space, one that is private and special. Commence your meditation by visualizing yourself there and will it so that no one or no thought interrupts you. If thoughts enter, be disappointed and disinterested in them.

8. *Creating a Lack of Interest*—Perfect concentration is possible when the objective of our concentration is upon a subject that, in

our perception, is singularly and overwhelmingly important. There is something within all of us that enables us to switch off voices, noises and other external impulses during critical moments. For instance, when we are engrossed in a movie or a sports game on television, we just do not hear certain sounds and intrusions. Try calling out to your teenagers when they are in the middle of a video game and see if your voice is blocked out! There is a something within us that enables us to block out everything when we are pre-occupied with an important task. Hence, by making the subject of our concentration overwhelmingly important, we will automatically be disinterested in all other thoughts, making perfect concentration possible.

The Death Warrant—A traveler passed through a kingdom where the grand Vizir gave lectures on the occult. He decided to attend one and heard the Vizir explain that perfect concentration was possible. The traveler could not help but laugh at this claim. The Vizir was not happy with the way this stranger ridiculed him in public and instantly condemned the stranger to death. The stranger was in shock as he was taken to the dungeon. The next day, he was summoned by the Vizir who informed him that there was only one way that he could avoid death. He gave him a bowl of water filled to the brim and a path upon which he must travel. If he was able to return without spilling any water, his life would be spared. Since this was the only chance the stranger had of saving his life, he took the bowl of water and went on his way. An hour later, he returned and not a drop of water had been spilled. The Vizir asked him what he had seen or heard along the way, but the traveler had no recollection. The Vizir smiled and told him that he had walked through a noisy marketplace and yet the traveler had not spilled any water, proving that, under certain circumstances, perfect concentration was possible. The traveler was set free instantly.

By creating a lack of interest in everything except the object of our concentration, we are able to block out all intrusions. This means we have to make our meditation an uncompromised practice. These, then, are the defenses that we can use during our meditation. They can be personalized and used in combinations; therefore, become familiar with them.

The Bhagavad Gita states:

> For the sage who seeks the heights of spiritual
>> meditation,
> Practice is the only method, and when he has
>> attained them
> He must maintain himself there by continual self
>> control.

The secret of attainment is in the practice, not in the study, because we cannot experience the imperishable without the constancy of practice.

Sri Aurobindo writes:

> Transform your efforts into the controlled and
>> powerful stream of your soul
> Let everything in you be a conscious force
> For such is your destiny
> Transform your mind into controlled intuition
> Let everything in you be the light
> For such is your destiny

Let us now look at the two approaches to meditation. The first approach is the one most used in the Western world. If you have never meditated, it is recommended that you begin here and then move to the second approach.

MEDITATION: FIRST APPROACH
In Search of the Self

This method of meditation is designed to help the practitioner discover the real self. Who are we? What are we? What is the quintessence of our real identity? More important, this practice can take us to the experience of our real spiritual self. In this respect, it is a meditation that may not take us all the way; however, for the beginner, it is one that awakens us to the existence and the experience of the greater reality that lies ahead.

This meditation will set you on a journey to the discovery of the self that will ultimately bring you to the self realization of your spiritual personality. This, in turn, will open up new vistas and horizons to the transformation of your being from physical to spiritual. The technique for this meditation is to use "themes" as the object of the meditation. The themes are carefully chosen and designed to expand the consciousness to the point where our meditation makes us receptive to the different states of experience.

I have mentioned previously that, when an idea or thought prevails in our mind, all other thoughts will submit to it. We can only have one thought in our focus at a time. Therefore, with the use of concentration, we can insert into our mind a "theme" that encompasses ideas and thoughts which we have carefully selected. By holding our attention to this theme, no other ideas or thoughts will enter. Our meditation can than provide the leadership and creativity to develop this theme in a manner that allows input from the wellspring of our higher self.

By closing our mind to all worldly thoughts and meditating on the theme, the responses and impulses of the higher self can slowly emerge to inform and guide us on the subject of the theme. The five spiritual insights that I introduced at the beginning of the book are all designed to become meditative themes that the reader can use. Let me give you an example of how a theme can be used and developed in meditation.

Theme: If I know my death is tomorrow what would I do today?

Development: The theme represents a starting point for your inner journey. However, unlike other journeys in our physical world, for which we have predetermined our route and destination, this inward way has no end point. Develop the theme and expand it through inward reflection and contemplation. This theme is taken from the first chapter; read and reflect upon it prior to commencing this meditation.

Read the theme numerous times, memorize it and visualize it on the black screen in between your two eyes, returning to it every time you get distracted. Then concentrate on this theme at the exclusion of all other thoughts, and allow your meditation to provide leadership to develop ideas and thoughts associated with it.

For instance, *what happens to all of my relationships*, my spouse, children, family and friends? All these would end. I would be missed for a while, but that's all. People just disappear, and in time, so does their memory. *What happens to my work and career?* My employer will hire someone else to do my job. I invested so much time in it, yet it can give me no reward now. *What about all the things I worked so hard to accumulate?* They all get left behind. The title on them changes, others will live in my home, drive my car, own my investments. But they were the goals I strived for! Everything is repossessed at death So *what part of me does not get buried?* Only my soul. *What happens to my soul after death?* The journey continues. *What can I take with me in this journey?* All the good I did. But if I am going to die tomorrow, and I have but one day, *what can I do with this time?*

- Spend some of it with the ones you love and tell them you love them.
- Do something worthwhile, so that those assisted would send some blessings to you.
- Pray that the God of all forgives you.
- Forgive others who have hurt you.

These are just some ideas and thoughts that can be developed from the theme. Remember, it is your journey, and therefore the development of the theme must occur from your meditation and emerge from your higher self. Of course, it will take some practice, but encourage your inner being to help you, and when all else is silent, you will be quite surprised.

Also, often our meditation will take a direction that is decidedly away from the theme. This happens either because our concentration becomes weak, which allows worldly thoughts to infiltrate our meditation, or it could happen because we have allowed our meditation to stray from the theme. In either case, it is important to stay alert by bringing up the theme as if it were written on the black screen between your two eyes. By revisiting and visualizing the theme, we are able to end this thought development as it diverts away from our chosen path. Our meditation gives us control and choice to do this.

Let us now look at a practical application of this theme in a meditation.

- Begin the meditation by finding your most comfortable posture and keep your back straight. Sit without any expectation and tell yourself, with belief and assertiveness, "I am not interested in anything during my meditation save the theme and nothing is going to happen during it. I do not wish to be interrupted by anything, any thought or anyone."
- Close your eyes and slow down your breathing to reduce the mental activity and relax the body. Look inward at the black screen that exists in between your two outer eyes at the center of your forehead.
- Visualize the theme on the screen, It reads: "If I knew my death is tomorrow, what would I do today?"
- Remember to revisualize the intermittently to ensure that your meditation has not gone astray.

Now commence meditating on this theme. Stay concentrated and allow your meditation to develop its own ideas and thoughts. Merge your breathing into the gentle meditation so that you become unaware of the breathing rhythm. Create a dialogue with your inner self; speak to it and ask questions, but most of all, listen in the silence from where the intuitive energy will emerge. Be patient; if you put out a thought or question, just wait in the stillness. Wait in patience and a belief that your question does not need an answer because stillness is an answer in itself. As long as you have been successful in eliminating the thoughts from without, every moment you sit in that silence is an energy that is expanded but never wasted. It is creating small ripples in your interior pond that one day, with enough expansion of such energy, will become an ocean.

Fill your whole interior self with that silence. Keep focused on the black screen and allow the theme to be visible on it. Every now and again, look at it, focus on it and push on it and allow it to melt away with the ideas that emanate from the meditation. Be sincere and humble in your meditation, and remember that silence and stillness in meditation when no thought or idea exists is a great place to be; revel in that space with sincerity and humility. As the wise saying goes: "Action is thy duty, reward is not thy concern."

If distractions do emerge, as they inevitably will, eliminate them as quickly as possible using one or more of the defenses I outlined earlier in the chapter. Be sure to remember that intrusive thoughts can come dressed in great ideas and inspirations, but once you attach to them, they will betray you and distract you from your meditation. It is a battle to tame the mind and, once won, the victory must not be taken for granted. Expect a mutiny, because the mind is rebellious by nature. Be alert; close yourself to all thoughts that come from outside and, with practice, your intuitive faculty develops so that you are able to discern which idea is from the stillness and higher self and which is from the Trojan horse.

At the end of this chapter, I have put together some themes taken from the five insights in this book. They are a great starting point for the beginner. In time, the reader can develop his or her own themes from the writings of prophets, scriptures and mystics that have inspired them.

SECOND APPROACH
Meditation in Search of the Invisible Light

The meditation in search of the real self, which I outlined in the previous section, can only take us so far, because the themes that we introduce and meditate upon create boundaries and internal limits. This is understandable, since the themes we introduce come from our own limited perception. Nevertheless, they serve an important purpose, especially for beginners and agnostics. Furthermore, they will take this practioner quite some way toward self-realization and the experience of the real.

The meditation in search of the Invisible Light goes far beyond the first meditation and represents the quintessence and purpose of this book. The Invisible Light, as we have learned, is our divine self that sits within each one of us. The real journey, which is the journey of our soul, ends when it awakens to its own divinity. This meditation is about our disintegration to the physical world and reintegration to the divine reality. This is when all personalities and identities dissolve in the stream of the Invisible Light and merge with God. As we learned earlier in the chapter, our journey from our lower self through the innumerous veils toward the Invisible Light brings us to Point C in our diagram. Here at this furthest point, in patience and reverence, we wait, because our entry into the sacred space depends on an invitation, a grace that calls us onto itself. Therefore, any meditation that limits this will restrict the journey. The meditation in search of the Invisible Light is the deepest meditation there is because it is one that seeks God and nothing less. There are two very important tools that this meditation requires: understanding the power of breathing and mantra. Let us look at both because this meditation would be impossible without them.

Breathing—A serious student of meditation will realize the importance of breathing and the power it conceals. When we examine the word *spiritual*, it comes from the Latin word *spiritus*, which refers to the breath of life. For plants, animals and humans alike, breathing represents life, and therefore it is perhaps the most sacred act that we perform. Mystics have long understood the spiritual power of our breathing.

The mystic Ansari writes:

> O you who have departed from your self
> and who have not reached the friend
> do not be sad for,
> he is accompanying you in each
> Of your breaths.

We go through our life completely unaware that each breath we take actually gives us life, and we are alive because of it. Furthermore, each moment of our aliveness is followed by our death, when the breath of life leaves us. We are alive because the soul within this limp body enters through this breath and our body dies when this soul leaves it with the outgoing breath. Our breathing is absolutely the most sacred activity we are involved in on a constant basis. Our life, however, passes in our attachment to the world of the profane while we are oblivious to the sacredness that enters our real self in every moment.

Some of the most sublime moments of meditation occur with the rhythm of our breathing. The life energy of the divine sustainer enters into us and gives us life, and this soul is, with grace, able to leave the body through the breath and experience the dimensions of the higher realms. Indeed, as the prophets of old tell us, it is this soul that, when invited, is graced with the union of the divine. The *now* moment of aliveness that I explained earlier occurs with our breathing, and this meditation practice is our entry point into the timeless realm.

A part of our inner work must be to experience this breath, and the more we meditate, the greater is our understanding of the sacredness of breathing. During our meditation, there are four stages of breathing that we must be constantly aware of.

Stage One: The Moment of Life—As we inhale, the life energy enters into us and makes us alive. Feel this energy as it enters, because it is pure and sustaining. Focus on the qualities of the air as it fills your whole self and makes it spring to life, and in the process purifies the soul.

Stage Two: The Moment of Aliveness—Hold this life energy within you momentarily. Feel the divine energy as it fills your complete body, rising from your abdomen to your forehead. We exist because of it.

Stage Three: The Moment of Dying—Feel the life energy leave your body as you exhale. It carries with it all the toxins and impurities from your body. The time of dying is at hand in the out-breath, and one day it is such a breath that will shift your soul back to the spiritual realm of its origin.

Stage Four: The Moment of Death—Once you have exhaled, momentarily hold your breath in the exhale. Now feel the empty space within you, for it is lifeless and dead without the life energy. Experience the lifeless moment.

On average we breathe 15 to 16 times per minute, and as we slow down, it naturally relaxes us and reduces our mental activity. It is important to practice some inner work on breathing in our meditation. Practice the stages I have outlined in the following manner.

When breathing in, visualize the breath as light, because it is sacred. Through the nostrils, let it go downward into your abdomen and halfway through, let it rise upward and feel the breath's pressure in your forehead at the location of your third eye. On your exhale, toward the end, feel the breath's pressure against the forehead at the location of the third eye (against the black screen described in the concentration section).

Once you have established your breathing rhythm, the inhale should represent the receding tide as it wells up with energy, and the exhale should represent gentle waves falling against the shore, which is the black screen. Later, try turning the rolling waves of the exhale into a laser-like surge of the ocean tide, focused on the shore, that is, the black screen.

Breathing is an important component of the higher meditations. Furthermore, it provides us a defense against the unwanted thoughts when we focus on it during the formative period of our meditation. Later, even though our breathing merges into the free-flowing rhythm and therefore becomes unnoticeable, it still regulates the waves of our flow.

Mantra—This is another matter that a serious student of the higher meditations must become familiar with. A mantra is a word of power used as an object of meditation, and it is derived from Sanskrit, referring to "man to think and to liberate." Hence it is associated with our liberation from the mind and its thoughts. References to mantra are found in some of the oldest sacred works, such as the Vedas, where they are connected to the divine. We also see a reference in one of the more mystical verses in the gospels:

>   In the beginning was the word
>   And the word was with God
>   And the word was God.

We can see from the above that not only do words have power, but certain words are not ordinary words; they are sacred. If the divine intelligence can be concealed within a single word, then it is a source of creative power and transformation. Therefore, from my perspective, the mantra we use has to have one primary quality: *It should be connected to God.*

Since the purpose of our meditation is to search for and attain the Invisible Light, which is our divine self, any mantra disconnected to the divine will create limitations. Most of the wise mystics will confirm that the meditation that initiates our quest of the divine source must commence with some connection with that source to begin with. In this sense it is like a seed or invisible rope by which we can move towards fulfillment.

In this way, the mantra or word has spiritual properties that lead us to the unfolding of the deeper spiritual levels within.

The mystic author of "The Cloud of Unknowing" writes:

And if any thought rise and will press above thee
    betwixt thee
and that darkness and ask thee saying what seekest
    thou and what
wouldest thou have? Say thou, that it is God that
    thou wouldest have
"Him I covet, him I seek, and nought but him."

Therefore, in this meditation, if you do not have a mantra that has a connection to God, then acquire one. The best way to do this is to go within your own devotional tradition and seek it there with the help of your intuition. If you lean toward Christianity, find one from the many that appear in the Christian texts. Similarly, if you lean toward Hinduism, Judaism, Islam and others, all of them have some very sacred words connected to God. However, if you have built up a resistance toward using any connection to God in your meditations, certainly use a neutral word. At the end of this chapter, I have provided some suggestions and sources for the reader to find a suitable mantra or neutral word. It is important that this mantra is two syllables and one the reader finds easy to pronounce, understands the meaning of and feels comfortable with.

A mantra that comes from a divine origin will awaken the divine within. These words may be new to us, but they create a vibration and resonate with the soul within, which has a cosmic memory of primordial existence. Sacred words allow us to enter the sacred space.

The mystic author of "The Cloud of Unknowing" writes:
>   And fasten this word to thine heart
>   So that it never hence for thing befalleth.
>   This word shall be thy shield and spear,
>   Whether thou ridest on peace or on war.
>   With this word, thou shalt beat on this cloud and
>   this darkness.
>   Above thee, with this word thou shalt smite down
>   all manner of thought under the cloud of
>   forgetting."

The mantra becomes a shield, a defense against the thoughts emanating from our lower self. However, it is also a spiritual conduit that can take us to that place where we can be receptive to the grace we long for.

Once you have selected a mantra of your choice, it becomes important to entrench it in your meditative practice. This can be done as follows:

1. Understand thoroughly the connection of the mantra to the divine. (If the reader is using a neutral word, be openminded when meditating).
2. Practice your mantra by speaking it aloud.
3. Whisper the mantra.
4. Practice your mantra by reciting it mentally.
5. Listen to your mantra within.
6. Insert your mantra with the breathing practices outlined above.
7. Slowly allow your breathing focus to fade and allow the mantra to pulsate with the rhythm of breathing.

Let the mantra become the dominant sound and thought so that the minute you sit in meditation, the word will automatically be heard rhythmically and effortlessly. Feel the empty space by contemplating the mantra and merge it into a personal dialogue with the divine.

Now we are ready for the meditation in search of the Invisible Light.

Having looked at some of the individual components of meditation in search of the Invisible Light, let us now look at the whole picture. Prepare to sit in meditation in the usual way that I have described previously.

Step 1. Begin by deep breathing to reduce mental activity and find relaxation.

Step 2. Find your natural breathing rhythm and focus on the breathing. Look at the black screen in between your two eyes.

Step 3. Insert your mantra into your breathing rhythm and slowly move your focus away from the breathing. The mantra should be a part of the breathing rhythm. Keep looking at the black screen; see the mantra etched on it.

Step 4. Allow the mantra to fade into the background as if it is heard and pulsating with the rhythm. Go deeper and deeper into the stillness.

Step 5. Feel the inhale as if it were the back swell of a receding tide and gently roll out the waves with the exhale upon the black screen. Create a gentle rolling rhythm and keep sight of the mantra in the background.

Step 6. Every few minutes, gently merge the rolling waves of your exhale into a laser-like surge that pushes and expands the black screen. Keep pushing and expanding regularly before returning to the rolling wave rhythm.

Step 7. Follow through on the above. This time, just allow the black screen to melt away as you feel released and liberated. One day, if you are blessed, you will indeed be outside in the sacred spiritual realm.

Step 8. In this vast stillness, express an outpouring of love and yearning for the beloved. Pour out your most intimate longing and feelings. Make this conversation very personal and become aware of the divine presence beyond the black screen, because the divine reality always manifests when love is contemplated. Repeat this exercise from step seven with even more vigor and unleash those waves of longings, until one day the barrier breaks and you are released.

Every time you get distracted, go back to step three and start over. Remember to seek movement further and further into the silent darkness, aware and wide-eyed within. Finally, always be aware of the mantra, its meaning and sacred power. This meditation is in search of the divine; therefore, it is important to make it holy. Incorporate some personal feelings of happiness and sadness as you dialogue with the divine at opportune moments in the stillness and consider these moments as your time with God.

ADVANCED MEDITATION
In Search Of The Invisible Light

To develop our meditation in search of the Invisible Light toward its conclusion, other elements need to be incorporated into our meditation practice. A serious student, having traversed the previous meditative stage, will have come to the following conclusion as a consequence of personal experience and wisdom, informed by the wellspring of their higher self: This world of apparent multiplicity conceals a unity. Our physical world gives us an illusion of the separateness and independence of all things within creation. However, in reality, the interdependence of everything demonstrates that there is only oneness.

The Crow—The master explained the nature of this illusion to his students with the story about the crow. The crow, standing out in the open field, saw his shadow and, because of the position of the sun, the shadow appeared unusually large. When the crow moved, so did the shadow, and the crow concluded that the large shadow was him. Feeling very mighty and important, he ventured into the territory of the eagle, defiant and unafraid of the predator. The eagle was rather surprised that the crow would hand himself over as his next meal so easily. The crow, on the other hand, saw himself as the large shadow he had seen and expressed his greatness to the eagle. The eagle devoured the crow and so ended his illusion of greatness.

The master explained that people live like the crow; they believe themselves to be independent and creators rather than having been created. When the eagle's eye of man's real self awakens, the ignorance and illusion disappears. Thus, when we surrender our ego to the higher self, the light overwhelms the darkness.

We think we are independent and self-sufficient, but that is simply an outward form. Our meditation slowly awakens us to the fact that there is a divine reality and everything within creation is a part of it.

The late Aga Khan III explained this beautifully in his memoirs:

> In him we live and move and have our being. God is
> the sustainer.
> He sustains us always and everywhere.

There is a divine reality and, at the heart of it all, everything exists in unity. It is the uncovering of the veils through the process of meditation that awakens us to the wisdom of unity. The multiplicity and separateness we see is an illusion; we are actually all part of the one divine essence. This idea is beautifully illustrated in an old story about a fish that was informed that the most important thing to a fish was water. So it went in search of water!

The mystic Rumi states:

> He gazed upon the inward eye and gazed on the
> ideal form of that which he had only read in books.

The inward eye Rumi refers to is the third eye, which was discussed earlier in the book. This third eye is a primary faculty of the awakening soul, which begins to see the divinity in itself.

The sacred texts state, "In silence shall you possess your own soul." Having come to this realization from within and to continue toward the Invisible Light, our meditation practice must be converted into a 24-hour practice as follows:

1. Commence the physical meditation at two ends of the day. That is, practice a minimum of 40 minutes of serious meditation first thing in the morning, long before the working day begins, and the last thing before sleep.

The Mystic Rumi writes thus:
>   The breeze at dawn has secrets to tell you
>   Do not go back to sleep
>   You must ask for what you really want
>   Do not go back to sleep
>   People are going back and forth across the doorsill
>   where the two worlds touch
>   The door is round and open
>   Do not go back to sleep.

Since sleep takes up one third of our life, the meditation at night before retiring is particularly important for two reasons. First, since all words and objects have their own mental associations, what we input into our mind just prior to sleep will resonate within. By meditating on the divine word, that is, mantra, the mind will be filled with sublime spiritual thoughts. Remember, garbage in equals garbage out, and our meditation at night seeks to input those thoughts that will aid our spiritual development. Second, if the reader has previously ingrained the mantra into the pulse, this mantra will continue to circulate with each breath as we fall asleep.

Our meditation continues as we sleep. Since we spend such a large part of our life sleeping, this meditation before sleep will enable us to harness our sleep time as part of our meditation practice. Consequently, upon awakening at dawn, our meditation will have already reached an advanced stage, making the morning meditation very powerful. Once this morning meditation is completed and the work day begins, continue the inner recitation of the mantra throughout the day. It is important to make this mantra a part of your whole self so that, when you close your eyes in mediation, you can skip all the steps I outlined earlier and find yourself instantly in that stillness, regardless of where you are. Always remember that, once we put a seed in the ground, and water it, considerable activity is taking place beneath the ground though this is invisible to our physical sight. The 24-hour meditation will create powerful, yet unseen, inner transformations, which one day will manifest as an unthinkable blossom.

The Bhagavad Gita states:

> You will keep him in perfect peace
> Whose mind is fixed on you.

Thus, we need to start the day in meditation and end the day in meditation. In between, modify your meditation so that while you are at work, walking, standing and performing everyday life activities, there is an ongoing, active inner meditation. This inner meditation will consequently create a much more meaningful purpose in your worldly activities. The inward state of meditation must continue throughout the 24-hour cycle of the day. When the last thought at night and the first thought upon awakening are the word, it forms a sacred circle, and this sacredness will inevitably emerge into our life. The 24-hour meditation is about creating this sacred circle.

2. I have discussed at length the necessity to express our higher self at all times. At this stage, this idea becomes very much ingrained as a natural response emanating from the inside out.

Our understanding of the principle "Love thy neighbor," which exists in all sacred texts, takes on a new meaning. We begin to understand that, if we are all part of the one divine essence, then, in helping others, we are really helping ourselves. Similarly, when we hurt others with words, malice or otherwise, we are harming ourselves. Therefore we need to practice detachment as discussed previously. Failure to do this will result in our actions becoming obstacles in our path.

I knew a couple once who were having problems in their marriage, so they approached a marriage counselor for assistance. The marriage counselor wanted to see each spouse separately to understand the issues. He first met with the wife, who had kept a diary of all the husband's infringements. She outlined a long list of everything he had done wrong, all his shortcomings and also everything he should have done but never did. It was quite a scorecard, and the wife felt it was impossible to continue with the marriage. The marriage counselor then asked the husband for his perception and thoughts. He, too, pulled out his book that recorded all of the wife's shortcomings, the promises she had failed to keep, and again, it was a lengthy scorecard. He also felt that there were just too many problems and that the marriage could not survive. The marriage counselor called the two together and told them that there was nothing he could do to help. He said, "If you are going to keep score in your home and marriage, then it cannot survive. The only way to save this marriage is to throw out the scorecard and forgive one another, because marriage is not a game of golf." He explained that, in this sport, the whole game starts with a scorecard, which you take with you and fill out with every putt.

Similarly, a serious student of meditation wishing to make spiritual progress would see others as himself, a soul journeying toward consciousness in the one divine reality. Thus one needs to detach from the scorecard and learn to forgive the imperfections of everyone who comes into our life.

3. Beyond concentration and meditation is the stillness where the divine calls us unto itself in response to the love we emanate. Love is a vital part of the higher meditations, and the mystics that made significant progress were those that had an insatiable thirst for the beloved.

The mystic Attar writes:

> From each, love demands a mystic silence
> What do all seek so earnestly? 'Tis love
> Love is the subject of their inmost thoughts,
> In love no longer 'thou' and 'I' exist
> For self has passed away in the beloved
> Now will I draw aside the veil from love
> And in the temple of mine inmost soul
> Behold the friend, incomparable love
> He who would know the secret of both worlds
> Will find that the secret of them both is love.

Love is not an emotion we can manufacture, but when it manifests itself within, it is like a burning fire. In my own life, some of my most intense and sublime meditations have been those when the inward outpouring of weeping love has been so overwhelming that no object of love can resist its call.

The mystic Kheir writes thus:
> Piousness and the path of love are two different
>   roads
> Love is fire that burns both belief and non belief
> Those who practice love have neither religion
>   nor caste.

Love is perhaps the most important aspect of the higher meditation. Beyond religion and dogmas, it is love that awakens and finally unites the subject with the object because love is, in essence, a sacrifice and surrender. In most meditations, even those that call upon the divine, the meditation tries to draw God's attention to oneself with varying degrees. This becomes a barrier to the highest meditations, because it expresses a need that is an element of our ego. The deepest meditation goes beyond all needs into the stillness where we surrender, that which is love.

The mystic Araby states:
> O marvel! A garden amidst the flames
> My heart has become capable of every form
> It is a pasture for gazelles and a convent for
>   Christian monks
> And a temple for idols and the pilgrim's kaaba
> And the tablets of the Torah and the book of
>   the Quran
> I follow the religion of love; what ever way
>   love's camel takes
> That is my religion and my faith.

Everyone needs to develop their own personal meditation practice because we are all journeying toward awakening in the real. What I have written in this book represents insight drawn from personal experience, as well as from what I have learned from my teacher. It is by no means complete! We are all "a work in progress," and as I am reading my book, each reader needs to read their book. The only way to do this is through meditation. If there is just one book that you read, then let it be the one that is within you. May you be blessed on that quest and may you be touched by the divine fragrance of the Invisible light. This is my hope and prayer.

4. Our outer world if filled with considerable chaos and confusion. It is important to simplify our life so that we eliminate as much as possible the external impulses that become obstacles in our path. This means being selective about what television programs we watch, the books we read and the people we hang out with. It means being selective about what we put into our bodies, too. Alcohol, drugs and tobacco harm the body and will undoubtedly become a hindrance. Also, our eating habits have to be modified. For instance, eating a heavy meal late at night would affect the early morning and the night meditations. It is important to rearrange life and find time for reflection and walks during which the inner meditation can continue. Physical and spiritual calmness will create balance, which is important, because neglect and ignorance has shifted it. It is hard to incorporate an advanced meditation practice in a disordered and chaotic life.

OBSTACLES

We have discussed that the uncontrolled mind is the biggest obstacle to our meditation. This mind, however, is rooted in our material attachments, which are the source of all our inner obstacles. There are five categories of attachments, and overcoming these would eliminate most of the obstacles on the inward path.

The attachment of our physical body—From the time we are born, we create this illusion of our physical existence. We spend a whole life trying to become someone we are not. Young children see themselves as Disney characters and other icons created by savvy advertising companies. Teenagers put up posters of their favorite music artists and emulate their clothing and style. Adults are no different; everyone has an icon or some Hollywood star after whom they model themselves. We take time to follow their lives, off-screen successes and challenges and to live their dreams. From the time we are able to look in the mirror, we are never good enough to be us because we want to be someone else. We seem to be preoccupied trying to understand the struggles of others, but somehow never feel that understanding the self is worth our effort. We need to see ourselves as what we are—unique and latently divine—before we can remove this obstacle.

Attachments to the physical life—We live our lives as if we are never going to die. We escape from our own life by living other people's lives, which are readily found in soap operas and other television programs. We spend fortunes in shaping our bodies and modeling ourselves to the expectations of others because our outward form and image are vital to our self esteem. It never occurs to us that there is also an inward form, which is the source of all external images. We do not have the time to find meaning in our lives, but spend a lifetime trying to find meaning in the lives of others. I have known people who have been to the same pub for 30 years and watched the same soap opera for 20 years. We are so absorbed in the lives of others because we consider our own life unworthy of serious reflection. One day, tragedy strikes, and we are jolted into becoming our real self. Then we realize that we know much about everyone's life but nothing about our own. Unless we recognize the importance of our spiritual life, our physical life will remain an obstacle.

Attachment to our mind—We are confused and assume mistakenly that we are our mind. The mind drives us to achieve and conquer, and in the process, meaningless things have become important to us. Engrossed in a materialistic world, we are ruthlessly driven to own and possess and are vaccinated against feeling the pain of others. Our life is one big rush, and our ego is inflated with an image of self-importance. One day, this mind and body will decay and die, but a part of us that was neglected lives on. We need to let go of our attachments to our own greatness and instead recognize the greatness of the creator in whom our neglected self lives.

Attachment to our knowledge—We are under the illusion that, as physical personalities, we are important because we appear to have acquired so much advancement in science and technology. Worldly knowledge is a small part of the greater divine knowledge, yet we exist as proud egos, believing that we know a lot and are important. But one day, we realize that we were living in an illusion based on what we thought was real, and this illusion carries on within and becomes a barrier. We are ignorant until we discover the spiritual knowledge that forms the foundation of the physical one.

Attachments to pleasure—We have become creatures of pleasure whose sole objective is to seek enjoyment and gratification. When we are born, a bottle of milk and a hug are enough, but somehow things change, and soon nothing ever satisfies us. We spend our lives seeking pleasure outside of ourself, in people, places and things. It never occurs to us that the greatest of all pleasure is within us. The more we strive to find pleasure in the attachments to people, things and places, the greater become the obstacles to the interior path.

The Bhagavad Gita states:

> Passion engendered by thirst for
> Pleasure and attachment binds the soul
> Through its fondness for activity.

The above five obstacles represent an illusion we have created about our own life and purpose. These determine our actions and intentions, and since they are rooted in an illusion, we are grounded to our lower nature because of them. The mind takes our attachments to these illusions and turns them into formidable barriers to our inward journey. Every thought that enters our mind invariably has a source in one of these five categories of attachments. If I had to identify the worst form of the attachments, these would be lust, anger, pride, greed, malicious gossip and excessive materialism. These external experiences become significant internal obstacles.

The Katha Upanishad states:

> When all desires that surge in the heart are renounced
> The mortal becomes immortal
> When all the knots that strangle the heart are loosened
> The mortal becomes immortal
> This sums up the teaching of the scriptures.

A meditation practice will slowly dissolve these illusions that, in turn, will reduce our blind attachments to material things, leading to a gradual awakening of the soul.

CHAPTER 11

Some Final Thoughts

As a civilization, we have come a long way in understanding the nature of things in our tangible world of matter. In an effort to comprehend our physical landscape, we have explored every square inch of our earth, marking every piece of land, ocean and mountain, and have given each a name and identity. We have used this inquisitive nature to discover all aspects of the human body, defining every organ, every passage, every cell and all the diseases and ailments that hinder it. Furthermore, we have taken the natural abundance in our planet and turned the minerals, metals and oils into consumer staples and durables that can allow us to live our life in comfort. The cars we drive, the homes we live in and the television we watch are a testament to mankind's ingenuity in turning natural resources into items of luxury.

We also have become excessive, for it is not enough to have a car that transports us; we dedicate professions to making a hundred models, each one different in color, shape and feature. Our grocery stores have long isles where a bar of soap can come in over 30 brands, each packaged differently in terms of shape, size and fragrance, although all of them do the same thing. Our furniture stores sell dining tables that come in square, oblong, round, rectangular, and octagonal, made of glass, pewter, marble, aluminum, and a host of different finishes so that we can eat a meal; these offer yet more evidence that the caveman has indeed arrived! We know much about our world, yet what do we know about ourselves? Very little. Consequently, we are agitated, forever struggling and unhappy. Despite all the outward progress, we are primitive when it comes to understanding our real nature. Our lives are filled with discontentment, disillusion and confusion, which are rooted in the ignorance of our spiritual essence. This inner conflict has manifested itself in our so-called "advanced world," which is filled with violence, wars, terrorism and poverty.

Although mankind has lost its compass it is ironic that, when the human being was developing, we came with an instruction manual. It came in parts and phases brought to us by the divinely inspired prophets of old. Zoroaster, Krishna, Buddha, Abraham, Moses, Jesus and Mohammed are just a few of the 124,000 enlightened souls who have graced our planet. Of the vast wisdom they brought to us, one simple message stands out explains our current situation:

> Everything in our created world has two sides.
> There is a wrong side and a right side,
> A positive and a negative, a dark side and a
>   bright side,
> There is good and bad; inward and the outward,
> Male and female. There is the visible and the
>   invisible.

To find the Invisible Light, we have to change sides from the outward to the inward. This single change in our focus turns the conflict into peace and the darkness into light. The process to make this change is meditation. When you read about the yogis, Zen and Buddhist monks and others who renounced the world to spend their life in meditation, these sacrifices seem to demonstrate great courage. However, in my view, the greatest sacrifices and acts of courage are being made by people who live in a modern world surrounded by distractions and temptations, yet fulfill their responsibilities to their families and community and are still able to find the solitude to walk along the Invisible Way and practice meditation.

The Ancient Knowledge—There was a civilization that was

spiritually advanced beyond any other, where the esoteric truths transmitted through the generations was the substance that informed and guided the members of the society. The practice of meditation as passed on to them by the wise people of old, was central to their lifestyle. It enabled them to live as enlightened beings because it allowed them to draw from the fountain of wisdom and light within them. One day, a wise soul came to their elders and informed them that they should henceforth stop drinking water from the wells of the villages. He warned them that if they did not do this, they would slowly become ignorant. At first, this advice was taken very seriously and great effort was made by everyone to go further away and use the water from the rivers instead. Years went by and slowly, as the elders passed away, the new generation began questioning these old traditions, and many started drinking the water from the wells. Others followed this path, for it was very convenient to drink water from the wells rather then the river, which took days to fetch. Soon the warnings of the wise soul became folklore that few took seriously. One by one, however, the people of the village started down the slope of ignorance, and these ignorant ones were often easy to identify because they acted without any understanding of the truth. Slowly the numbers of the ignorant swelled until there remained just one person in the whole village who had not drunk from the well. All the people of the village thought he was the ignorant one because he had no understanding of the truth, so he was shunned and ridiculed. Such is the way of our world, that those who stand apart from the masses and are true to the ancient wisdom are marginalized.

All of us had the ancient knowledge, but in time, we became like the people in the village—ignorant, because we chose to drink from the well of our lower nature. In time, the esoteric practice of meditation was stopped because it was inconvenient and time-consuming, and this disconnected us from our higher self. Soon the messages of the prophets of old became folklore, that could be disregarded, and the few that continued the ancient practice were called mystics. All of us had this ancient knowledge, and all of us still have this knowledge locked up deep in the vaults of our soul.

Veils of ignorance formed a crust around this self, and meditation was the key that slowly dispersed the ignorance of darkness surrounding the real self. Meditation was the essential practice of every enlightened soul whose purpose was to awaken our consciousness, and they taught this to their closest disciples in the expectation that it would be transmitted to all the people in all times. This spiritual knowledge was conveyed through the ages at first as a sacred and valuable revelation that was centered in the lives of people. Later, these revelations and spiritual truths were given form by way of religious expression.

Religion itself had a noble beginning, for it was the way in which human beings tried to understand the creator and their own origin. The politics of power, unfortunately, birthed orthodoxy, and everything changed. As mankind progressed, there was a new focus on the rites and rituals, the outward form of that deep, inherent desire people had to understand their origin. As long as these external expressions were connected to their inherent desire to know God, it was a positive development because it allowed them to express the inner emotions outwardly through religious expression. Unfortunately, power and politics ensured the introduction of strict dogmas that served to cut the umbilical cord of religion's outward appearance from the wellspring of the ancient knowledge. Not only were those who stayed focused on the esoteric dimension ridiculed and marginalized, they also were persecuted and killed. This has been evident in history, and it forced the adherents who had the conviction to practice the essence of the ancient ways to go into hiding.

We can see that, in all three of the major monotheistic faiths, there were mystical orders and groups who continued to exist in secrecy. The Jewish faith had their mystics, and today, one of the better-known esoteric dimensions of Judaism is the Kabbalah, which teaches the inner dimensions of the Torah. It is not a coincidence that meditation is an integral part of this philosophy. Abraham, who is a central figure in Jewish mysticism, is also known as the father of all prophets. Abraham had a very personal relationship with God and, through meditation, Abraham learned the spiritual laws of creation. The ancient manuscript Sefer Yetzirah, known as The Book of Formation, was the product of Abraham's meditation. This closeness between God and Abraham occurred through meditation and is confirmed by these words from Chapter 6 of the manuscript:

> Then God appeared to him unto himself, kissed him,
>   called him his friend,
> And made a covenant with him and his descendents
>   forever.

In Chapter 8 of the same ancient manuscript, we learn of the union and graduation that took place, again validating the role meditation played in the life of Abraham:

> And when Abraham, our father, had formed and
> combined and investigated and reckoned and
> succeeded, then He-Qof-Bet-He, "the holy one
> blessed be he," was revealed to him, and unto
> Abraham he called the convocation.

However, the most profound wisdom is found in Chapter 3 of the ancient manuscript of Abraham:

> Stop your mouth from speaking; stop your heart
>   from thinking....
> Their end is infused with their beginning, and their
>   beginning with their end.
> Like a flame attached to a glowing ember
> Know, meditate and imagine that the creator is one
>   and there is nothing apart
> From him and before one, what do you count?

If ever there was an imperative to silence the mind with concentration and become receptive to the grace emanating from the Invisible Light and become one with the divine, it is found in these meditations of Abraham. Yet how central is meditation to the practice of Judaism today? Such esoteric practices have been left to the mystical movements, such as the Kabbalah, while the mainstream Jews have become very secular.

Indeed, if we were to venture into the time before the advent of Abraham, we would find in the oldest scared Hindu texts in existence very clear and precise directives about the importance of meditation. Vedantic scripts are replete with spiritual knowledge of profound depth on the role of meditation in our quest for liberation. I have used some inspiring words from the Bhagavad Gita in this book because of all the Vedic scriptures; they have a lot to offer the serious student of meditation. The earliest teachings of Krishna remain free of censorship, most likely because many did not understand their depth and therefore remained untouched by so-called protectors of religion. Hence, some of the concepts I have written about in this book exist in much clarity. The concepts of rebirth, the spiritual body as a separate entity to the human one, and that of the spiritual eye has existed in these texts far longer than our knowledge about our physical world.

For instance, the Bhagavad Gita states:

> He who leaves the body with the mind unmoved
> and filled with devotion
> By the power of meditation gathering between his
> eyebrows
> His whole vital energy attains the supreme.

The knowledge that meditation empowers us to change our fate, leave the body and define the role of the third eye exists in its raw simplicity as it has for thousands of years. We have done so much to discover our outer nature but have invested next to nothing to determine the essence that makes all things possible. Meditation is also very central to the practice of Buddhism. The life of this prince who appeared to be wealthy outwardly demonstrates how much poverty was concealed within him until he was awakened through the process of meditation and ennobled.

When we look at the advent of later religions, we find the wise souls who preached them taught the same things once we were able to dismantle their outward form. The life of Jesus, for instance, prior to his ministry, is hardly ever discussed at the pulpit. The discovery of the fourth century manuscripts, buried 1600 years ago by monks who feared their destruction by the church near Nag Hammadi, Egypt, tells us a lot about Jesus and the spiritual dimensions he was aware of and taught. Jesus belonged to the Essene order, in which the practice of meditation was central, as was the belief in rebirth. In fact, the council of Nicea is known to have removed the concepts of reincarnation from the church's theology. There is a lot of evidence available today that connects Jesus' early life with the key issue of meditation and spirituality. All of his closest disciples were taught this and in fact witnessed Jesus' encounter with God. For instance, Jesus led three of his apostles, Peter, John and James, to pray at the top of the mountain when Jesus became transfigured and experienced the divine light. Also, Paul put into practice some of the esoteric teachings of Jesus and, in the process, had an out of body experience, described in two Corinthians 12:24:

> I knew a man in Christ above fourteen years ago,
>   (whether in the body, I cannot tell, or whether
>   out of the body, I cannot tell. God knoweth)
> such as one caught up to the third heaven. And I
>   knew such a man, (whether in the body, or out
>   of the body, I cannot tell: God knoweth)
> How that he was caught up into paradise and heard
>   unspeakable words, which it is not lawful for a
>   man to utter.

Paul had meditated and his soul had left the body to reach the third spiritual realm. Ironically, much of this knowledge was stifled and marginalized. Clearly the esoteric dimension was at the root of Jesus' real ministry, one that had meditation as its center.

Islam was the final of the three monotheistic faiths. Mohamed, the prophet of Islam, spent 30 days each year in a cave in Mount Hira meditating, and this was long before he was declared a prophet. Meditation was intrinsic, not only to the way Mohamed lived his life, but also to the manner in which he received the revelations from God. The angel Gabriel came to him during his moments in meditation and revealed the messages that became known as the Holy Quran. In fact, there were a number of ecstatic moments in meditation that are mentioned in the Holy Quran. For instance, the night of Miraj is known to be the moment when Rasul (the prophet) left his physical body and journeyed to what has become a holy shrine for the Muslims, The Dome of the Rock in Jerusalem. Subsequently, his spiritual journey took him to heaven, where he met the earlier prophets before experiencing union with God; quoted in 17:1:

> Glory to God
> who did take his servant
> for a journey by night
> from the sacred mosque
> to the farthest mosque
> whose precincts we did bless
> In order that we might show him
> Some of our signs: For he is the one
> Who heareth and seeth all things.

What is also evident from the Holy Quran is that there is validation that the previous prophets all communicated with God through the internal prayer of meditation.

It is written in Chapter 16:43:

> And before thee also
> The apostles we sent
> Were but men, to whom
> We granted Inspiration; if ye realize this not,
> ask of those who possess the message.

Islam also has much in its holy book on the concept of rebirth. For instance 22:66:

> It is he who gave you life will cause you to die
> And will again give you life
> Truly man is a most ungrateful creature.

In addition to the above, Islam empowers the adherents to change their fate from the inside out 13:11:

> Truly God changeth not the conditions of a people
> Until they change the condition of their own soul.

In the same way that the mainstream Christian Church marginalized much of this spiritual wisdom from use in the church, as did the Jewish people from their synagogues, the Muslim faith marginalized it from the mosques. Since meditation was so intrinsic in the prophets' lives, and also in the way the message of Islam was revealed, one wonders why it is not one of the pillars of Islam.

Instead, meditation became the province of those that held onto the convictions of the esoteric dimensions. Thus, Ali, cousin and son-in-law of the prophet of Islam, became the source that birthed the mystical dimensions of Islam in which meditation became an essential element.

Ali wrote:

> Watch the world go by, it is a two-day spring
> King, fakirs lesser and greater no one is at peace here
> Realize it and beware as long as the signs of autumn
> do not come
> Till then draw from the water of true meditation
> Thus the garden of your life will always blossom.

A beautiful simile describing meditation as the wellspring that can transcend time and empowers us to change our fate.

When we look at latter day religion, we find that the practice of meditation is also rooted in their origins. For instance, Guru Nanak who founded Sikhism, was known to have spent long hours in meditation as a young man herding the family cattle. His ministry began with inspiration he received in meditation. Guru Arjan, the fifth Sikh prophet, explained the purpose of life thus:

> Having gained a body this time, a rare opportunity
> you have got;
> This is your chance to meet God.
> Your other pursuits will be of no avail at the end.
> Seek the company of holy men, and learn to
> meditate on God.
> Set your mind on crossing the sea of life;
> Life is being wasted away in pursuits of sensual
> pleasures.

The reoccurring themes of the world of lower desires and the role of meditation are very apparent. Finally, when we look at Taoism once again, we see that this ancient tradition of philosophy and religious belief is deeply rooted in Chinese customs and doesn't make a rigid division between body and spirit. It regards physical activities, such as yoga, meditation and martial arts, as an important way to spiritual growth and a long life.

One thing we now know with absolute certainty is that the esoteric knowledge of the divine laws and practices, though not visible in most religions today, was transmitted to the closest and most trusted confidantes of the prophets and was passed on from generation to generation as the Invisible Way; meditation was a central practice for all of them.

Ironically, this misuse of the sacred texts by the extremists in all religions was alluded to in the Bhagavad Gita;

> As a man can drink water from any side of a full
>   tank
> so the skilled theologian can wrest from any
>   scripture that which will serve him.

The mystics who have followed the practices of the Invisible Way have continually reminded us:

> All that is left
> To us by tradition is mere words,
> It is up to us to find out what they mean.

It is not my intention to discuss religion at any great length, because this is an old subject and one on which the debate never ends. I have the utmost respect for all religions; at the core, they are simply man's attempt to understand and communicate with God. What I have tried to explain is that, at the very heart, all of the religious traditions at inception incorporated the practice of meditation, and this is apparent in the way the personalities who introduced these religions lived and taught. Today, however, this aspect, and indeed the connections to the esoteric dimensions, generally have been removed from most but not all of the major religions and it is my view that, as a consequence, religion has lost its compass.

Therefore, there are numerous barriers to our ultimate liberation, but we need to look past the dogmas and get into the quintessence, for all religions have at their source the same wellspring. The mystics did this and found unhindered spiritual freedom.

The mystic Attar writes:

> What are "I" and "you"
> Just lattices in the niches of a lamp
> Through which the one light radiates
> I and you are the veil
> Between heaven and Earth;
> Lift this veil and you will see
> How all sects and religions are one
> Lift this veil and you will ask
> When "I" and "you" do not exist
> What is mosque?
> What is synagogue?
> What is Fire Temple?"

There is a light beyond everything, beyond time and form, beyond image and reflection.

It is the light that sustains all the realms in creation, and it is a fountain within us.

The Bhagavad Gita states:

> When the intellect, bewildered by the multiplicity
> of holy scripts, stands unperturbed in blissful con-
> templation of the infinite, then thou hast attained
> spirituality.

Precious things are always concealed, like the pearl found in an oyster shell at the bottom of the ocean or the diamonds found hidden deep inside the mountains. Similarly, the blueprints of our life and the treasure above all treasures, the genome of the creator, is concealed within our soul. Meditation enables us to go beyond the din of the world, the impulses of our lower nature and the tenets of religion into the very bosom of our soul. It is here in con-templation that we find the cause that creates our fate and shapes our destiny; it is here that we find the Invisible Light and the power to create change. This, then, is the sacred and timeless path of old, known as the Invisible Way.

MEDITATION THEMES

The themes from the meditation are a starting point for an inner journey that has no predetermined conclusion. Before a theme meditation commences, prepare yourself as follows:

1. Read the chapter on that theme. Refer to the stories and quotes and reflect upon them. Beginners may need to open their eyes and read some of the quotes during the meditations.
2. Read the theme numerous times and memorize it.
3. Visualize the theme written upon the black screen that you can see in between your two physical eyes (when they are closed).
4. Develop the theme seeking to go inward and allow its development to occur from within.
5. If your thoughts become captive to your wondering mind, go back to the black screen, visualize the theme and use some of the defenses I outlined to rein in the unruly mind. It is important that the wellspring of meditation on a theme emerges from within, rather than the mind.

THEME: CHAPTER 3
Everything in the physical world is repossessed
Development:

- I am born naked without possessions and will die similarly. Why do I try to possess all the physical things that I can only use while I am alive? Everything I care about in life, including my family, will be repossessed.
- Everything that comes into my life is an abundance, yet do I see it as such, or am I too busy looking ahead to getting that which I do not have?
- Everything that comes into my life comes for a reason; do I stop to understand why?
- Am I simply collecting green golf balls like everyone else? Is this the purpose of life? Is this supposed to give me happiness?
- Am I who I am and defined by what I own? What remains at death? I can see myself old and close to death. How would I live my live if given another chance?
- What is this mind that distracts me and why will it not be silenced when I ask?
- In the silence of the mind, will I discover the answers?

THEME: CHAPTER 4
We are spiritual beings in the midst of a temporary human experience
Development:

- There is a part of me that does not get buried at death and that is the real me. My physical body is temporary, and at death, I will know my real self. But in meditation I can know the real me now.
- What is the origin of my spiritual self? In my meditation, I can experience that origin. My soul will outlive physical death; how can I care for it?
- First I must remove the physical mask. In my meditation, I can remove the mask and experience the soul that gives me

life. Life is like a hotel; we check in and out, but the life of
the soul is timeless.

- Deep within me, my soul lives, and in my meditation, I can
experience it.
- The unseen world is the root of everything; my physical life
is short. How can I use it to discover the unseen?

What was I before this physical life and what will I be after?

THEME: CHAPTER 5
We have two centers

Development:

- There is a physical and a spiritual center, that which is seen
and that which is unseen. Balance between the two creates
harmony.
- I am physical and spiritual. Are they both balanced, and is
there harmony in my life or chaos?
- Am I aware of my spiritual self or is my ego overwhelmingly
dominant?
- Am I overly attached to material goods and possessions?
Everything I can see is an illusion because it will all disappear.
- What are my spiritual needs? Do I hear their anguish? What
do I do to nurture my soul?
- In my meditation, I can feel the real self and nurture its
needs.In this silence, shall I discover my real self?

Develop Similar Themes from Chapters 6 and 7:

Going further, readers can develop their own themes for meditations. Take your pick from your favorite verse, from a holy text
to the poetry of the mystics. There are some powerful themes
awaiting the reader both in this book and out in the expansive
world. Even sitting by a river or lying down and watching the stars
on a dark night can become a meditation theme.

MANTRA DISCUSSION

A mantra, sometimes referred to as "shabda," is a sacred word which is repeated in meditation. When we examine the lives of the great prophets, such words chimed with every beat of their heart, inwardly in meditation and outwardly in their every act.

The Bhagvad Gita states:

> Closing the gates of the body, drawing the forces
> of his mind into the heart and by the power of
> meditation concentrating this vital energy in the
> brain, repeating "ohm," the symbol of eternity,
> holding me always in remembrance, he who
> thus leaves his body and goes forth reaches the
> spirit supreme.

The Bhagvad Gita, one of the older sacred texts, introduces one such word, "ohm," which is a symbol of the absolute. This word and many others can be found in the Vedic scriptures, and each one symbolizes an aspect of the divine self. Buddhism followed from the Vedic society, and many of the mantras used by Buddhists are rooted in the Vedas.

During the time of Abraham, we find a similar use of sacred words that were always connected to the absolute God. For instance, Shaddai, (almighty god); Shalom (peace); and Yahweh (personal name of God). These are found in the Old Testament, as are many others, and Abraham used their mystical potential in his ministry. The Kabbala, representing the mystical dimension of Judaism, has 72 sacred names it has identified, all of which are rooted in Hebrew.

Since the origins of Christianity are also rooted in Hebrew, many of the sacred words Jesus used can be also found in the Old Testament. For instance, we find in the book of Mathew 27:46:

> Eli, Eli Lama Sabacthani (My God, My God, why
> have you forsaken me)?

Jesus used Eli as a personal name of God. There are others like Elohim (God the creator) and Jehovah.

Islam was revealed in Arabic, and the Quran contains 99 beautiful names of God, all of them connected to the divine. For instance, Allah (The God), Al Ali (the sublimely exalted), and An-noor (the light).

Sikhism also has sacred words. For instance, Wheguru (wonderful lord), and Satnam (true name).

Finally, there are those who prefer a neutral word. I have explained the inherent power of using a mantra connected to God; however, ultimately, the power of our intentions will determine the word's strength. Therefore, readers wishing to use a word that is neutral with respect to any association can select a suitable word, preferably with two syllables. One mantra I have come across often is the phrase "I AM." Follow your own heart and intuition in picking something suitable.

Throughout history, people have used sacred words to merge their physical selves into their divine selves. I am not qualified to recommend what mantra you should pick; however, I would suggest that you use the following six guidelines in choosing one.

1. Go into your own tradition; there is a reason why you were born a Christian, Jewish, Muslim, etc. Therefore, it is a starting point. Let the journey begin here; who knows where it will take you?

2. In seeking out a mantra, use a name or attribute of God. These are known with certainty to have spiritual powers.

3. Stick to the original root language in which the word was originally conveyed. For instance, by translating Allah

(Arabic), Shadda (Hebrew), and Eli (Hebrew) into English as "God," the sacredness is lost.

4. Use a word you are comfortable with, one which flows easily from your lips and resonates within.

5. Do not keep changing words; stick with the one, personalize it and keep it secret.

6. Do not go out looking for another person to give you the word. Remember, when you are ready, a teacher will come into your life. No one ever needs to find a master; the master will find you. Too often we have come across people who have readily trusted meditation teachers, gurus and others and, in the process, have been taken advantage of. A true master only asks that his pupil follows the disciplines of the meditation with conviction. Finally, this meditation is private and should be performed by you in the sanctity of the place you consider sacred.

Spend a little time finding the right word. The Internet is a wonderful tool and will put countless options within reach.

Always remember, "In the beginning was the word, the word was with God, the word was God." Creation flowed from the sacred word. It is this sacred word that enables us to connect with the Invisible Light within.

In my own experience, I followed this path and chose my own mantra from my own tradition. One day, a master appeared to me and my own intuition validated his authenticity; subsequently, he gave me a shabda that could accompany me in my journey to the Invisible Light. It is important to remember that I did not wait, nor did I seek the master. Instead, I accepted my journey in receptiveness. I have known people who have waited many soul rebirths before the master came, and there is no need to rush this process. For this reason, the starting point is your own current tradition; this you cannot change. In fact, you have gone through much in your previous soul births to arrive at it.

One enlightened soul explained that, in his life, he was born close to a master and served him. That was not a coincidence but a process of gradual soul development. Too often we ignore the fact

that the journey starts within our own backyard rather than someone else's. Our personal journey must start with who we are, where
we are born and the tradition and culture of our birth. From here,
place the sacred word within you and follow your heart.

RESOURCES

Anonymous, *The Cloud of Unknowing*

Attar, 1984. *Conference of the Birds,* Penguin

Balagha, N., *Sermons of Ali*

Bell, G.L., translated by, 1979. *Teachings of Hafiz,* The Sufi Trust

Borysenko, J., 1993. *Fire in the Soul,* Warner Books, Inc.

Bruce, C., 1977. *Bhagavad Gita Shri Purohit,* Random House

Brunton, P., 1986. *The notebooks of Paul Brunton—Meditation,* Larson
    Publications

Brunton, P., 1984. *The notebooks of Paul Brunton—Perspectives,* Larson
    Publications

Fadiman & Frager, 1998. *Essential Sufism,* Cashe Books

Giga, A., *Seven Colors,* SterlingHouse Publisher, Inc.

Hunsburger, A., 2000. *The Ruby of Badakshan,* I.B. Tauris Publishers

Hunzai, F., 1997. *Shimmering Light,* I.B. Tauris Publishers

Khan, A., 1954. *Memoirs of Aga Khan 3rd,* Cassell and Co. Ltd.

Johnson, W., 2003. *Rumi,* Inner Traditions Int.

Maclaine, S., 1989. *Going Within,* Bantam Books

Maclaine, S., 1983. *Out on a Limb,* Bantam Books

Nicholson, R., 1926. *Mathnawi of Rumi Books 1-6*, E.J.W. Bibb
    Memorial Trust

Sadhu, M., 1977. *Concentration*, George Allen and Unwirv

Sadhu, M., 1976. *Samadhi*, George Allen and Unwirv

Sadhu, M., 1967. *Meditation*, George Allen and Unwirv

Schimmel, A., 2001. *Make a Shield from Wisdom*, I.B. Tauris Publishers

Schimmel, A., 1992. *Rumi World*, Shambhala Publications, Inc.

Shah, I., 1974. *Way of the Sufi*, Penguin

Tolle, E., 2002. *The Power of Now*, Namaste Publishing Inc.

Ward, T., 2001. *Meditation and Dream Works*, Arcturus Publishing Ltd.

Zukav, G., 1989. *Care of the Soul* Simon and Schuster

The New Testament and Psalms

The Quran

The Old Testament

Internet Resources—Miscellaneous